P9-CKN-700

THE VIENNA OPERA

THE VIENNA OPERA

Edited by Andrea Seebohm

With contributions by
Wolfgang Greisenegger,
Wilhelm Holzbauer, Riki Raab,
Andrea Seebohm, Egon Seefehlner
and Otto Strasser

RIZZOLI
NEW YORK

English translation:
Copyright © 1987 by Office du Livre S.A., Fribourg, Switzerland

English translation published in 1987 in the United States of America by:

Rizzoli International Publications, Inc.
597 Fifth Avenue/New York 10017

All rights reserved:
No part of this book may be reproduced in any manner whatsoever without permission
of Rizzoli International Publications, Inc.

German language edition, *Die Wiener Oper: 350 Jahre Glanz und Tradition* Copyright
© 1986 by Office du Livre S.A., Fribourg, Switzerland, and Verlag Carl Ueberreuter,
Vienna

Photodocumentalist: Ingrid Hänsel

Translated from the German by Simon Nye

Library of Congress Cataloging-in-Publication Data

Seebohm, Andrea.
  [Wiener Oper. English]
  The Vienna Opera.

  Translation of: Die Wiener Oper.
  Bibliography: p.
  Includes index.
  1. Wiener Staatsoper.   I. Greisenegger, Wolfgang.
II. Title.
ML1723.8.V62S853 1987   782.1'09436'13   86-43187
ISBN 0-8478-0811-4

Printed in Austria

CONTENTS

Andrea Seebohm: Preface   7

Andrea Seebohm: Opera in Vienna before 1869   9

Wilhelm Holzbauer: The Architecture of the Vienna Opera House   31

Egon Seefehlner: The Directors and their Ensembles   57

Franz von Dingelstedt   58 · Johann von Herbeck   64
Franz von Jauner   66 · Wilhelm Jahn   72 · Gustav Mahler   77
Felix von Weingartner   86 · Hans Gregor   90 · Richard Strauss/
Franz Schalk   96 · Franz Schalk   103 · Clemens Krauss   107
Felix von Weingartner   115 · Erwin Kerber   115
Heinrich Karl Strohm/Lothar Müthel   119 · Karl Böhm   122
Franz Salmhofer   127 · Karl Böhm   133 · Herbert von Karajan ˙ 141
Egon Hilbert   150 · Heinrich Reif-Gintl   154 · Rudolf Gamsjäger   157
Egon Seefehlner   162 · Lorin Maazel   168 · Egon Seefehlner   174

Wolfgang Greisenegger: Set Design and Costumes   175

Riki Raab: The Vienna Opera Ballet   211

Otto Strasser: The Orchestra   239

Premiers and World Premiers of Major Opera at the Opera
House on the Ring since 1869   263

Select Bibliography   266

Index   268

PREFACE

There are many histories of the Vienna Opera; nevertheless anyone who intends to describe its history will have to dig deeply into the past. When I started research in Vienna's libraries and archives into the origins of opera at the imperial court I found four versions giving five different dates. Most baroque operas did not give the name of the composers; some accounts claimed that works by Claudio Monteverdi and Francesco Cavalli were performed at the Viennese court, while others said no such thing; information was confused as to the early years of the Kärntnertor theater and its performances in the eighteenth century—even details of the repertoire of the old Burgtheater in Michaelerplatz (where operas by Gluck and Mozart were first shown) were patchy.

All the more credit, then, should go to my five colleagues, who agreed immediately to offer their specialized knowledge in the form of individual contributions:

Egon Seefehlner is the former director of the Vienna State Opera, who took on the task of writing the long chapter on "The Directors and their Ensembles" in spite of his responsibilities during his last year at the Vienna Opera and a major tour of Japan. One additional attraction is the chance to read his comments on his predecessors!

Wilhelm Holzbauer is a prominent Austrian architect who recently designed the new opera house in Amsterdam. He has a wide knowledge of European theater in general and the architecture of the Vienna Opera house in particular.

Wolfgang Greisenegger, professor of theater studies at the University of Vienna, takes a keen interest in stage design and costume, and his enthusiasm is reflected in his contribution.

Otto Strasser is eighty-five years old and previously a member of the Vienna Philharmonic. His knowledge of the history of the State Opera's orchestra is second to none—he was a violinist there for over forty years and was on the board of the Vienna Philharmonic between 1958 and 1969.

Riki Raab began dancing at the Court Opera in 1914, becoming a solo dancer in 1921. Since retiring she has written about the Vienna Ballet on many occasions.

It remained for me, as a former musicologist, to write the introductory chapter describing opera in Vienna until 1869, the year when the opera house opened on the Ringstrasse, Vienna's great circular boulevard.

My thanks go to all the friends and colleagues who assisted me with my research and by answering question, and to my five co-authors, who stuck at it and delivered their manuscripts on time in spite of the pressing deadline and the painstaking nature of the work. Particular thanks are due to the untiring efforts of the musical historian Ingrid Hänsel, who gave up much of her time in order to help me gather source material. Without her support and friendly advice my job as editor of this, my first, book would certainly have been a good deal harder.

I am also grateful for all the cooperation I received at the National Library's theater collection and picture archive, the Art History Museum, the Vienna History Museum, the Setzer-Tschiedel archives and those of the Vienna Philharmonic, and from the photographers Lillian Barylli-Fayer, Johanna Feigl, Alex Zeininger, Alfred Janderka, Viktor Harrandt, Margit Münter, and Elisabeth Hausmann.

I dedicate this book to opera lovers all over the world and would ask them to forgive me if I have left out or neglected any of their favorite singers who have performed in Vienna. Space had to be found to describe three hundred fifty years of the splendor and tradition of an art form that attracts no less enthusiastic support today than it did in the past—not to mention what it costs. Lucky the country that can still spend millions on opera, rather than on arms!

Vienna, summer 1986

Andrea Seebohm

OPERA IN VIENNA BEFORE 1869

Andrea Seebohm

Vienna was one of Europe's leading operatic centers long before the new opera house on the Ring opened in 1869. It is true that little Salzburg had won the race to stage the first opera on Austrian soil–in 1614 *Orfeo* was performed at the Residenz, followed by *Andromeda* in 1616–but at the imperial court in Vienna they also knew how to hold theatrical celebrations with music. More than one emperor imported, direct from Italy, the birthplace of opera, not only his wife but also this new art form and attendant singers, musicians, theater architects and designers. Emperor Maximilian I had already brought over his second wife from Milan and Ferdinand II, who became emperor in 1619, also married a princess from Mantua, Eleanore Gonzaga.

It was the latter who initiated the first modest performances of music drama at the Viennese court in 1622; called *Invenzione*, they were always combined with a ballet. On the occasion of the emperor's birthday on 9 July 1625, she arranged a performance in the great hall of the imperial palace, the Hofburg, of an Italian verse drama with music, in which six court musicians– dressed as a Roman, a Genoese, a Neopolitan, Doctor Graziano, Pantalon, and Zanni (personages from *commedia dell'arte*)–recited, played, and sang. There then appeared twelve ladies of the empress's court and twelve noblemen, who either danced, sang, or played the lute.

Many historians consider this comedy given in the Amalientrakt as the first performance of an opera in Vienna, although other experts do not agree and maintain that the occasion only consisted of a comedy with madrigals. Be that as it may, the performance proved such a success that, before long, music dramas of this kind were being given on all the birthdays and holidays of the imperial family. In this way an increasingly rich and grand style of court opera quickly developed; from a modern standpoint it was marred in only one respect–in contrast to opera in Venice, the people and the bourgeoisie were excluded in Vienna.

The first reliably attested opera performed at the emperor's Viennese court took place in November 1627 at Hradčany castle in Prague, where Ferdinand II resided for six months of the year with his retinue. The title of this *pastorale in musica* is given as *Callisto et Arcade* but the composer's name has not survived.

Two years later the empress gave orders for a "new hall or place for dancing" to be built at the Hofburg in Vienna. The site chosen was that of the present ballrooms. Operas were performed at the Hofburg in this Grosser Comoedi Saal (great hall of comedy)–first called the Ballroom and later the Great Court Theater–until 1744. The smaller antechamber, later called the Small Court Theater, was used for more intimate performances of music drama after 1659. When Crown Prince Ferdinand married Maria Anna of Spain in 1631, a ballet, at which two archduches-

1 Emperor Ferdinand II married his second wife in 1622–Princess Eleonore Gonzaga, the famous beautiful daughter of Duke Vicenzo I of Mantua and Eleonore de Medici. The art-loving new empress was twenty-four when she went to Vienna, and she supported music and theater in the city until her death in 1655.

2 The opera *La Gara* was performed at the ballroom of the Hofburg on 8 January 1652 on the occasion of the birth of the Infanta Margarita Theresa of Spain. The stage machinery and scenery were the work of Giovanni Burnacini. The picture shows the auditorium of the old court theater and a tournament scene from *La Gara*.

ses and twenty-two court ladies danced, was held in the great hall; there was an equestrian ballet in the palace courtyard and numerous other theatrical performances. The wedding opera *La Caccia Felice* (composer unknown) took place, however, in the great chamber of the Imperial Diet of Lower Austria (in the Minoritenplatz).

In 1633 Ludovico Bartolaia, tenor in the court orchestra, performed two opera scores at the Viennese court–*Gli Inganni di Polinesso* and a few months later *Il Sidonio*–on Ferdinand II's birthday in the great hall of the Hofburg. Recent research has established that operas by the two major musical dramatists of the age–Claudio Monteverdi and Francesco Cavalli–were also performed at the Viennese court until the end of the Thirty Years War in 1648. The next big operatic event in Vienna was certainly *La Gara* (the music possibly by Caspar Freysinger), which took place in 1652 on the birth of the Infanta Margherita of Spain, who was later to become empress. The

work was given three subsequent performances to which nobles and clerics who were not part of the imperial court were also admitted.

In 1651 Ferdinand III–himself a gifted composer, chiefly of church music–married his third wife Eleonore Gonzaga. It was thanks to her irrepressible joy in the theater, particularly opera, that the imperial court in Vienna was overrun by Italian artists. Thus, in 1653, on the orders of the emperor, the architect Giovanni Burnacini built a wooden theater for the Regensburg Imperial Diet, where Antonio Bertalli's carnival opera *Ingannno d'Amore* was staged in the same year.

When the festivities in Regensburg were over, the theater was dismantled, shipped down the Danube and stored in the arsenal in Vienna. In 1659 Leopold I (who was probably a more enthusiastic lover of music and theater than any other Austrian emperor in the baroque period) gave orders for the theater to be re-erected in the Tummelplatz in front of the court Riding School, and on 4 January 1660 the theater opened with an Italian *commedia dell'arte*. A spectacular accident occurred during the performance: three inquisitive court ladies who had leaned too far forward fell from the balcony, taking the balustrade with them. Miraculously no one was seriously hurt, but as early as 1662 the emperor had the theater pulled down again, no opera having been presented there.

Leopold ordered the building of a new theater on the occasion of his marriage to Margherita of Spain in 1666. To outdo even the Sun King's magnificent theatrical celebrations at Versailles, he constructed a splendid wooden theater, which the architect Lodovico Ottavio Burnacini designed with three tiers in the "Cortina" (now the courtyard behind the administrative wing of the National Library). Today it is estimated that it could have accommodated 1,000 people. In 1668 the oft-recounted performance of Antonio Cesti's *Il Pomo d'Oro* took place there on the empress's birthday. Burnacini's production was a theatrical sensation in Europe, with its flying machines and trap doors, adjustable scenery and backdrops, seascapes and vessels, starship and fire engine.

The emperor continued to spare no expense on his magnificent operatic displays. In 1667 and 1668, for example, an envoy criticized Leopold I's extravagance over his musical displays at a time when no money was available to provide Spain with the military support it needed. Again in 1685, a Venetian ambassador complained about the massive expenditure of the court on the marriage celebrations of Archduchess Maria Antonio (four performances of music drama in two months!) at a time when ressources needed for the war against Turkey were lacking.

Nowadays we would find the auditorium of Leopold's time rather disorderly during opera performances at court. The presence of the imperial couple admittedly had some effect on the behavior of the audience composed of nobles, but their chattering, eating, and drinking provided an incessant backdrop to the show. Important business was transacted in the opera house, and diplomatic

ELEONORA RÖM. KAISERIN

affairs were often discussed at great length, not to mention court gossip.

During the forty-seven-year reign of Leopold I alone (1658–1705), almost four hundred operas, ballets, requiems, and oratorios were performed in Vienna. The opera house in the Cortina was the site of extremely lavish productions by that genius of baroque theater Burnacini; *Il Pomo d'Oro* was followed in 1674 by Antonio Draghi's *Il Ratto delle Sabine*, with ballets by Johann Heinrich Schmelzer. In the same year Draghi's *Il*

3 Eleonore Gonzaga, born in 1628 the daughter of Prince Karl von Mantua-Nevers and Maria Gonzaga, became Emperor Ferdinand III's third wife in 1651. The portrait was probably painted shortly after the wedding and shows the young empress in the costume of Diana with her hunter's bag.

12

4, 5   Emperor Leopold I and his
wife Margarita of Spain dressed in
lavish, fanciful theater costumes.
The paintings are probably from
1667, the year after their
wedding, which Vienna had
celebrated with a large number
of musical performances. The
official wedding opera, *Il Pomo
d'Oro*, had to be postponed.

13

6 Antonio Bertalli's opera *L'Inganno d'Amore* was performed in Regensburg in 1653. Giovanni Burnacini built a wooden theater especially for the occasion which was later errected in Vienna. He also designed the sets for the opera's six scenes, including this dramatic sea tableau.

Fuoco Eterno (with thirty-five singing parts, six choruses, and twelve groups of supernumeraries) was performed, and in 1678 another work by Draghi, *La Monarcha latina trionfante*, with ballet music once more by Schmelzer. Cesti's *La Dori* (whose theme was an early precursor of *Fidelio*) remained a favorite at the court for some decades: twenty-eight productions are known of this opera alone.

A veritable "theater colony" gradually grew up around composers such as Bertalli, Cesti, Ziani, Sances, and Draghi, and librettists Sbarra, Miniata, and Pariati. It comprised musicians, singers, architects, designers, dancing-masters, and dancers, who were answerable to a powerful musical overlord. There was music and dance in the "Favorita" (now the Theresianum, the empress's former summer residence), in the Amalienburg, in the small and the great halls of the Hofburg, in the Cortina, in the imperial family's private apartments, in the palace gardens and the Burgplatz, in Laxenburg, Schönbrunn, the Augarten and—after the Turks had destroyed Vienna—for a time in the bastion of the empress's Bell'aria pleasure gardens, where a theater was constructed in 1687.

The theater in the Cortina was demolished in 1683 because of the risk of fire. The great hall in the Hofburg, which had been completely renovated in 1666–67, was damaged during the seige by the Turks and no operas were performed there until 1697. A year later the emperor commissioned Francesco Galli-Bibiena to reconstruct the theater. The new palace of Schönbrunn was built at the same time. The new Court Theater opened in the Hofburg on 28 January 1700 with Draghi's *Alceste*, followed immediately on 16 February by Johann Joseph Fux's *Il Fato Monarchico*. On 18 April, Carlo Agostino Badia's *Diana rappacificata con Venere e con l'Aurora* was staged in a hall

7 Antonio Cesti's opera *Il Pomo d'Oro* was a theatrical sensation in Europe in 1668. Lodovico Ottavio Burnacini built the new theater in the palace courtyard, the Cortina. The auditorium seated some one thousand spectators for the special performance of the opera before the emperor.

8 In 1678 Antonio Draghi's *La Monarchia latina trionfante* was performed in the Cortina, with ballet music by Johann Heinrich Schmelzer. The sets were by Burnacini—here we see a lively army scene with elephants and (just visible in the background) camels.

9 A theater festival around the pond of the Favorita (now the Theresianum, the empress's former summer residence). In the foreground are the imperial family under a canopy, surrounded by an audience of nobles.

in the palace of Schönbrunn. This was to be the only performance in the new palace during Leopold's reign.

The newly restored Court Theater reopened under Joseph I (1705–11) with Giovanni Bononcini's *Il Natale di Giunone* in 1708. A year later architect Antonio Beduzzi completed the new theater near the Kärntnertor (the Corinthian Gate), the first home of the indigenous Vienna Volkstheater. Its leader, the clown Josef Anton Stranitzky, had been entertaining the public since about 1705 in a "comedy hut" in the Neumarkt, which was a perennial thorn in the side of the local Viennese authorities because it was a fire hazard. The city authorities, therefore, obtained the emperor's permission to build a new theater. It was Stranitzky who moved in as leaseholder of Vienna's first municipal theater in 1710. His repertoire consisted of Viennese folk plays and comedies, but he also performed arrangements of operas in German.

In 1726 he was succeeded as director of the Kärntnertor theater by Austria's first theatrical manager: the singer Francesco Borosini and the dancer Josef Carl Selliers.

Emperor Karl VI, however, refused them the right to perform operas on the grounds that the genre was "not to the taste of the common man." He himself appointed Pietro Metastasio Court Poet, and composers such as Bononcini, Porsile, Conti, Caldara, and Fux were also now working for the city of Vienna. Outstanding among the operas produced at the time were Fux's *Angelica Vincitrice* in 1716, which proved horrendously expensive to put on (one chronichler mentions a figure of 300,000 gulden), *Costanza e Fortezza* by the same composer in 1723 for the coronation of the emperor in Prague and a festival of opera in 1724, which included Caldara's *Palladio* and Conti's *Grossmogul*.

Members of the imperial household had taken part in operas and ballets in Vienna from the very start. Two of the emperor's daughters as well as Prince Pio of Savoy and Count Ferdinand Harrach are said to have sung in Caldara's *Euristheno*, while the offspring of the Lobkowitz, Piccolomini, Herberstein, Hardegg, Truchsess, and Trautmansdorff families played in the orchestra.

10, 11 Scenery designs by Giuseppe and Ferdinando Galli-Bibiena for the opera *Angelica Vincitrice* by Johann Josef Fux, which was staged in the Favorita in 1716. The magnificent proscenium of the *Festa Teatrale* (top) and the arrival on one of the islands populated by wild animals (bottom).

Veduta del PROSCENIO nella Festa Teatrale intitolata ANGELICA VINCITRICE di ALCINA.

ISOLE orride e disabitate occupate da diversi Mostri per incanto di ALCINA.

12 The theater next to the Kärntnertor, the first home of Vienna's own Volkstheater, built during the reign of Joseph I and completed in 1709 (architect: Antonio Beduzzi). The projecting porch was later added when the house was enlarged in 1762–63.

13 The old Burgtheater on Michaelerplatz. Christoph Willibald Gluck's *Semiramis* was performed here in 1748 on Maria Theresa's birthday. His great reforming operas *Orfeo ed Euridice, Alceste,* and *Paride ed Helena* were also premiered in the old Burgtheater.

14   After about 1705 Josef Anton Stranitzky from Hanswurst performed at the "Comedy Hut" in the Neuer Markt playing a harlequin. In 1710 he took a lease on the Kärntnertor theater, performing with his troop on this, the city's first stage to the delight of middle-class audiences.

Viel Orth hab ich durchreist zu Wien will ich verbleiben
Ich bitt mein Herr laßt mich in eüre Bande schreib

15 Performance of the opera *Costanza e Fortezza* by Johann Josef Fux to celebrate the coronation of Karl VI in Prague (1723). The sets were again by Guiseppe Galli-Bibiena.

Maria Theresa grew up in this musical atmosphere. Herself a talented singer as a girl, she introduced radical reforms to Viennese theater from 1740. The courtly pomp of baroque opera came to an end in the Age of Enlightenment and also as a result of political and financial difficulties. Smaller stages and more intimate styles of production were, in any case, more suited to the rococo period. Other changes in court life saw the cultural influences of Italy curbed and French became the spoken language. The great Court Theater in the palace was replaced temporarily in 1747, and permanently in 1752 by the present ballrooms, which were used for dances at first and later also for concerts.

The most important reform under Maria Theresa, who recognized the love of the Viennese for show and theater (she once sighed, "There has to be spectacle.") was opening theaters to the common people. The original leaseholder of the Kärntnertor theater, Franz Selliers, was given permission to stage operas for the court, and then for the paying public. In addition to the Kärntnertor theater, the empress in 1742 also let the shrewd Selliers have the unused court ballroom that adjoined the Hofburg, hence its name "Burgtheater." So now Vienna found itself with two prestigious court theaters where henceforth operas, ballets, and plays were performed. Often there was rivalry between the old Burgtheater in Michaelerplatz and the Kärntnertor theater.

Christoph Willibald Gluck's *Semiramis* was performed on 14 May 1748, the empress's birthday, on the reopening of the magnificent, newly restored Burgtheater. Shortly afterwards Count Esterhazy (known as "Quinquin") was given supreme imperial and royal authority by Maria Theresa for all court opera and theater in Vienna. He named Count Durazzo director of the Burgtheater, and in 1752 Durazzo engaged a Parisian theater company, which introduced the Viennese to French *opéra comique* and vaudeville among other things.

16 A performance in the theater at the palace of Schönbrunn to mark Joseph II's marriage to Isabella of Parma in 1760. The theater was built to the plans of Nikolaus Franz Leonhard von Picassi and opened in 1747, later being decorated in the style of the late rococo in 1766–67 by Johann Ferdinand Hötendorf von Hohenberg.

Gluck eventually established a new style at the Burgtheater with his ballet *Don Juan* (1761) and his reforming Viennese operas *Orfeo ed Euridice* (1762), *Alceste* (1767), and *Paride ed Helene* (1770). The librettist and producer Ranieri Calzabigi, the *maîtres de ballet* Gaspar Angiolini and Jean Noverre, and the designer Giovanni Maria Quaglio played a decisive role in this theatrical revolution.

In spite of such artistic peaks there were frequent financial crises at the Burgtheater. As a consequence, Maria Theresa had to allow Count Durazzo to introduce the *Pharaospiel* (a type of gambling) to the Burgtheater. Some rooms in the playhouse were especially set up for this game, to which only the nobility and those who were "acceptable at court" were admitted. Half the proceeds went into the theater's coffers (in 1762 this was said to have been 110,000 gulden), while the other half was donated to Vienna's poor.

The Kärntnertor theater had burnt down in 1761, but only two years later it was rebuilt–larger and more beautiful this time. On the death of her husband François in 1765, Maria Theresa ordered a period of court mourning and closed theaters, but within six months the Viennese nobility began protesting. Subscription lists were circulated and those who signed pledged to contribute an annual sum of one hundred ducats to maintain the two court theaters. The empress reluctantly gave in, and in autumn 1766 the Kärntnertor theater resumed productions, followed shortly afterwards by the Burgtheater. Both theaters were now under the direction of the *maître de ballet* Franz Hilverding van Wewen for ballets, plays, and operas.

In 1763 Florian Gassmann became Kapellmeister (a prestigious post) at the Kärntnertor theater, where his operas were shown in repertory with those of colleagues of his such as Galuppi, Piccini, and Hasse. Gassmann was the favorite composer of Maria Theresa and her son Joseph II, and in 1765 he brought his fifteen-year old pupil Antonio Salieri to Vienna, where the latter became the artistic director of the Kärntnertor theater in 1780.

17–19 Wolfgang Amadeus Mozart's operas were also staged in the old Burgtheater: *Die Entführung aus dem Serail* in 1782, *The Marriage of Figaro* in 1786, and *Cosi fan tutte* in 1790. *Don Giovanni* had its world premiere in Prague and was seen later in the Burgtheater in May 1788.

20–23 Costume designs (Papageno, the Queen of the Night) and contemporary engravings showing scenes from Mozart's *The Magic Flute*, which was first seen in the suburbs of Vienna in 1791 in Emanuel Schikaneder's public Theater auf der Wieden. Schikaneder sang and played the role of Papageno himself. In 1801 he took over the running of the newly built Theater an der Wien, where Mozart's successful operas were soon put on again. (The two engravings are by the Schaffer brothers).

The Viennese were introduced to Lessing's *Emilia Galotti* at the Burgtheater in 1772. In 1776 Joseph II decided to found a national theater for German language productions as a counterpart to the German national *Singspiel*—a form of opera, usually comic, in which musical numbers are separated by dialogue. This initiative came only two years after a particularly successful attempt at the genre with Ignaz Umlauf's *Die Bergknappen* had been performed at the Burgtheater. Joseph II installed a German opera company with a thirty-seven-piece orchestra and a choir at the Burgtheater, in deliberate opposition to Salieri's Italian opera company at the Kärntnertor theater.

In the first year about fourteen *Singspiele* were performed at the Burgtheater, the works of Umlauf, Gassmann, Aspelmayer, Gluck, and others, including German translations of French comic operas by composers such as Greftry, Guglielmi, Gossec, and Philidor. It is worth noting in passing Maria Theresa's famous allusion to Joseph Haydn: "If I want to hear a good opera, I go to Esterháza" (the summer residence of Count Esterházy, Haydn's patron). The empress was forever disparaging Viennese theater.

The German national *Singspiel* found its apotheosis in Wolfgang Amadeus Mozart, who came to Vienna in 1781. His *Entführung aus dem Serail* (first performed at the Burgtheater in 1782, and joyfully received by the Viennese) certainly provoked the envy of his rivals. Soon afterwards, in 1783, Salieri and his Italian opera company from the Kärntnertor theater were given permission by the emperor to appear at the Burgtheater too. Mozart was hardpressed from now on and had to struggle against his rival Salieri, who was to dominate musical life in Vienna for thirty years, in order to have his operas—*The Marriage of Figaro* (1786), *Don Giovanni* (1788, following its premiere in Prague), and *Cosi fan tutte* (1790)—performed at the Burgtheater. Salieri's *Axur* (original French title was *Tarare*, libretto by Beaumarchais and translated into Italian by Lorenzo da Ponte) was said to have been one of Joseph II's favorite operas and, along with

his *Les Danaïdes*, remained in the Viennese theatrical repertoire for many years.

In Vienna many composers such as Paisiello, Sarti, Martin, Cimarosa, Dittersdorf, Süssmayer, as well as others, were achieving great success with their work, which were frequently being performed. Mozart, however, had to take *The Magic Flute* to the suburbs—to Emanuel Schikaneder's public Theater auf der Weiden,

24 Prison scene from Beethoven's *Fidelio* at the Court Theater, taken from a book published in 1815.

where popular support for opera had been providing great competition to court theater for some time.

The Leopoldstädter theater (which opened in 1781) had already attracted the public in the suburbs with Wenzel Müller's musical farces and also with *Singspiele* by Dittersdorf, Gassmann, and Martin. The Theater auf der Weiden was built in 1787, two years before Schikaneder took over as director. *The Magic Flute* played there· two hundred twenty-three times before the theater closed on 12 June 1801. In 1792 Schikaneder also produced Mozart's *Don Giovanni* there in German.

Initially Joseph II's death in 1790 led to a decline in both court theaters, for Leopold II showed little interest in running and maintaining them. Although Mozart had composed *La Clemenza di Tito* for his coronation in Prague in 1791, it was not heard at the Burgtheater until four years later. Under Francis I the theaters were leased by the banker Baron Braun in 1794. The court withdrew gradually, leaving the patronage of the fine arts to the nobility and also, before long, to the bourgeoisie. (Prince Lobkowitz had already offered such patronage to Gluck, and Prince Auersperg had had Mozart's *Idomeneo* played in concerto form in his palace in Vienna.)

Salieri continued to choose the programs at the Kärntnertor theater, where his own operas and those of Weigl, Schenk, Gryowetz, Winter, and others were performed in addition to works by Gluck, Umlauf, Süssmayer, and others previously mentioned. Costs were high and artistic returns were low. As a result, when the Theater an der Wien opened in 1801 with Schikaneder as director, it became the Kärntnertor theater's fiercest rival. Schikaneder overextended himself financially, however, so in 1804 Baron Braun, the leaseholder of the Court Theater, also bought the Theater an der Wien. This now became the sister stage of the Kärntnertor theater·sharing singers and, in turn, new operas.

Luigi Cherubini's *Les deux journées* had already been performed in the Theater an der Wien in 1802, and in 1805 he presented *Finisca* at the Kärntnertor theater. The same year witnessed the premiere of Beethoven's *Fidelio*, which played, unsuccessfully, to a half-empty theater at the Theater an der Wien. These were sad times, for Napoleon's troops had just occupied the city. Baron Braun even contemplated closing down the theaters, though orders from the emperor prevented him from doing so.

Kavaliersgesellschaft, consisting of eight members of the high nobility, took over the running of the Court Theater in 1807. Prince Lobkowitz was responsible for opera, Count Palffy for plays. Reorganization took effect on 1 October 1810; from then on the Burgtheater was to be the home of German plays exclusively, and the Kärntnertor theater of opera and ballet.

Gasparo Spontini's *Vestale* (1810) was produced shortly before the national bankruptcy in 1811, and in 1812 Vienna heard his *Fernand Cortez* for the first time. In 1813 the premiere of Carl Maria von Weber's *Abu Hassan* took place at the Theater an der Wien. The Kärntnertor theater (now known as the *Hofoper*, or Court Opera) achieved a notable triumph for German opera in 1814 with the third version of Beethoven's *Fidelio*. In the same year Count Palffy took charge of Vienna's three great theaters; he appointed the first German romantic composer in Vienna in the person of Louis Spohr, who soon proved to be stiff competition for the "Italians" at the Theater an der Wien.

In 1816, when the impresario Domenico Barbaja's company made a guest appearance at the Kärntnertor theater, Vienna caught Rossini fever. (Barbaja's leading soprano was Isabella Colbran, who later became Gioacchino Rossini's wife.) Beginning with *Adelina*, then *Tancredi, Otello, The Barber of Seville*, and *La Gazza Ladra*, Rossini's operas were received with great enthusiasm by audiences, paving the way for Barbaja to lease the Court Opera for eight years in 1821. An Italian age had been ushered in, and was to last until the revolution of 1848. The philosopher Hegel wrote to his wife: "As long as I have money to see Italian opera, I am not leaving Vienna."

It was a difficult time for devotees of German opera. In 1817, nevertheless,

25, 26 The Viennese first heard Carl Maria von Weber's *Freischutz* at the Kärntertor theater in 1821 and loved it. He was commissioned by the same theater and composed *Euryanthe*; although he conducted the work himself, it only enjoyed moderate success. Wilhelmine Schröder-Devrient sang the title role.

27 Richard Wagner's *Tann-häuser* had its premiere on 28 August 1857 before a sold-out house at the Thalia theater in Neulerchenfeld. Of wooden construction, the theater was said to seat 3,000 people. The work was such a success that eight more performances were given there and almost thirty at the Josefstadt theater.

Kaiserl. Königl. privilegiertes

Thalia-Theater

der Direction des Eigenthümers — Johann Hoffm.

Heute Freitag den 28. August 1857.
Zum ersten Male:

Tannhäuser
und
Der Sängerkrieg auf Wartburg.

Große romantische Oper in 3 Akten. Text und Musik von Richard Wagner.
Gruppirungen vom Balletmeister Stöckl.
Die neuen Dekorationen „Die Venusgrotte im Hörselberge,"
„Thal mit Ansicht der Wartburg," „Saal auf Wartburg"
sind vom Dekorateur Kautzky.
Die gänzlich neue Garderobe nach den Original-Figurinen des k. Hoftheaters in
Dresden, angefertigt vom Obergarderobier Krampa.
In Szene gesetzt vom Oberregisseur Forst.

Personen:

Heemann, Landgraf von Thüringen	Hr. Reichmann	Elisabeth, Richte des Landgrafen	Frl. Friedlowsky
Tannhäuser,	Hr. Kaminski	Venus	Frl. Lieven
Wolfram vom Eschinbach,	Hr. Eghart	Ein junger Hirt	Frl. Altani
Walter von der Vogelweide,	Hr. Patzelt	Erster	Frl. Seemann
Biterolf,	Hr. Abich	Zweiter, Edelknabe	Frl. Michel
Heinrich, der Schreiber,	Hr. Groß	Dritter	Frl. Oberhuber
Reinar von Zweter,	Hr. Nadler	Vierter	Frl. Kohler

Fürsten, Grafen und Edelleute. Thüringische Ritter und Edelfrauen. Aeltere und jüngere Pilger. Pagen. Sirenen.
Nymphen. Bachantinnen. — Thüringen. Wartburg. Zu Anfang des 13. Jahrhunderts.

Preise der Plätze in C.-M.:

Eine Loge für 6 Personen	6 fl.	— kr.	Ein Sperrsitz in der 2. Gallerie		40 kr.
Ein Sitz in der Fremdenloge	2	—	Eintritt in das Parterre		40
Ein Balconsitz im 1. Stock	1	20	Eintritt in die 1. Gallerie		40
Ein Sperrsitz im Parterre	1	—	Eintritt in die 2. Gallerie		24
Ein Sperrsitz in der 1. Gallerie	1	—	Eintritt in die 3. Gallerie		10

Die vorgemerkten Logen und Sperrsitze sind in den bekannten Verkaufslokalen
gefälligst abzuholen.

Die Textbücher sind an der Kassa das Stück zu 20 kr. CM. zu haben.

Anfang um 6 Uhr.
Logen und Sperrsitze sind bereits vergriffen.

Der Clavier-Auszug mit Text dieser Oper, sowie die einzelnen Gesangsstücke daraus, dann die
Ouverture für Pianoforte zu 2 und 4 Händen, Potpourris, Fantaisie's, sind zu haben in der
k. k. Hof-Musikalien-Handlung des Herrn Carl Haslinger.

28 The Theater an der Wien during an opera performance in 1832. The copperplate engraving depicts an overflowing theater—the audience is tightly packed down the sides as far as the orchestra and is even standing in the center aisle. Vienna during the craze for Rossini?

Spohr's *Faust* was performed successfully at the Theater an der Wien, and in 1821 Carl Maria von Weber's *Freischütz* delighted audiences in the Kärntnertor theater. Barbaja responded shrewdly: he appointed Konradin Kreutzer, a German devotee, to the position of Kapellmeister at his theater and commissioned a composition from Weber. In spite of this, however, *Euryanthe* did not enjoy much success when first performed at the Kärntnertor theater in 1823.

Almost all Rossini's operas were produced at the Court Opera under subsequent leaseholders and directors until 1848. Vincenzo Bellini's success in Vienna, by contrast, was based on relatively few works: *I Montecchi e i Capuletti* (1832), *Norma* (1833), and *La Somnambula* (1835) were played the most often. Gaetano Donizetti, who, like Rossini and Weber, came to Vienna and even became Kapellmeister to the court—against the wishes of Robert Schumann—was repre-

sented by *Linda di Chamonix* (1842 in Vienna), *Don Pasquale* (1843), *Maria di Rohan* (1843), and many other operas. A total of no less than thirty-two of his works are said to have been staged in only ten years! Giuseppe Verdi also enjoyed early success at the Kärntnertor theater, with *Nabucco* (1843), *Ernani* (1844), *I Due Foscari* (1845), and *I Lombardi* (1846).

Apart from the Italians Cherubini and Spontini, the musical program during these years was dominated by Frenchmen: Mehul (*Josef* and *Uthal*), Boieldieu (*Jean de Paris, La Dame Blanche*), Auber (*La Muette de Portici*), Herold (*Zampa*), Halévy (*La Juive*), and Meyerbeer (*Les Huguenots*).

In addition to Weber, German opera was represented by Louis Spohr (*Zemire und Azor, Jessonda*), Peter Lindpaintner (*Der Vampyr* in 1829, *Die Genueserin* in Vienna in 1839), Konradin Kreuzer (*Das Nachtlager von Granada* and *Melusine*),

29 Costume designs by Girolamo Francescini for *Lohengrin* in a production seen by Wagner in Vienna in 1861. For a while the Kärntertor theater was the leading theater in Europe for Wagner's operas, staging *Lohengrin* in 1858, *Tannhäuser* in 1859, and *Der fliegende Holländer* in 1860. Wagner was delighted by the productions, at which he was present.

Heinrich Marschner *(Hans Heiling)*, Albert Lortzing *(Zar und Zimmermann, Der Waffenschmied, Undine)*, and Friedrich von Flotow *(Allessandro Stradella* and *Martha*, in 1847). Otto Nicolai, Albert Lortzing, and Friedrich von Flotow came to Vienna as Kapellmeister and settled there for a time. Schubert's attempts at opera–*Zauberharfe* (1820) and *Rosamunde* (1823)–failed at the Theater an der Wien, whereas Gluck and Mozart remained in the repertoire at the Kärntnertor theater.

Mention should also be made here of the Josefstädter theater, which staged operas from 1825. Konradin Kreutzer worked there before going to the Court Opera, and Weber's *Oberon* and Auber's *La Muette de Portici* had their Viennese premiere in this theater. Adolphe Adam's *Le Postillon de Longjumeau* was a hit at the box office. This period spawned numerous operatic parodies in the theaters in Vienna's suburbs, such as *The Barber of Severing*, *Othellerl*, and *The Postillion of Enzersdorf Barn*, which were greeted with gales of laughter by audiences.

The 1848 revolution brought profound changes that affected even the Court Opera. A rekindled sense of national pride brought Mozart's operas new glory, and works by foreign composers were presented in German for a time. This xenophobia was not to last long, however. In 1850 Viennese audiences were introduced to Meyerbeer's *Le Prophète*, Otto Nicolai's *The Merry Wives of Windsor*, and Verdi's *Rigoletto* in 1852, *Il Trovatore* in 1854, and *La Traviata* in 1856.

The great artistic revolution following the upheavals of March 1848 brought Richard Wagner's operas to Vienna. His *Tannhäuser* was unusual in that it opened in the new Thalia-Theater and then in the Josefstädter theater, before the Court Opera became, for a time, Wagner's premiere theater in Europe. *Lohengrin* opened there in the autumn of 1859, followed in November of the same year by

Tannhäuser and a year later *Der fliegende Holländer*.

In 1861 a new director, Matteo Salvi, took charge of the Court Opera. In 1862 he presented Charles Gounod's *Faust* and in 1864 Verdi's *Un Ballo in Maschera*. There were no further premieres for almost two years. The war in 1866 took its toll, as did the construction of the new opera house on the Ring, which made rapid progress after work had started on 16 December 1861.

On 1 July 1867 the last director of the Kärntnertor theater, Franz von Dingelstedt, took up his post. A year later he presented *Roméo et Juliette*, again by Gounod, and Ambroise Thomas's *Mignon*. He then had to prepare for the opening of the new opera house and plan the program for his first season. Mozart's *Don Giovanni* inaugurated a new era of Viennese opera at the theater on the Ring on May 1869. Only a year later on 17 April 1870, after a performance of Rossini's *William Tell*, the Kärntnertor theater closed its doors forever.

30 Opera parodies in Vienna's suburban theaters: *Othellerl, der Mohr von Wien* by Ferdinand Kringsteiner was one of the farces that amused the Viennese.

THE ARCHITECTURE OF THE VIENNA OPERA HOUSE

Wilhelm Holzbauer

When the Vienna State Opera, the former royal and imperial Court Opera, suffered large-scale destruction during the last days of the war in March 1945, the damaged edifice (like St Stephan's Cathedral) was to a very great extent a symbol of Vienna and the Viennese way of life. When the opera house opened on 25 May 1869, however, the building's subsequent popularity seemed hard to imagine. The story of the tragic fate of the architects–one committed suicide as a result of the bitter criticism of the building and the other died a few weeks later, grieving for the loss of his friend and colleague–is still used by many architects to justify buildings which are heavily criticized by the public. The facts can admittedly be given a different interpretation, since at the time of his death Eduard van der Nüll had long been suffering from severe depression and August Siccard von Siccardsburg had been ill and bed-ridden for some while. It is surely also a legend that criticism of the building reached such a level that the two men were even pursued by children shouting "Siccardsburg and Van der Nüll have got no style, have got no style." Nor is it easy to establish whether there is any truth in the story that Emperor Franz Joseph's remark that the building looked "as if it was about to sink into the ground" was the cause of Nüll's suicide. The story continues that the emperor was so shaken by this that from then on he could only bring himself to make his well-known comment: "It was very nice, I enjoyed it very much."

It is certainly true, nevertheless, that both during construction and following completion criticism was leveled at the building from many quarters, but disapproval almost always centered on the opera house's height proportions and the way it failed to fit in with the city's architectural style. When Emperor Franz Josef talked of "sinking in," he was either repeating a widely held opinion, or he had expressed it intuitively. The new opera house may have been labeled an architectural disaster, but this rebuke was never extended to the building's interior, which was described almost unanimously as impressive, magnificent, and a great success.

When the Vienna Opera was designed, the form of construction the complex took was rooted in the traditional style of Italian theater. By that time it no longer made functional sense to incorporate the auditorium and the stage under one great roof. Such a design made it inevitable that the framework of the stage had to be restricted and that a huge empty space was left under the roof in the auditorium.

It was natural, perhaps, for architects to model their overall concept on the Italian basilica form. In fact the Fenice in Venice and in particular, of course, the Scala in Milan formed the basis of competition when it was announced. The architectural fraternity, however, drew their inspiration from the Basilica Paladiana in Vicenza. Since its construction in 1580 this building had been the automatic blueprint for numerous projects, espe-

31, 32 The two architects Eduard van der Null (left) and August Siccard von Siccardsburg (right) did not live to see the glamorous opening of their theater: Van der Null hanged himself on 3 April 1868 and Siccardsburg died on 11 June in the same year following an operation.

cially those with an official function. It is indeed remarkable when one witnesses the similarity of the proportions of the facades, the building methods used, the design of the plinth level, the main level, the broken main cornice in the form of a balustrade and the structure above, with the great, long, rounded roof. This likeness is even stronger when sections of the opera house are glimpsed in isolation, from Mahlerstrasse for example, rather than as a whole. The impression given by the ground-level colonnades (which ring almost the whole of the opera house) is that they are sinking into the earth. It was this effect that received so much attention and adverse criticism at the time, and which has an almost exact counterpart in Palladio's building in Vicenza. The State Opera's resemblance to this great prototype is reflected most clearly in the open balconies on the Ringstrasse.

There is no question about it–Palladio's work has had a greater influence over the

centuries than any other architect before or since. Even so, the second half of the nineteenth century saw no more radical a reinterpretation of Palladio's precepts than in the case of the Vienna State Opera.

Architectural forms were already subject in large measure to the influence of Italy; the same was true for stage and theater design. With their horseshoe-shaped auditoriums and wide, open stage areas, the early theater designs of Palladio, Scamozzi, and Serlio were a reinterpretation of the theater of ancient Rome. Palladio's Teatro Olimpico in Vicenza is of particular significance as the first theater with an interior which provided permanent seating and a permanent stage in the ancient tradition. It was the Galli-Bibienas family above all who had most impact on the development of theatrical architecture.

The Galli-Bibienas were unique in the field of theater and set design. No other family in the history of Western art can

33 The Vienna Court Opera in 1869. The building was severely criticized by the Viennese, who considered it an architectural disaster.

34 Franz Alt: the Ringstrasse near the opera house (a chromo-lithograph from the 1870s). The architects agreed that their theater's location enclosed by streets and lacking a square in front was a mistake.

35, 36 The Vienna Opera's architects based their design on the Basilica Palladiana in Vicenza (top, seen from the Piazza dei Signori). Bottom: the Vienna Opera with its open balcony overlooking the Ringstrasse.

match their creative power. From 1680 to 1780 eight members and three generations of the Galli-Bibiena family brought Italy's achievments in the field of stage engineering, theater design, and decoration to the attention of the whole of Europe, from Naples to Stockholm, Barcelona to St Petersburg. Their influence affected not only the development of theater at court, but also laid the foundations for the development of the theater as we know it today. Francesco Galli-Bibiena was commissioned by Emperor Leopold I in 1700 to reconstruct the opera theater in the Hofburg, and Antonio Galli-Bibiena gave the great ballroom its final shape, which was essentially as it remains today. The Teatro Communale, which he built in Bologna in about 1775, already had all the essential elements which were to feature in the great opera houses one hundred years later: four tiers of boxes arranged in the shape of a horseshoe, a vaulted ceiling that was almost if not completely flat in the middle and joined the exterior walls, and the inevitable sumptuous decor.

The Teatro Farnese in Parma, the first theater in the world with a proscenium stage, had seating in the form of a horseshoe and an elaborate false wall behind the boxes, even though for structural reasons its basic shape was rectangular. Although this theater offered imperfect visibility and acoustics, it had considerable influence for quite some time. It became the forerunner of a trend towards breaking up the stadium style of seating and replacing it with a flat wall with several tiers of boxes and barely raked stalls. This design was first seen at the Scala Milan—it was both the culmination of Italy's two-hundred-year tradition of baroque theater and a sudden foretaste of the pattern which the theater was to take throughout the nineteenth century. The Scala is Grand Opera par excellence, in all its positive and negative aspects.

A performance at the Scala can be a total theatrical experience for the eyes and ears, but it must be said that little more than half of the audience is able to derive full enjoyment from the opera because of the position from which they see and hear. The bad visibility from the side boxes in horseshoe-shaped auditoriums was admittedly improved in later theaters, but the difficulty was never to be completely overcome.

Problems associated with viewing eventually led to attempts to move away from the constricting influence of Italian theater architecture. The scene of this movement was Germany, where attention concentrated on the search for technological solutions to problems of visibility and in particular to seating arrangements.

These efforts towards reform—which also brought about a new relationship between the proscenium stage, the orchestra pit, and the auditorium—came slowly and only after several solutions had failed. The first really new theater was the Bayreuth Festival Theater, which opened in 1876 and was inspired by just one man: Richard Wagner.

Almost all the world's major opera houses originated in the second half of

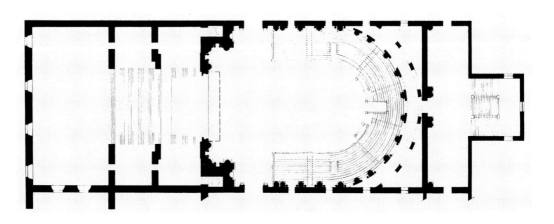

37   The Teatro Farnese in Parma, built in 1618, was the first proscenium theater to be rectangular in form, although the seats were raked and arranged in a horseshoe shape.

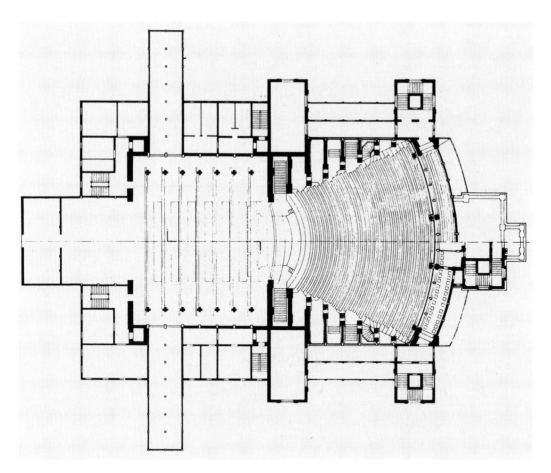

38 The Bayreuth Festival Theater of 1876 introduced a completely new concept to theater. A wedge-shaped auditorium, a seating plan in the form of an amphitheater and the orchestra out of the audience's sight—all this improved the view of the stage.

the nineteenth century. It is interesting how the principles that had guided Italian theatrical traditions were developed at more or less the same time—in the opera houses of Paris and Vienna, for example. In a parallel trend, however, theaters were being built which arose out of attempts at reform that were initiated by Carl Ferdinand Langhans, Friedrich Gilly, and Karl Friedrich Schinkel and taken up by Wagner and Semper.

This dual evolution is embodied most clearly in the person of Gottfried Semper, one of the most creative and brilliant architects of the nineteenth century. The conflict was not simply a question of architecture and art; it was just as much a reflection of the new social pressures which were being applied by an emerging and independant bourgeoisie, who did not see the theater simply as a social convention. To them it was no less important than an educational institution, and it was largely for this reason that thea-

ters were built in the latter part of the nineteenth century.

Semper made an extraordinary contribution to the development of a theater for the middle classes, even though his most radical and far-reaching plans in this field got no further than the drawing board. The designs he created which were actually realized all relied heavily on the system of tiered boxes seen in baroque auditoriums. In his design for a festival theater in Munich, which was built in 1864–67 (the same time as the opera house in Vienna), Semper tried one last time to realize his bourgeois concept of a classical theater. This he achieved, but there is little doubt that the last thing he had in mind was a return to the style of the great festival theaters of ancient Greece.

Richard Wagner wanted the seating in his theater to be arranged in the form of an amphitheater (his intention was "the greatest possible separation between the

39 The Vienna Court Opera in a drawing by Eduard van der Null. Architecturally, the building remained true to tradition and its Italian models.

ideal world on the stage and the real world as represented by the audience") and for optical and acoustic reasons he wanted the orchestra to be "invisible."

Not even Semper was able to resolve fully the functional contradiction between a wide, amphitheater-style auditorium and a proscenium stage.

It was only when the Bayreuth Festival Theater was built in 1876 (a mere seven years after the Vienna Opera opened) that a compromise was provided in the form of a wedge-shaped auditorium. Wagner had enlisted another architect, Otto Bruckwald, to build the theater, but it may have been some small consolation for Semper that Wagner wrote to him: "Clumsy and unsophisticated though it is, the theater is designed to your plans."

When the competition was held to design the Vienna Opera there was no hint of this kind of ideological and, at that time, *avant-garde* debate over a new form of contemporary theater. The same could be said of the competition to design the opera house in Paris. It was the emperor's wish that public competitions should be held for all the state buildings that were planned as part of the rebuilding of the city following the razing of its fortifications. It is difficult to argue that progress has been made when one considers how commissions are sometimes awarded today. The committee appointed by the emperor to organize the competition for the opera house respected his desire for an open, international contest. A decree to this effect was issued on 19 February 1860. By 10 January 1861, the last day for submitting entries, thirty-five projects had been received. By comparison, when a competition to design the new Opéra de la Bastille in Paris was held in 1984 seven hundred forty-three projects were submitted.

It is staggering when one compares this with the time allowed for the international competition for the nineteenth century opera house in Paris. The Paris competition was announced on 29 December 1860 and anyone could take part, irrespective of profession or nationality. The deadline was set for 31 January 1861, so there was only one month to work on the plans. Furthermore, the announcement only called for one idea, which was to be presented in three drawings—a ground plan, a side elevation, and a front elevation. The number of entrants for the Paris competition was also correspondingly higher, with one hundred seventy-one projects being submitted.

For both Paris and Vienna the competition was part of a construction program that would lead to the fulfillment of long-cherished wishes. It should be seen first and foremost in the context of both cities' plans to open out and enlarge their streets. In Vienna, particularly, the building of a new opera house was part of such a program, and the site chosen was a sloping area where a new opera house had been envisaged ever since the end of the Napoleonic wars in the 1820s. These plans had always been a part of changes which were to affect the city's fortifications.

The choice of a site for the new opera house had always centered on the area around the Kärntnertor. In 1844 Emperor Ferdinand decided that an enlargement at the Kärntnertor should be limited to the site allocated for the new opera house. But changes brought about in 1848, the year of the revolution, meant that the military authorities had the final word in all building matters; the fortifications and the slope in front of them were held onto even more fiercely than before, though now they were to be protected against the enemy within and "revolutionaries" rather than from external forces. The pressure from the inner city to break out of its confining walls became so urgent a problem, however, that even the military could not ignore the call to expand.

A decree issued by Emperor Franz Joseph now approved, in principle, the moving of the garrison on the slope in front of the fortifications, the construction of a new city gate, and an opera house. Paul Sprenger was made responsible for planning. Private areas were subject to compulsory purchase (as they were later when the Ringstrasse was constructed) and the proceeds from their sale offset the costs incurred by the work.

While this was going on, attempts were being made to join the Court Opera to the Hofburg, the imperial palace. In 1851 the director of the theater, Bartolomeo Merelli, issued a memorandum suggesting that the opera house on its site by the fortifications should be linked to the Hofburg by bridges. In line with the architectural style of the Hofburg, the lay-out was to be modeled on the three most well-known Italian opera houses of the time—the Scala in Milan, the Teatro San Carlo in Naples, and the Fenice in Venice. There are plans in existence which show the Court Opera alongside the gardens of the Hofburg. In 1857 it was even reported that the new building had definitely been decided upon. This coincided, however, with another announcement—the famous handwritten imperial notice of 20 December 1857, which ordered the complete abandonment of the fortifications and the development of the slope.

In the competition to design the new enlarged city center of Vienna, which was to start after 30 January 1858, one item already on the agenda was the site of the new opera house: an "area of land of some 2000 to 2400 square fathoms." The text of the competition did specify, however, that the area between the palace and the court stables should not be built on, an architectural requirement laid down by the military authorities. This was not really a curtailment as most competitors did not favor the idea of joining the new court opera house to the Hofburg.

Until the competition to design the opera house was actually announced in July 1860, the question of where it was to be built was discussed by a whole series of committees: the wishes of the First Court Chamberlain's office, of the body in charge of the enlarging of the city, and of court circles were all made known. The new building was finally accorded the site on which it stands today, and it was left up to the competition entrants whether they designed the facade to overlook either Kärntnerstrasse or the Ring.

40   A design by Bartolomeo
Morelli for an opera house in
front of the "Leopoldnischer
Trakt," a wing of the imperial
palace, the Hofburg.

Although the projects were entered for the competition with code names to preserve anonymity, an unofficial list of competitors became available. It does not make particularly impressive reading. Only a few architects of any standing were represented, such as Edward Barry and Hector Horeau from London, and above all Carl Hasenauer, who won third prize and whose design could have been the only feasible alternative to the winning entry by van der Nüll and Siccardsburg.

Between these two projects came the winners of the second prize, a pair of architects from Dresden called Giese and Schreiber. Their success may be due to the kind of mysterious mechanism which we still see operating today among juries when two strong factions, having failed to agree, decide to award a prize to one project that is still acceptable to both parties.

Charming though it was in its architectural conception, Hasenauer's scheme had serious functional faults. The stage would have been some eight meters above street level, and given that the already existing city moat was twelve meters deep, the basement would also have had to be the same depth. It could not have been too difficult a decision to accept the recommendation of the opera house's building committee to entrust the commission to van der Nüll and Siccardsburg. After all, the two architects were professors at the Academy of Fine Art and had been responsible for some notable buildings, for example the Altlerchenfeld church, the Carltheater and, in particular, the arsenal. Hasenauer, a pupil of theirs, was in the early stages of his career, and in partnership with Gottfried Semper, he was later given the responsibility of building Vienna's second court theater, the Burgtheater.

It is inevitable that entries for competitions, because they are submitted anonymously and without consultation with the commissioning party, are often subject to considerable amendment as work progresses. When a commission has been secured, plans can be contemplated (and this is known or assumed) that would not have met with the approval of the jury in the context of a competition. But in this case the two architects spent only a few more weeks developing their competition entry into a final blueprint that could then be built. In so doing they managed, without departing from the framework that had been laid down, to simplify the structure radically, to improve architectural harmony, and above all to respond in a new way to the environment.

The overall composition of the building was now better defined, its cubic structure more clearly delineated. In the competition version the whole length of the facade had hardly been set back from the Ring at all and the box motif looked as if it had been "stuck on" to the front of the building. Now, by contrast, the balcony became an independant architectural element, held by nothing more than narrow structures set into the building. It was becoming clear that the intention was to leave an area at the corners free, creating open squares there. The reason for this was undoubtedly that the architects felt it would be unsatisfactory from a planning point of view if a building as important as the Viennese opera house were shut inside a block of closely packed streets. When one thinks of the grandiose symmetry displayed by the Paris Opera, which was built at about the same time, it is difficult not to feel that it is a shame that the Viennese opera house cannot be seen from a great perspective. The theater gives the slight impression that it is at an angle, leaving a relatively large open area and a sense of rather strained compromise. Hans Christoph Hoffmann pointed out the similarity of its proportions to Theophil Hansen's imperial council building (the present-day parliament) "whose disparate components hold together in superficial, but not in architectural terms." He also referred to Karl Friedrich Schinkel's Berlin theater, which the Viennese architects "had met on their travels while studying, but did not appreciate that there were ideas in its design which they could incorporate in the freestanding Viennese opera house until they toured with members of the Court Opera committee."

The rigid, rather modern effect of the proportions of this block create difficulties for the eye—it stands perpendicular to the Ring but is separated from it by two adjacent stretches of road. There is insufficient distance between the facade facing the Ring and the Heinrichshof—a piece of speculative real estate—for the structure to be appreciated. The most exalted architectural works were mixed with purely speculative buildings paid for by private capital, which was why it was quite possible for the huge Heinrichshof to be constructed at all.

When the architecture of the State Opera is judged today by visitors or onlookers they should bear in mind that the destruction that took place in 1945 represents a decisive break. The opera house was nothing more than a building site. Its rebuilding in the early 1950s was seen as the greatest of all the symbols of postwar regeneration. It is difficult to imagine today that at the time an exact reconstruction of the opera house (or, as it turned out, the broadly similar reconstruction) was not considered by young, budding architects to be by any means a foregone conclusion.

When I arrived in Vienna from Salzburg, the competition to design the new opera house had already been held and the project had been put in the hands of Erich Boltenstern. He had to put up with a lot of complaints and criticism, and I can remember one emotional discussion taking place in public in which (admittedly in another connection) the elderly Josef Hoffmann exhorted young architects to shed the burden of the past and give their support to the present. Erich Boltenstern, who was clearly annoyed and deeply hurt, gave a memorable reply to his many critics: "I have lived for this building with every fibre of my heart." At that moment I do not think that anyone in the room doubted the integrity of the architect's intentions. Even so, many colleagues of both the younger and older generation felt that Boltenstern's plans to reconstruct the opera house were a wasted opportunity. Their reasons, however, differed widely. Some argued for the complete reconstruction of both the original auditorium and the two huge foyers on either side; whereas young architects were of the opinion that the only worthwhile approach was to design a completely new opera house incorporating highly radical ideas.

The latter considered that any of the *avant-garde* theatrical styles of architec-

41, 42 Front view and ground
plan at the height of the first tier
of the Court Opera by van der Nüll
and Siccardsburg.

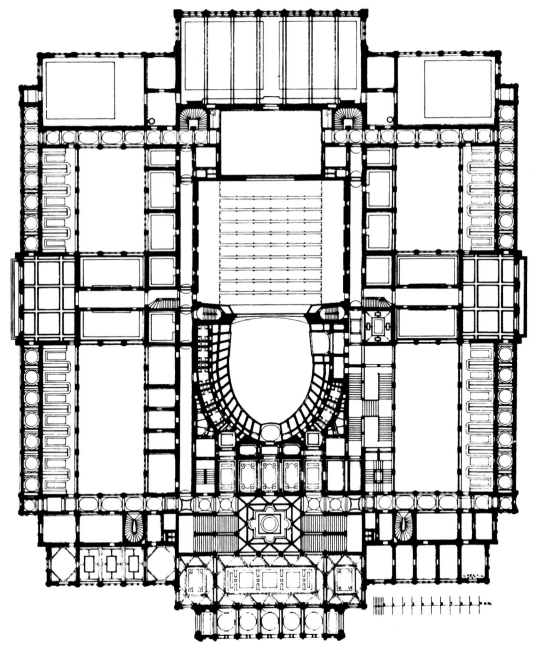

ture–from Oskar Strnad's circular stage of the "total theater" of Walter Gropius–would have been more appropriate to the age they felt to be dawning rather than reconstructing the Vienna State Opera in a style that represented all that was typical of the architecture of the Ring, which was by that time out of favor.

Joseph Gregor, a leading expert on theater, reports that during this period careful consideration had to be given before even the slightest detail was allowed to be reproduced. He relates how he asked the theater architect Karl Witzmann whether he thought it possible for the State Opera to be restored in such a way that one day a visitor might imagine it was the same opera house that had been destroyed on 12 March 1945 (once allowances were made for obvious improvements). After pondering for a short while, Witzmann answered "I daresay."

All decisions taken at that time as to the rebuilding of major buildings gave rise, inevitably, to arguments; this happened in the cases of the Burgtheater, the Haas-Haus (a music archive in the Vienna National Library containing original manuscripts) at the corner of the Graben (one of Vienna's main shopping streets) and Stock-im-Eisen-Platz, and the Heinrichshof. I remember, that as a student of the architect Clemens Holzmeister, joining forces with a number of my classmates (we later formed a work group known as *Arbeitsgruppe 4*) to argue forcefully for a modified reconstruction of the Heinrichshof. Our plan was to leave a spacious square in front of the opera house, and to ensure this we wanted the rebuilding of the Heinrichshof restricted to only one of the narrow blocks set back from the Ringstrasse along Elisabethstrasse. It is a matter of debate whether this suggestion would have enhanced the overall effect of the opera.

It was no great surprise, in view of Vienna's cultural climate as a whole (nor would it be any more of a surprise today), that Erich Boltenstern's project was chosen. He was a cautious man who was able to adapt to situations skillfully.

Holzmeister's competition entry was of a different order. Although his arrangement for the boxes in the opera house

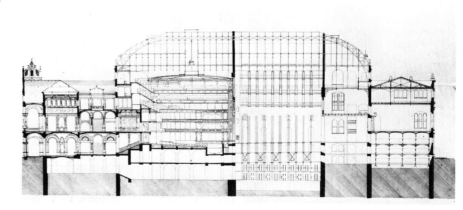

was similar to Boltenstern's–both proposed tiers in an amphitheater formation and avoided pillars in the upper level which would have impaired visibility–Holzmeister wanted the overall effect of the auditorium to convey a new sense of space. Josef Gregor gave this description of Holzmeister's auditorium: "The ceiling has an important and unusual feature. Lighting equipment for the stage is set into a huge, bright flower-like unit and the ceiling is fitted with special acoustic devices (for choirs, bells and so forth). But the best idea is the stage. The two proscenium boxes in the stalls and dress circle have been left out, creating an apron–an idea that has been in the offing

43 Longitudinal section taken from van der Null and Siccardburg's plans.

44 Celebrations surrounding the laying of the foundation stone of the Court Opera.

45 The State Opera on fire after the American bombing on 12 March 1945. In less than an hour and a half they dropped 1667 tons of bombs on Vienna.

for as long as Holzmeister has been designing for the theater. The back of the stage can accommodate all sorts of advanced technical systems. The alternative forms of proscenium stage are supplemented by a third arrangement: the fourth upper-circle extends round the whole of the auditorium to form a gallery over the stage, which can be used by members of the public who do not consider a view of the stage to be important (during concerts, for example), and which can itself be incorporated into performances. A great number of operas (such as *Palestrina* by Pfitzner, *Parsifal*, *Die Meistersinger*, *Fidelio*, and Carl Orff's *Carmina Burana*) would benefit from the completely new dramatic possibilities offered by using three new sources—apron, proscenium stage and gallery. The theater would cry out for innovative productions and ideas."

Clemens Holzmeister worked on several theater construction projects in the course of his years of exile in Turkey during the war. Together with the producer Carl Ebert he developed plans for an "ideal theater," in which a whole

46 The extent of the damage: A good part of the auditorium and the stage facing the Sacher Hotel were the worse hit. The facade and elegant stairway escaped destruction.

47 The State Opera during reconstruction. The Heinrichshof had been leveled but the opportunity to create a great square in front of the opera house was missed.

range of new ideas were to be put into practice–particularly with a view to uniting the stage and auditorium visually, and opening up the proscenium stage. It is not surprising that at the earliest opportunity on his return Holzmeister should try to realize at least some of these ideas, insofar as this could be achieved within the restricted framework offered by the burnt-down section of the State Opera. When the decision was announced that Erich Boltenstern was to be responsible for the rebuilding, Gregor wrote: "I am not afraid to say straight away that I consider it a major setback for architecture and Viennese theater that Holzmeister's inspired version has been passed over. I can only hope that events prove me wrong."

No one can say categorically whether this turned out to be the case. It is certain, however, that the restrained classicism of Boltenstern's auditorium comes closer to the original than Holzmeister's version.

In the meantime it has probably turned out just as Joseph Gregor predicted so gloomily: most visitors to the opera house are unaware that the original theater was destroyed in an Allied air raid on 12 March 1945. The decision to com-

48 A project by Clemens Holzmeister that was never realized.
Holzmeister made use of the
proscenium, extending the
gallery round above the stage to
provide seats without a view of
the action where opera fans
could read the score.

mission Erich Boltenstern to reconstruct
the auditorium set the stylistic tone for the
design of other parts of the theater, for
example the side rooms and, in particular,
the decoration of the safety curtain. Further heated discussions centered on the
choice of an artist to design the curtain.
Once again the modernists were at odds
with the forces of conservatism: Fritz
Wotruba had submitted a tapestry design
in the Gobelin style which, with its
gigantic and mesmeric expressive power,
would without a doubt have utterly
disrupted the formal homogeneity of the
restored interior.

The design depicted a frieze of five
enormous figures, typical examples of
Wotruba's work. His unchallenged status
as Austria's foremost artist made it difficult
for the decision-makers (principally politicians and officials in the government
department responsible for the rebuilding
program) to justify their preference in
favor of the painter Rudolf Eisenmenger,
whose reputation had been somewhat
tarnished as a result of his role in the artistic scene during the Third Reich. It
should be said that the pleasant, yet artistically bland, composition that now adorns
the safety curtain fits in better with the

49, 50 Before, and after. The old auditorium with its rich ornamentation and pointed arches over the gallery (top) and the new, classically restrained design by Erich Bolternstern (bottom).

51 View of the stage, orchestra, and auditorium during a performance of *Die Meistersinger* (watercolour from the thirties by Oskar Laske).

46

52, 53 Before, and after. The old auditorium looking towards the stage (top) and the new design with the safety curtain by Rudolf Eisenmenger (bottom).

54 Fritz Wotruba's design for the safety curtain, which was not chosen.

stylistic tenor of the house than would have been the case with Fritz Wotruba's mighty creation. In artistic matters, reticence and conservatism (which was interpreted as elegance) were what mattered when the State Opera was rebuilt.

Tragic though the destruction of the opera house in 1945 was, there was reason to look on the bright side. The bombs and the resulting fire affected in the main only the auditorium and the stage area, while the great, magnificent staircases and the richly decorated foyer remained intact for the most part. The wrecking of the stage area made it possible for the rebuilding plans to include the modernization of the stage and lighting equipment, the opening up of the main stage backwards and the installation of a spacious rear stage. To the right of the main stage they were able to create an area for assembling scenery that had direct access to the main stage. The old machinery under the main stage area was replaced by a modern system of hydraulic ramps divided into sections. Great technical changes were introduced in the new rear stage area. The space beneath this stage was now just as extensive as the area above the stage, allowing sets and props to be kept there in readiness and then lifted up to stage level by means of hydraulic platforms. Opera productions as we know them today would be inconceivable without such technical innovations.

Large new foyers could now be added at the front of the building, to the right and left of the auditorium and stairwell. These rooms, which were designed by the architects Otto Prossinger (the Marble Room) and Zeno Kossak (the Gobelin tapestry room), are among the few things to have been retained from the early fifties: most of the others were subsequently demolished as it was believed that this was an impoverished artistic era. The auditorium, designed by Erich Boltenstern, has elements of this period (which is very recent in terms of the history of art), but the architect managed to give it an impression of near-timelessness by the use of extreme restraint. He achieved this principally by doing away with all figurative elements and by drasti-

cally reducing the ornamentation on the balustrades of the rows of boxes, on the ceiling, and the proscenium. The most noticeable change compared with the interior of the earlier building is the removal of the pointed arches in the gallery and their obstructive pillars.

Most visitors who are not conversant with the recent history of the opera house forget that the opulence and decorative richness of the great stairway used to be matched in its extravagant ornamentation by the auditorium itself. Nevertheless, the stairway, which was a major part of the nineteenth century opera house, cannot be compared with the excessive splendor of the staircases in the Paris Opera, which was conceived at the same time. It has none of the baroque dynamism and unrestrained vividness of its Parisian counterpart, nor does it take up as much space, proportionally, of its total size. The staircase in Vienna is redolent of chamber music, moderate and well-proportioned. In spite of its limited size, the three-dimensional projections and vistas afforded by the staircase and the line of the decorative border on the round, open arches and ribbed domes produce an almost unreal, sensuous interior.

The Imperial Hall and the empress's room, the opera house's rooms of state before 1945, were both destroyed. Only the foyer and the ceremonial room attached to the imperial box remained. In terms of their proportions, building materials, and decorative design, these areas are the quintessence of "romantic historicism" and were to serve as a stylistic model until the development of the *Jugendstil* (or art nouveau).

The great balcony facing the Ringstrasse also survived in its original form. It is not only the main architectural theme of the whole design, but it also represents the bridge linking the architectural elements contained in the facade with the forms and structures within. The balcony motif had been a structural feature since the early Italian renaissance and its purpose was to underscore the public nature of a building. The structure of the facade is echoed in the arrangement of architectural elements in the open area of the balcony. The architects paid particular atten-

55 The good news among the bad: the magnificent staircase and the richly embellished loggia with its frescoes remained intact after the bombing.

56, 57 Moritz von Schwind created the frescoes in the loggia–a decorative highlight of Ringstrasse architecture.

tion to the form and embellishment of the balcony and a minutely-detailed model was made of all the refinements and ornamentation which the balcony was eventually to contain. The balcony is a highlight of Vienna's Ringstrasse, with its strict but generously structured architecture and its decorative relief, notably the statues under the arches of the balcony (by Ernst Julius Hähnel) and the painted medallions and domes (by Moritz von Schwind).

The Vienna Opera was built at a turning point. It took almost ten years, from the first draft until completion, for an architectural style to finally establish itself, rooted in late classicism and drifting towards romanticism. It must be the most typically Viennese of all the buildings on the Ring–less classical than the Parliament building, less monumental than the Burgtheater, less dramatic than the Neue Hofburg. One thing is certain: it is not merely the function and physical reality of the building that makes the Viennese consider the State Opera, after St Stephen's Cathedral, to be the embodiment of all that is most cherished about the Viennese way of life, a sentiment visitors quickly sense.

58 The tea room in the opera house, formerly the banquet room attached to the imperial box.

THE DIRECTORS AND THEIR ENSEMBLES

Egon Seefehlner

The position of Director of the Vienna Opera seems to be shrouded in mysteries that particularly interest and intrigue the public. For some time now, in fact, he has been simply a civil servant who is paid a salary that is generally lower than that of, for example, the person in charge of Austria's Post Office, Railways, or Forests (his pension is smaller, at any rate). In terms of official status he has always been their inferior. I can remember one typical instance, the occasion of a ceremony in the Hofburg to celebrate the jubilee of the second republic, when the director of the State Theater sat with members of the *Kunstsenat* (a body concerned with the arts) some rows behind politicians and senior officials. Art, after all, is vulgar.

And yet, directors of the Opera in this city do have a particular aura. If you look at the history of the Vienna State Opera, which enjoys a special position among the ranks of the world's opera houses, you will find that hardly any of these men are exceptions in this respect.

The cycle began with Franz von Dingelstedt, who was the first of these public figures to occupy this special podium when the Court Opera opened in 1869. Choosing the director was the same in the days of the monarchy as it is today. It used to be the emperor or his First Court Chamberlain and later, in the republic, it was the government or even the head of government who assumed responsibility for selecting and appointing the director. The emperor took this upon himself for obvious reasons, since he financed the court theaters and in particular the Court Opera (which was not inexpensive even in those days) out of his own private funds. Today the appointment is made by the government through its Education Department, because the state theaters are of far greater importance to the country's standing and to individual politicians than their actual power would indicate. In the past the splendor of the court, and the esteem in which the monarch was held, depended on the impression created by the emperor and by the palaces, horses, and works of art (and also theaters) with which he surrounded himself. The extraordinary interest shown in opera in Vienna can be traced with some certainty back to the prestigious involvement of the imperial line, above all Leopold I and Joseph I. They were outstanding musicians and loved opera most of all. There is no doubt that the financial straits and crises which the Hapsburg courts found themselves in can be attributed in no small measure to their considerable expenditure on the arts. Criticism was certainly leveled at operas and ballets when entertainments of this kind took place in difficult times, but the passion for the theater was not merely a courtly enthusiasm—on the contrary, it was shared, on another level, by the people as a whole.

In France the lavish nature of court opera and court theater was constantly denounced as extravagance and was one cause of its decline. It never occurred to anyone in Austria to condemn the imperial family's love of the arts. Given this attitude, it was only natural that the emperor should commission a grand new opera house with all imaginable refinements, and following the demolition of the fortifications he should errect in their place buildings that put the monarchy in a prestigious light. Thus, he constructed the Ringstrasse. The decision to do so was also a response to the thriving middle-classes. The new opera house, which exceeded the estimated cost of construction, was on the one hand admired for its magnificence and architectural significance, and the immediate butt of criticism on the other hand for being set back too far from the Ringstrasse.

Franz Freiherr von Dingelstedt

Born Halsdorf (Oberhessen) 6. 30. 1814; died Vienna 5. 15. 1881.
Director of the Court Opera from 7. 1. 1867 to 12. 18. 1870.

The celebrations that accompanied the opening of the new Court Opera under the directorship of Franz von Dingelstedt were as lavish as those that took place when the theater reopened in 1955. At that time, too, the position of director was the subject of great intrigue. Dingelstedt, who was born in Oberhessen in Germany, was neither a musician nor a man of the theater–he had been a teacher and then made a name for himself as a liberal journalist. His connection with the theater, and with Vienna, had its origins in his marriage to Jenny Lutzer, a singer at the Court Opera. He was already a well-respected author when he became drama advisor at the court theater in Stuttgart in 1846, theater manager at the court theater in Munich by 1851, and in 1857 director of the Weimar court theater and orchestra, which then held a leading position in the field of music and German-language theater.

Dingelstedt was a proponent of a sumptuous theatrical style and it was probably for this reason that the theater director Friedrich von Halm suggested him for the position of leader of the new opera house, in an age when everyone wanted to see the colorful grandeur typified by Makart (an influencial and exuberant Viennese painter) in all spheres of cultural life and public performance. The incorporation of the repertory of the modest Kärntnertor theater in the new house on the Ring involved an enormous outlay, and Dingelstedt, the orchestral director, was assisted in the arrangements by Franz Gaul acting as artistic advisor. All the sets for the new opera house had to be remade, and the major part of the work was to be tackled by the scenery painter Carlo Brioschi, whose style was based on Makart's. Dingelstedt became director of the Court Opera on 1 July 1867, but his secret aim was to take over the Hofburg theater (which von Halm had also more or less promised him). On 25 May 1869 performances at the new Court Opera on the Ring started with Mozart's *Don Giovanni*. Dingelstedt had not allowed himself to be hurried into an early opening. He knew that he needed to have a repertoire of twelve new productions ready for performance–otherwise the theater would have had to close as soon as it had opened. It was not possible simply to transfer productions from the Kärntnertor theater, because the dimensions of the new stage were completely different.

The situation was utterly different for Karl Böhm and me in 1954–55, the year in which the State Opera reopened. There will always be initial problems when a new and prestigious state opera house opens for daily performances. I know this from personal experience because, along with my work on the Vienna Opera, I also played a part in the reopening of the Berlin opera house in 1961. The first problems is the practice of installing the latest stage technology, untested, and it almost invariably proves to be unreliable. Although the public will not notice, this

59 The auditorium of the new Court Opera for the opening performance on 25 May 1869 (a wood engraving by Bruno Strassberger).

puts an enormous strain on the machinery. Secondly, a minimum number of productions is required in order to cope with a repertoire to cover at least three hundred performances a year. When the new Court Opera opened, Dingelstedt could not fall back on any of the productions from the Kärntnertor theater. He asked accordingly for the opening to be delayed until such time as he had twelve operas ready for performance. It is true that Dingelstedt had unlimited use of the large and famous vocal ensemble of his predecessor Salvi (who, like almost all his successors, was much maligned). But Dingelstedt was also criticized from the very start for wanting too much money. He managed to get increased funding by referring to the well-supported Paris Opera and declaring: "The emperor of Austria must be in a position to spend as much on his opera house as the French emperor spends on his." He was also criticized for the time it took before the Viennese had their fully operative opera house. Nonetheless, Dingelstedt had the great advantage of having an exceptional ensemble at his disposal and of being able to tailor his productions to the requirements of the new building.

It is interesting to compare this with the rebirth of the State Opera in 1955 (and it was the same for the opera house in Berlin) when seven new opera productions and an evening of ballet were required for performance within a short period, as the reopening was to take the form of an opera festival of the very highest artistic standard. All this was to take place in a theater which was still not ready four months before it was due to open—work on the auditorium, most noticeably, was still in progress during stage rehearsals. In view of the fact that seven operas are not enough to keep a repertory theater in productions—and, on top of everything, they had to be cast out of resources which were only available for a limited time—we had to adopt new productions from the Theater an der Wien and use singers from there who had not actually been given leave of absence. This approach proved a severe handicap to Böhm's job as director. When the in-

60 Play-bill for the theater's first performance: Mozart's *Don Giovanni,* following the prologue by Franz Dingelstedt.

61 Louise Dustmann as Donna Anna in the inaugural production.

62 Carlo Brioschi's set design for *Don Giovanni* (act II, scene 1), "A street in Seville."

63 Costume designs by Joseph Hoffmann for *The Magic Flute*—the Queen of the Night, Sarastro, Pamina, Tamino.

augural festival was over, not only did Karl Böhm leave to undertake a long-standing engagement in America, but the star performers also departed, having fulfilled their stipulated four-month contracts.

A further parallel with the opening under Dingelstedt's leadership was the difficulty of satisfying the demand for tickets. Dingelstedt tried to skirt round the problem by scheduling *Don Giovanni* on three successive opening nights, each with a different cast. Nevertheless he still had to turn down many requests for tickets, including one from a popular actor in the Dresden court theater–there was simply no ticket available for the young matinee idol, who was also his admirer, Franz Jauner. Little did Dingelstedt know that he had just turned down one of his successors as director of the Vienna Opera.

The distribution of tickets for the opening performance was certainly not carried out in his time with as much strategic planning as was shown in 1955. The office of Ernst Marboe, administrator of the State Theater, was filled with a vast number of seating plans, on which the names of meticulously selected personalities were neatly entered, and in some cases crossed out again. Debates raged for some weeks over whether Secretary of State John Foster Dulles should sit in the dress circle in box 10 or box 12. One point was agreed: that honorary members should be given seats in the right-hand proscenium box. There was only room, mind you, for the honorary members and not for their spouse or partner. For this reason it was not possible to accommodate the husband of Maria Jeritza in the same box. So what happened? To our chagrin the great soprano Maria Jeritza, surely the most famous honorary member of all, failed to appear.

We are often amused today by how desperate the high nobility during Dingelstedt's time was to be seen. But when similar events are held today it is not unusual to see certain successful figures showing just the same concern to be seated in accord with their status.

When Dingelstedt was director the musical side was the responsibility of Johann Herbeck (or, more properly, *Hrbeck*), who was later knighted von Herbeck. His youth had been spent as a choir boy at the Heiligenkreuz (Holy Cross) cathedral school, and after studying law he went on to become director of the choir of the Piarists (Roman Catholics), choir master with the Vienna Men's Choir, professor at the Academy of Music and, in 1859, artistic director of the *Gesellschaft der Musikfreunde* (Society of Music-lovers). By 1866 he had become principal court conductor and on 8 July he was appointed for a year "to play a part in organizing the musical activities of the imperial and royal Court Opera." His debut at the new opera house on the Ring took place on 16 October 1869, when he conducted a performance of Ambroise Thomas's *Mignon*. By engaging a conductor who was so well-loved in Vienna, Dingelstedt acquired not only an exceptional musician but also his ostensible successor.

Herbeck's appointment brought a confirmed Wagnerian to the court theater. It should be remembered that although Wagner was already a major figure in international music, he was also vigorously rejected by a sizeable portion of the musical community in Vienna–led by the feared music critic Eduard Hanslick. Dingelstedt's repertoire kept largely to works which had already been in the program at the Kärntnertor theater, but on 15 October 1869, with the help of Herbeck, he managed to obtain a contract with Wagner for the first performance in Vienna of *Die Meistersinger von Nürnberg* (which was eventually performed on 27 February 1870). Herbeck's mediation was needed because Wagner's links with Vienna had been severed following dismally unsuccessful attempts to produce *Tristan und Isolde* at the Kärntnertor theater.

The most-performed opera on the Ringstrasse while Dingelstedt was director was Mozart's *Magic Flute* in a production designed by Josef Hoffmann (sets) and Franz Gaul (costumes) in the style of pure Makart. This version alone was performed twenty-five times in Dingelstedt's reign. But this figure was far exceeded by the much-admired and spectacular ballet

64, 65 Bertha Ehnn as Gretchen and Karl Adams in the title role in two scenes from Charles Gounod's *Faust*.

66 Amalie Materna as Valentine and Karl Adams as Raoul in Giacomo Meyerbeer's *Les Huguenots*.

67 Caroline Tellheim as Susanna and Carl Mayerhofer as Figaro in Mozart's *The Marriage of Figaro*.

Sardanapal, which appeared on the program forty-seven times during the same period and gave Dingelstedt the opportunity for opulent staging.

Dingelstedt's leading singers were the baritone Johann Nepomuk Beck (who played Don Giovanni in the opening production), the lyric tenor Gustav Walter (the opening Ottavio, Stolzing, and Lohengrin), and the baritone Angelo Neumann. Neumann later became well-known as a result of a tour of Wagner's complete operas which he took throughout Europe between 1882 and 1888, going down in history as a director of the German State Theater in Prague. Other singers included the bass Hans von Rokitansky (Leporello), sopranos Louise Dust-mann (Donna-Anna, Elsa, Elisabeth, Senta, and Leonore in *Fidelio*) and Maria Wilt (Donna-Elvira, Leonore in *Il Trovatore*, the countess in *Figaro*, the Queen of the Night, and Elisabeth), and the mezzo-soprano Bertha Ehnn (Zerlina, Selica in *Königin von Saba*, Agathe, Pamina). Dingelstedt also took on the dramatic soprano Amalie Materna (who sang all the Wagnerian roles in her range during the course of her career), although she developed more fully under his successors. In 1876 she sang the role of Brünnhilde in Bayreuth in the original rendition of the tetralogy *Der Ring des Nibelungen*; in 1882 she played Kundry in the first performance of *Parsifal*, and in 1894 she left the Court Opera.

Johann Ritter von Herbeck

Born 12. 25. 1831; died 10. 28. 1877, Vienna.
Director of the Court Opera from 12. 19. 1870 to 4. 30. 1875

When Dingelstedt left the opera house happily a few months after it opened to take up a post at the Hofburg theater, his successor was already there; on 19 December 1870 the general intendant (the functionary who held the theater's purse-strings) Rudolf Count Wrbna appointed the court conductor Johann Herbeck as the new director of the court opera theater.

Herbeck's directorship was a typical example of a phenomenon we still find today, where a practicing artist (whether he be conductor, singer, or producer) is more able than an ordinary administrator would be to give a theater an unmistakable artistic profile. On the other hand, since his principal concern is with artistic matters he is less adept at coping with duties which many people would consider to be no more than red tape. In the end Herbeck's downfall was the result of constant friction with the First Court Chamberlain's office and the general intendant. An ardent admirer of Richard Wagner, he also failed in his plan to produce the *Ring des Nibelungen* at the Court

Opera. Wagner had at one time signed a contract to have his works performed at the Court Opera, and he believed that this should only cover operas which had been composed up to the time when the contract was arranged. The court officials took the view, however, that the contract included all his works, in other words even those which had not yet been composed when the contract was arranged. This dispute with Wagner, who was already annoyed by the planned cuts to his *Tristan*, was not settled until Jauner became director.

The major events under Herbeck were the extremely successful Viennese debut of Wagner's *Rienzi*, Verdi's *Aida*, and Thomas's *Hamlet*, and the premiere of Goldmark's *Königin von Saba*. He also had to admit to several failures, such as the first performances of Schubert's *Genoveva* and Weber's *Oberon* and *Abu Hassan*, which were found unsatisfactory on both an artistic and commercial level. Herbeck's period as director was brought to an end by the general intendant, not least because the economic situation as a

68, 69 Two set designs by Hermann Burghart for Verdi's *Aida* in 1874: Act I "Room in the King's palace," Act III "By the Nile."

70 Marie Wilt as the Queen of the Night in Mozart's *The Magic Flute*.

71 Amalie Materna as the Queen of Sheba in the opera of the same name by Karl Goldmark.

72 Costume sketches by Franz Gaul for the Viennese premiere of *Aida* under Herbeck in 1874: Aida and Amneris.

whole was catastrophic following the stock market crash in May 1873, and because funds were not flowing into the court theater quite as abundantly as they had under Dingelstedt.

Herbeck's success was largely attributable to singers who had been engaged by Salvi. One exception was Amalie Materna, whose star was now in the ascendancy. She was joined by Pauline Lucca, who later achieved world fame. Herbeck's most important appointment, which only bore fruit when he had ceased to be director, was the one that brought the conductor Hans Richter to the Court Opera house. Herbeck's successful operatic productions included Gounod's *Faust* with sixty-five performances and the ballet *Fantasca*, which had one hundred fourteen.

Franz Ritter von Jauner

Born 11. 14. 1832; died 2. 23. 1900, Vienna.
Director of the Court Opera from 5. 1. 1875 to 6. 19. 1880

It was a sign of the times that the man sought to replace Herbeck as director of the Court Opera was someone who would set the cash tills ringing and sooth angry opera fans (there were fans even in those days). The choice fell on the hugely successful director of the Carltheater in Vienna, Franz Jauner, who was responsible for one sell-out production after the other. Jauner had to be asked no less than three times whether he would be willing to take over the running of the Court Opera. This tactic brought him exactly what he wanted: the removal of the inhi-

409

73 Rosa Papier as Sieglinde in Wagner's *Die Walküre*.

74 Play-bill for the premiere of Wagner's *Götterdämmerung* on 14 February 1879.

biting presence of the general intendant, an increase in the subsidy to 500,000 gulden and a reconciliation between the court authorities and Richard Wagner. Jauner thus achieved his aim of making Vienna a Wagnerian city. He also managed to persuade Wagner onto the conductor's podium, when the master conducted *Lohengrin* at the Court Opera.

The only major work that Jauner introduced apart from Wagner's operas was the first performance in Vienna of Bizet's *Carmen*, which in its new, final version made triumphant progress throughout the world. Pauline Lucca, who now made only guest appearances, sang the title role.

Jauner's ensemble was practically the same as it had been in the time of Salvi, Dingelstedt, and Herbeck, since it was not yet necessary to search for the next generation of performers. Jauner complemented his ensemble by adding the coloratura soprano Bianca Bianchi and the tenor Anton Schittenhelm. Amalie Materna could now triumph as Brünnhilde.

Hans Richter was the leading conductor of Wagner's work at that time. He finally managed to have them performed in Vienna, did Wagner's bidding in his absence, and ensured that the master's works were performed with hardly any cuts. Jauner was always on the look-out for attractions and, having had Wagner perform his *Lohengrin*, he now arranged for Giuseppe Verdi to make an appearance on the platform, where he conducted his opera *Aida* and his Requiem. Johannes Brahms conducted his *German Requiem* at the Court Opera; before this work (which is today considered sufficient for a whole evening) Hans Richter conducted Mendelssohn's *Athalia* overture and finished with Beethoven's *Eroica*. The visit of Bizet to conduct *Carmen* never went ahead—the composer died suddenly on 3 June 1875.

The engagement of these famous composers as conductors was a spectacular idea and was typical of Jauner's approach. His Valkyries were instructed by the Empress Elizabeth's riding instructor; the horses which they rode onto the stage belonged to the imperial court; eight Polish riders were taken on to act as understudies. All his other productions were also spectacular by virtue of the splendor of their décor and costumes.

75 Scenery design by Anton Brioschi for Wagner's *Rheingold* in 1878.

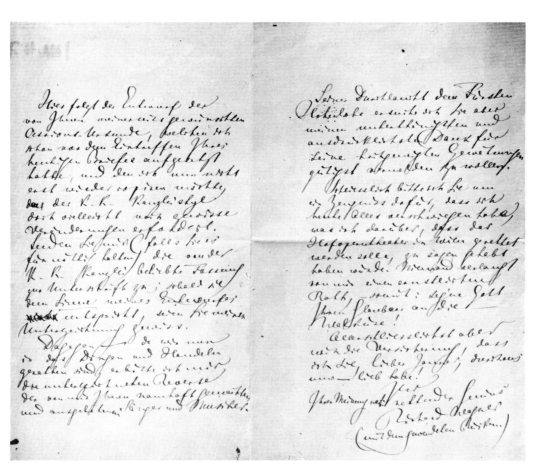

76 Letter from Richard Wagner to Franz Jauner regarding the Viennese production of the *Ring des Nibelungen*.

77 Amalie Materna as Brünnhilde in Wagner's *Walküre*.

78 Emil Scaria as Wotan in Wagner's *Ring*. He was one of the best Wagnerian singers of his time.

79 Pauline Lucca as Carmen in Georges Bizet's opera (oil painting by Gustav Wertheimer, 1879).

The opera most often performed under Jauner was *Les Huguenots* by Meyerbeer, which made forty-eight appearances.

While director of the Court Opera, Jauner made a name for himself as a man who liked theater to be sensational, with a tendency towards the comic opera of the kind seen at the Ringtheater, where he took charge in 1881. This move had tragic consequences–his career never recovered after the fire at the Ringtheater on 8 December 1881 during a performance of Offenbach's *Tales of Hoffmann* in which a considerable number of people died. The scandal cast a shadow over his life which was tragically ended by suicide on 23 February 1900.

In spite of Jauner's sensationalism the receipts at the Court Opera sank to a new low. His expensive productions were criticized and the public realized that the reappointment of a general intendant might provide a way out of the crisis. As a result Leopold Friedrich Freiherr von Hofmann was hired, whereupon Jauner, who had insisted in his contract that he should be able to dispense with such a post, resigned. Until his successor was chosen the Court Opera was run by a committee consisting of the singers Emil Scaria, Carl Mayerhof, and Gustav Walter. Emil Scaria, who had been engaged by Herbeck in 1873, was the premier bass baritone of the time, singing the roles of Wotan, the Landgrave, King Heinrich, and Gurnemanz.

80   Anton Schittenhelm in Wagner's *Der Meistersinger von Nürnberg.*

81   Carlo Brioschi's set design for Wagner's *Tristan und Isolde* in 1883.

Wilhelm Jahn

Born 11. 24. 1835, Moravia; died 4. 21. 1900, Vienna.
Director of the Court from 1. 1. 1881 to 10. 14. 1897.

The committee's interregnum lasted six months until 1 January 1881, when Wilhelm Jahn took over the post of director. He was to hold office for almost seventeen years, the longest tenure in the history of the Vienna Opera (as it is likely to remain). Hans Richter had been offered the job but he wanted nothing to do with administration and turned it down. Besides, he had all the influence he needed during the reign of his friend Jahn. Jahn was born at the court in Moravia (now in Czeckoslovakia) in 1835 and had started out as a singer. He then made his name as a conductor and also ran the opera house in Wiesbaden as music director to the king. He was considered an outstanding company manager, and specialized in discovering and fostering young singing talent.

He was the director public and artists alike had been looking for–"Papa Jahn" was sociable and friendly, and he had a lovable nature which made him admired and respected everywhere. No one instilled more of the typical atmosphere of Vienna into the Court Opera than he did. These factors explain why Jahn

could stay on as director for seventeen years, far in excess of all who came both before and after him.

He benefited from a general upswing in the economy which was now taking place in the empire. His period as director only came to an end when after seventeen years he had become tired and ill—when, in other words (as it is so cruelly put) he was "used up." By that time it was not just the end of his era, but gradually the *fin de siècle* period and an age dominated by the Ringstrasse of Makart had given way to a new artistic direction. A new generation, the "Secession," was waiting in the wings.

Jahn's era laid the foundations of the operatic repertoire we have today. He produced first performances of the following works: *Tristan und Isolde* (1883), *Mephistopheles* by Boito (1882), Mascagni's *Cavalleria Rusticana* (1891), and Leoncavallo's *Bajazzo* (1893). Verdi's *Otello*, Massenet's *Le Cid* (1887), *Manon* (1890) and—the world premiere, no less—*Werther* (1892), *Die Drei Pintos* by Weber/Mahler (1889), *Der Barbier von*

82 Theodore Reichmann as Wotan in Wagner's *Ring*.

83 Amalie Materna and Hermann Winkelmann as Kundry and Parsifal in Wagner's *Parsifal* in 1889.

84 Marie Renard as Manon in Jules Massenet's opera *Manon Lescaut* (a pastel drawing by Clemens von Pausinger).

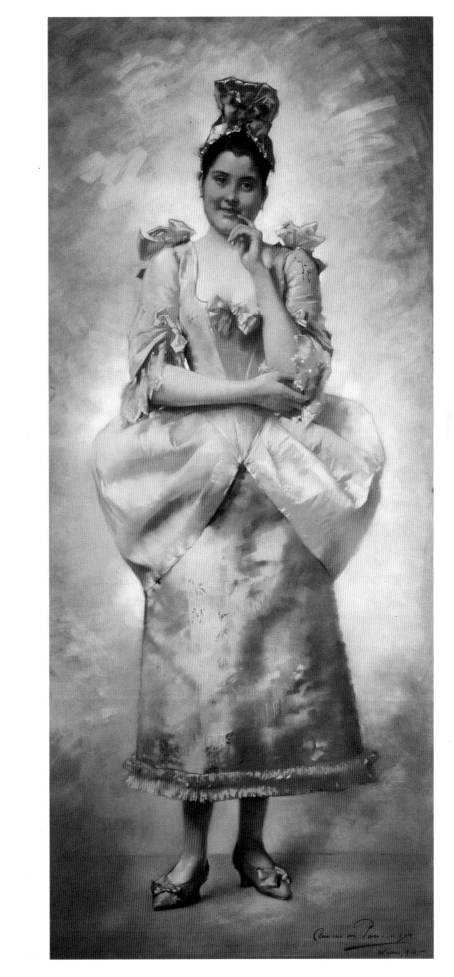

85   Marie Renard (Hänsel) and Paula Mark (Gretel) with Lily Lehmann (witch) in Engelbert Humperdinck's fairy tale opera *Hänsel und Gretel* in 1894.

86   Group portrait with witch. During Jahn's directorship *Hänsel und Gretel* became the traditional Christmas offering at the Court Opera.

87   The closing scene in Verdi's *Otello* with Antonie Schläger as Desdemona and Hermann Winkelmann in the title role.

88 Paula Mark as Marie in Gaetano Donizetti's *La Fille du Régiment.*

Bagdad by Cornelius (1890), *Hänsel und Gretel* by Humperdinck (1894), *Der Evangelimann* by Kienzl (1896) and—coming finally to the Court Opera—Smetana's *The Bartered Bride.* In 1893 Jahn organized the first performance of the *Ring* cycle in Vienna.

Wilhelm Jahn put his energies into reviving the singing ensemble. His most important appointments were the soprano Marie Renard who had started out as a deeper mezzo-soprano and who played Manon in Jahn's time, the sopranos Paula Mark, Elisa Elizza, and Rosa Papier (who became a leading teacher and figured largely in the appointment of Mahler), the tenor Hermann Winkelmann (all the Wagnerian roles, as well as Otello, Radamès, Prophet), the baritone Theodor Reichmann (Dutchman, Sachs, Wotan, Don Giovanni, Amonastro, Escamillo, Rigoletto), the Belgian tenor Ernest van Dyck (Tannhäuser, Werther, Des Grieux, Lohengrin, Canio), the baritone Josef Ritter (Don Giovanni, Almaviva, Pizarro, Figaro), the bass Wilhelm Hesch (comic roles—a famous Kezal, who could also play Hundung and Frosch!). These singers were also the mainstays of Bayreuth and they could be said to be known throughout the world.

The most frequently performed operas while Jahn was director were *Cavalleria Rusticana* (178 times) and *Lohengrin* (174). These figures were far exceeded by ballet, which was becoming extraordinarily popular during this period. Even today *Die Puppenfee* (The Fairy Doll) is the most produced work of all at the Vienna Opera with 296 performances, while the spectacular ballet *Excelsior* has been staged 243 times.

A whole era came to an end with Jahn's departure—an age characterized by a highly visual style and a life of splendor and passion. Jahn was responsible for all of this. But he was also proof that directors of theaters (and especially of opera houses) should be changed every ten years or so.

One of the basic rules of theater is that it cannot allow itself to be boring for a single moment, and the daily business of running a theater can become routine very quickly. Particular interest is taken in the director precisely because he—no less than conductors, producers, set designers, and singers—is supposed to entertain the public. When he stops doing that because his ideas have become old and tired, either he must step down as director, or the theater goes into decline.

Gustav Mahler

Born 7. 7. 1860, Kalischt (Moravia); died 5. 18. 1911, Vienna.
Director of the Court Opera from 10. 15. 1897 to 12. 31. 1907.

Jahn's period as director had been too long and the time was ripe for a radical change. Everyone looked to a new guiding spirit. Credit must be given to the First Court Chamberlain Prince Liechtenstein, and a number of well-known commentators in the world of art and music (in particular the opera singer Rosa Papier and her husband, the influential music critic Hans Paumgartner) for recognizing that the only possible choice was Mahler, the right man at the right time. Born in 1860 in the region of Moravia, Mahler came to the Budapest opera house by way of Bad Hall, Olmütz, Lyublyana, Kassel,

Prague, and Leipzig. From Budapest he went to Hamburg, where he exceeded all expectations in successfully breathing new artistic life into its stagnating opera house. Anna von Mildenburg, a pupil of Rosa Papier, sent enthusiastic reports from Hamburg where she had an engagement. Enquiries were made in Budapest, where the young conductor received no less praise.

Everything now happened quickly. Mahler made his debut at the Vienna Opera in May 1897 with *Lohengrin*, and on 8 October he was named director. Until that date the ailing nephew of Jahn, the chorus master Wondra, had been temporarily in charge.

Jahn had looked on the opera house fundamentally as a place of tradition and above all as a singer's theater. The result was that insufficient attention had been paid to production values and to the music, to the extent that the visual and musical standards expected by audiences were no longer being met. Alongside the dominating presence of Richard Wagner and Giuseppe Verdi there had emerged a strong, almost revolutionary movement which wanted to develop the spirit of Wagner but also to harness it; without Vienna noticing, it was Mahler who was to lead this movement and bring it to triumphant fulfillment.

Gustav Mahler's achievement after his appointment, which was made in spite of great opposition (particularly from Richard Wagner's wife Cosima), was to initiate all those measures which are considered the norm in modern opera. He zealously set about ridding the imperial opera of its intolerable sloppiness, which masqueraded as "tradition." He realized that opera requires more than beautiful voices; a great singer can only achieve world renown if he is able to bring a new interpretation to his various roles, just as Wagner had insisted. Mahler ruthlessly replaced older singers and created a new ensemble of his own.

It was even more significant, however, how much importance Mahler attached not only to the musical interpretation but also to the sets, the costumes, and a new form of lighting—in other words to all aspects of the work. He took on the brilliant set designer Alfred Roller, who created designs that were still effective in the late 1930s and which made some of the most forceful impressions on me in a lifetime of opera-going. The style of the imperial opera had until then largely come about by accident (with the possible exception of Jahn's period as director), but under Mahler there was a definite policy of thorough planning and rethinking where necessary.

Before Jahn's time conductors used to stand at the front on the apron of the stage, and while he was director they still only had a view of part of the orchestra.

Mahler was the first director to put the conductor's platform where it is today, in a position which offers the only full view of an opera performance. He was also the first to dim the lights in the auditorium and to refuse admission to latecomers until the first interval, two innovations which a section of the public found utterly shocking—they wanted to be seen even while the performance was on and liked to come and go as they pleased.

Even during Mahler's time, nevertheless, neither the conductor nor the producer was mentioned in the program; it was as if the composer himself was conducting the work. Mahler was very strict and made great demands both on himself and on everyone who worked with him. Over a period of time this led to opposition, not only from people who had been against his appointment in the first place, but also from those whom he had "treated badly" for artistic or any other reason.

Every opera premiere which took place during Mahler's reign was greatly influenced by him. His arrangement of Beethoven's *Fidelio* is as valid today as it was then; it was he who inserted the third "Leonore" overture between the prison scene and the final scene.

It was no doubt the strong influence Mahler had over everyone and every aspect of the opera which caused the most famous conductor of the age, Hans Richter, to become increasingly angry and finally in 1900 to resign from the Vienna Court Opera. He went to England and never again conducted at the Court Opera, dying in 1918. He has faded from Vienna's memory by comparison with the illustrious name of Gustav Mahler to such an extent that I was most surprised when in the early eighties an English lady approached me and introduced herself as Hans Richter's granddaughter.

We can probably attribute the excitement caused by Gustav Mahler's personality not only to his role as director but also to the fact that his stature as one of the greatest composers of all time was by no means recognized during his lifetime, at least not in Vienna. He was greatly respected as an orchestral leader (as his subsequent appointment in the United States proved), but his compositions were

89 Alfred Roller's set design for Wagner's *Rheingold* in 1905—"In the open, high up in the mountains."

90 Costume sketches by Alfred Roller for Wagner's *Rheingold* in 1905: Donner, Fricka, and Fasolt.

RICHARD·WAGNER·RHEINGOLD·
DONNER·

RICHARD·WAGNER·RHEINGOLD·
FRIKA.

RICHARD·WAGNER·RHEINGOLD
FASOLT.

91 Erik Schmedes as Siegfried and Hans Breuer as Mime (plus bear) in Wagner's *Siegfried*.

92 A young Leo Slezak as Lohengrin in Wagner's opera of the same name.

93 Erik Schmedes as Tristan and Fritz Weidemann as Kurwenal in Wagner's *Tristan und Isolde* in 1905.

94 Puccini's *La Bohème* in 1903, with Marie Gutheil-Schoder as Musette, Gerhard Stehmann as Marcel, Fritz Schrödter as Rudolf, and Selma Kurz as Mimi.

95 Selma Kurz, the most celebrated coloratura soprano of her time, as Madame Butterfly in Puccini's opera.

hardly ever performed in Vienna. It was only after the Second World War that his position alongside Bruckner and Brahms was really acknowledged. Between the wars whenever one of Mahler's works was performed–with the possible exception of his *Lied der Erde* and the *Kindertotenlieder*–critics would often comment that it was "typical conductor's music."

This discrepancy between the appreciation of Mahler the conductor and Mahler the composer unsettled public opinion increasingly and made Mahler more and more bitter. His choice of repertoire was dictated very largely by his desire, together with Roller, to adapt major works which had previously been in the program to the modern age.

Mahler introduced a number of interesting new works, including *Eugene Onegin, Yolanta*, and *Pique Dame* (Queen of Spades) by Tchaikovsky, Richard Strauss's *Feuersnot*–he could not get *Salome* past the court censor, who refused the work on the grounds that it was an "unappetizing piece"–Puccini's *La Bohème* (which he had earlier recommended to Jahn and which had already been acquired by the Theater an der Wien and its director Alexandrine von Schönerer, leaving Jahn to make do with Leoncavallo's *Bohème*), and Verdi's *Falstaff*. Mahler's new production of Mozart's *Don Giovanni* was particularly sensational. Roller made first use in this production of the famous side portal towers which were effective for lighting and could be adapted for other works such as *Die Entführung aus dem Serail*.

Mahler's program was frequently affected by the availability of important singer-performers. The great singing names at the time were Anna von Mildenburg (later to marry the writer Hermann Bahr), the great singer and actress Marie Gutheil-Schoder, the most famous coloratura soprano of the age Selma Kurz, mezzo-soprano Laura Hilgermann, star tenors Erik Schmedes and Leo Slezak, the baritone Friedrich Weidemann, alto Hermine Kittel, soprano Lucie Weidt, bass baritone Leopold Demuth, and bass Richard Mayr. These singers were not only Vienna's favorites and dominated the repertoire–they could also soon be

heard at the Met, which was at the time a definite criterion of international fame for singers. For me the Vienna Opera is history up until the end of Jahn's era, but in Mahler's time it starts to be the living past.

The first reason for this is that in my youth I knew a lot of people who talked about the wonders of Mahler's era and criticized the present (much as they do today). If I talked in glowing terms about Lauritz Melchior's Siegfried, I was immediately challenged "What is Melchior next to Schmedes?" and when I enthused over Elizabeth Schumann, I was immediately made to understand that Selma Kurz had been better in every way.

Secondly, I find Mahler's era so familiar because I encountered singers from his period as director when I used to go to the State Opera (as it had become) in the thirties. I was able on many occasions to hear Leo Slezak as Otello and Stolzing as well as the *buffo* Hans Breuer, whose name still appeared in my program in a *comprimario* role or in the capacity of evening producer during my almost daily visits to the opera in the twenties. I can also still recall Hermine Kittel, the alto Bella Paalen, the tenors Hubert Leuer and Georg Maikl, the soprano Bertha Forster, and above all Lucie Weidt performing as the sexton (with Maria Jeritza in the title role) in the first production of Janáček's *Jenufa* I ever saw. I also witnessed Anna Bahr-Mildenburg's last appearance at the State Opera: she declaimed Klytemnestra's screams in Strauss's *Elektra* almost voicelessly and with expansive gestures, but still made a strong impression. Sometimes, it must be said, she would make an unintentionally comic impression when she gave her all in public performances, using gestural techniques learned during the time of Mahler and Cosima Wagner, which is why she was unkindly called *Reichsgebärdenmutter* (Reich's mimic-mother) during the Hitler era.

I can still vividly remember Richard Mayr, famous for his historical Baron Ochs von Lerchenau in *Der Rosenkavalier*. He was a member of the opera house until his death in 1935. Laying aside Leo Slezak's work in films, Richard Mayr was the only singer from Mahler's time still to

96 Anna von Mildenburg, who later married Hermann Bahr, as Isolde, a part she first sang in 1900 (oil painting by Franz Matsch?).

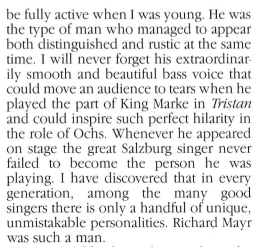

happened that can ever happen to a theater director: expenses went up and up, while receipts went down. It was at this point that there was criticism in high places, where gossip had until then been nobly ignored. The call to sack Mahler following the rejection of *Salome* by the censor had been resisted but the decision was now taken—albeit under protest from Vienna's intellectuals—to have Mahler removed.

He summed up his era best himself in his parting manifesto which he posted on the notice board:

98 Leopold Demuth as Hans Sachs in Wagner's *Die Meistersinger von Nürnberg*.

be fully active when I was young. He was the type of man who managed to appear both distinguished and rustic at the same time. I will never forget his extraordinarily smooth and beautiful bass voice that could move an audience to tears when he played the part of King Marke in *Tristan* and could inspire such perfect hilarity in the role of Ochs. Whenever he appeared on stage the great Salzburg singer never failed to become the person he was playing. I have discovered that in every generation, among the many good singers there is only a handful of unique, unmistakable personalities. Richard Mayr was such a man.

Gustav Mahler knew how to keep the daily repertoire at its best. It would not have been possible if he had not been able to call on the remarkable conducting talents of Alexander von Zemlinsky, Bruno Walter, and Franz Schalk. Walter and Schalk were later to play a prominent part in the history of the Vienna Opera.

Even Mahler, however, could not overcome the hurdle of the tenth year as director. He was increasingly hounded, precisely because he was such an exceptional man. In the end the worst thing

99 Wilhelm Hesch as the eponymous Falstaff in Verdi's opera, from 1905.

100 Margarethe Michalek as Chloë and Hermine Kittel als Daphnis in Tchaikovsky's *Pique Dame* in 1902. The costumes were the work of Heinrich Lefler.

101 Marie Gutheil-Schoder, seen here dressed as Carmen, was engaged at the Court Opera by Gustav Mahler.

102 Richard Mayr as King Mark in *Tristan und Isolde*. Mayr joined the Court Opera in 1902, a year before this picture was taken.

To the honored members of the Court Opera!

The hour has come when our work together must come to an end. I am leaving a place which I have grown to love, and this is my farewell to you.

Instead of something whole and rounded I am leaving behind me a fragmented and unfinished work, which is the fate of man.

It is not for me to pass judgment on what my work has meant to those people to whom it was dedicated. But I will say this about myself: my intentions were honest and I set my sights high. My efforts could not always be crowned with success. Nobody suffers more from the "intractability of matter," the power of matter over mind, than the practicing artist. And yet I have never given less than my all, sacrificing myself to the cause, my wishes to my duty. I have not spared myself and I therefore had the right to expect the same total commitment from others.

In the pressures of the struggle and the heat of the moment neither you nor I managed to avoid getting hurt or losing our way. But when a work was successful, a job well done, we would forget all trouble and strife and feel richly rewarded–even if there were no outward signs of success. We have all come a long way and with us the institution to which our efforts were devoted.

May I offer my heartfelt thanks to those people who supported me in my difficult and sometimes thankless job, who worked and argued with me. Accept my most sincere wishes for your future and for the prosperity of the Court Opera, whose fortunes I shall continue to follow with the very greatest interest.
Vienna, 7 December 1907

Gustav Mahler

He had conducted the Court Opera for the last time on 15 October. From 1908 until his death in 1911, Mahler, ailing, traveled restlessly in the new world and throughout Europe.

103 Alfred Roller's set design for Richard Strauss's *Elektra*, created by Anton Brioschi in 1909: "Inner courtyard of the king's palace at Mycenae."

Felix von Weingartner

Born 6. 2. 1863, Zara (Dalmatia); died 5. 7. 1942, Winterthur (Switzerland).
Director of the Court Opera from 1. 1. 1908 to 2. 28. 1911.

It was a foregone conclusion following Mahler's resignation that his preordained successor was the widely known Austrian conductor Felix Mottl. But the victor who emerged from skirmishes among the various interested factions was Felix von Weingartner.

Weingartner had been working as a conductor since 1884 in Königsberg, Danzig, Mannheim and, since 1891, at the Königliche Oper in Berlin. He was one of the leading figures in the anti-Mahler clique and had been associated with the Vienna Philharmonic for some time. He waited longingly for the seat of Court Opera director to fall vacant and "happened" to be in Vienna during the crisis surrounding the post. He was considered the ideal conductor of Beet-

hoven and was also a composer; his opera *Kain und Abel* was produced by his successor at the Court Opera on 4 December 1914. Weingartner's personality rebelled against Mahler's theatrical style. When he stood on the conductor's podium he always gave the impression that here was a highly elegant aristocrat who was not really moved by the music he was conducting. I myself always found his concerts and opera performances very balanced, somewhat cool, but never genuinely affecting.

Felix von Weingartner's choice of works was prompted fundamentally by a negative urge to reverse Mahler's legacy. Everything that Mahler had poured his heart into was now to be "put right again" as soon as possible. Thus, the third Leo-

nore overture was dropped from *Fidelio* again; when opposition to this interference proved irresistible Weingartner played the overture either in concerto form at the end of the opera or, on other occasions, at the beginning. He continued to reject Mahler's arrangement when he became director of the opera for the second time in the thirties.

Mahler's ensemble was left intact for the most part. Richard Mayr now displayed his abilities to the full, while the baritone Josef Schwarz and the bass baritone Victor Madin joined the company. Madin "survived" twelve directors and played an active part in the opera house until his death in 1968; as he was always proud to say, he sang in five thousand perfor-

104 Lucille Marcel, who became Felix von Weingartner's wife, as Elektra in Richard Strauss's opera in 1909.

105 Anna Bahr-Mildenburg as Klytamnestra in *Elektra*, a role which she sang to great acclaim between 1908 and 1930 (here with Roselotte Rudolf as Elektra).

Lucy Weidt

Opera, which had been scheduled by Mahler. This was reason enough for Weingartner to approach the project only half-heartedly. In typical fashion he did not study and conduct the opera himself, entrusting this difficult work instead to the conductor Hugo Reichenberger whom Weingartner had appointed to succeed Alexander von Zemlinsky. Reichenberger worked at the opera house until 1935, conducting fifty to sixty performances in a season, and was a typical musician of the old school. Richard Strauss supervised the rehearsals for *Elektra* personally.

Apart from Strauss's *Elektra*, the only works performed in Weingartner's era to remain in the repertoire were Puccini's *Tosca*, which had already been heard at the Volkstheater, and—to a lesser extent—*Basses Terres* by Eugen d'Albert. Weingartner's preference for comic opera was reflected in the number of works of this genre. One of the big hits was Richard Mayr in Cornelius's *Barbier von Bagdad*. The Austrian Julius Bittner was honored with the first ever performance of his opera *Der Musikant*, as was the thirteen-year old Erich Wolfgang Korngold with his ballet pantomime *Der Schneemann*. Weingartner's last premiere was Berlioz's *Benvenuto Cellini*. On 1 March 1911 he left the Court Opera because of serious attacks on him in the press.

Felix von Weingartner was strong enough to destroy the foundations laid by Mahler, but too weak to instill new life into the complex structure of the Court Opera. He did leave behind him one innovation, however, which we now take for granted: he started the practice of publishing the names of the conductor and producer in the program. This may be connected with the fact that as a bureaucrat he had little understanding of theater. As he did not get on well with Alfred Roller (who took the only logical step and left), Weingartner took on Wilhelm von Wymetal as producer.

After departing from the Court Opera Weingartner remained until 1927 as the Vienna Philharmonic's only conductor and also served as director of the Vienna Volksoper from 1919 to 1924. In Basel he achieved great success teaching conducting at the conservatory.

mances and never cancelled. He was the perfect example of the conscientious and outstanding member of a company, never seeking to join the ranks of the stars.

Weingartner's favorite female singer was Lucille Marcel, whom he later married. She achieved great success singing the title role of Richard Strauss's *Elektra* in its opening performance at the Court

Hans Gregor

Born 4. 14. 1866, Dresden; died 8. 13. 1945, Wernigerode.
Director of the Court Opera from 3. 1. 1911 to 11. 14. 1918.

It would appear that following the failure of Weingartner's directorship the view became widespread that the director of the Court Opera should not be selected as if the exercise was a party game. The First Court Chamberlain and the general intendant now had advisors to help them decide who should occupy the director's chair (a very progressive step). Advisors were considered better able to make suggestions than the ladies and gentlemen of Viennese society. They arrived finally at the name of Hans Gregor, who was the founder and leader of the Komische Oper in Berlin. He had made a name not only for this achievement but also as a producer. In those days opera producers were not yet looked on as artists (unlike in the spoken theater), so Gregor retains to this day the stigma of being no more than a manager. Even so, nobody can deny that with the exception of Gustav Mahler there had not been—and possibly has not been since, when one looks at his choice of repertoire—a more successful director of the Vienna Opera than Hans Gregor.

As a native Saxon working in Vienna he was certainly never going to have an easy time. He had a very bold tongue and often commented on Viennese sloppiness. The Viennese react badly when they hear remarks of this kind from a non-Viennese, let alone a non-Viennese from Saxony.

Gregor's period as director fell at the worst imaginable time. He was appointed in 1911 and departed at the end of the Great War. Yet Gregor managed to produce a number of Viennese and world premieres of major works. He also successfully conjured up excellent soloists almost out of thin air, and although they were not Austrians they were adopted as Austrians and even became honorary members of the Vienna Opera.

The world premieres were *Violanta* by Erich Wolfgang Korngold, the Viennese version of *Ariadne auf Naxos* by Richard Strauss, and *Notre Dame* by Franz Schmidt; the premieres were Strauss's *Rosenkavalier* (only three months after the world premiere in Dresden), Debussy's *Pelléas et Mélisande*, Puccini's *La fanciulla del West*, Wagner's *Parsifal* (immediately after the copyright expired), Leoš Janáček's *Jenufa*, and finally *Salome*, which Gregor managed to wring out of the crumbling Austro-Hungarian Empire's censor in 1918.

Gregor's arrival brought about the return of Alfred Roller to a position of influence and respect. As a producer Gregor knew Roller's true worth and under his directorship the hitherto neglected producer of opera came to the fore, achieving the status enjoyed in the spoken theater. Once again this incurred the displeasure of those whose interest was primarily in the music, for Roller's productions had a life of their own and did not simply illustrate the score. The singers were given ever greater freedom and increasing use was made of international stars such as Enrico Caruso and George Baklanoff.

Gregor's principal stars were without question Maria Jeritza (whom he persuaded away from the Volksoper and who made her debut at the Court Opera on 16 March 1912 as "Mitzi Jeritza" in Max Oberleithner's *Aphrodite* with Franz Schalte conducting) and Lotte Lehmann. In these two sopranos there is no doubt that Gregor had acquired the two most interesting German-speaking singers in the first half of the twentieth century.

Jeritza was the ideal performer of complex women such as Salome, Jenufa, the empress in *Die Frau ohne Schatten* and later in the title role of *Die Ägyptische Helena*. Puccini preferred her among all others as Tosca, Minnie, and Turandot, and she played in the Viennese premiere of *Jenufa* on 16 February 1918. Lotte Lehmann was by contrast the ideal Marschallin, the Dyer's wife, Desdemona, Manon (by Massenet), Lotte (in *Werther*), and also a most moving Leonore in *Fidelio*.

107   Richard Mayr as Ochs von Lerchenau in Richard Strauss's *Der Rosenkavalier* (oil painting by Anton Faistauer).

Although the two singers shared certain roles in the repertoire–for example Elisabeth in *Tannhäuser*–they differed widely in character and in the timbre of their voices. Jeritza had a glorious and unusually full voice, which enabled her to be heard with apparent ease above an equally booming orchestra, while Lehmann had a fervent and highly expressive voice that had a unique tonal quality. I am not embarrassed to say that Lehmann could move me to tears when she began to sing. Jeritza took complete control of every role with her temperament and sparkling appearance, while Lehmann put so much life into everything she sang. Jeritza was a theatrical *diva*; Lehmann a

great musician who was a triumphant success both on the stage and in the concert hall.

The lyric tenor during Gregor's time was the British singer Alfred Piccaver. He was born in Long Sutton, grew up in America and studied in Milan. He made his debut at the Court Opera in 1910 as a stand-in during an Italian *stagione*, was engaged permanently in 1912 and was to remain a member of the company until 1949 (though he spent the Hitler years in exile). He gave perfect interpretations of Italian and French works but also made an enchanting Lohengrin. His voice had a unique quality–he needed to sing no more than a couple of notes for the

108 Marie Gutheil-Schoder, the first Viennese "knight of the rose" in *Der Rosenkavalier* in 1911.

109 Lucie Weidt, Vienna's first Marschallin. The premiere of Richard Strauss's *Rosenkavalier* took place at the Court Opera on 8 April 1911.

110 Alfred Roller's costume sketches for Richard Strauss's *Der Rosenkavalier* in 1911: the Feldmarschallin, Baron Ochs, Oktavian, the little moor.

FELDMARSCHALLIN WARTENBERG
3.KOST.
3.AKT

BARON LERCHENAV
2.KOST.
2.AKT

OKTAVIAN
4.KOST.
2.AKT

DER KLEINE MOHR DER FÜRSTIN

listener to know who was singing. I saw him in all his roles from 1925. I will never forget his voice, and for me he has no equal in a number of parts, such as Canio (in *I Pagliacci*) and André Chenier. I would have seen him even more often if he had not, to our great regret, cancelled so many performances. Georg Maikl and Hubert Leuer acted as his stand-ins.

The dashing baritone during Gregor's directorship was Hans Duhan, a singer with an immensely beautiful voice who mastered every part with his persuasive musicality. He could also be seen at the end of his career conducting the Vienna State Opera, though unfortunately his conducting did not compare with his artistry as a singer.

I can also recall three singers from this period who were not the most prominent but who were outstanding performers in their fields: the *buffo* tenor Hermann

Gallos, the comic baritone Hermann Wiedemann, and the Croation bass Nikolas Zec. Hardly a single performance would have been possible without these three singers who appeared in conjunction with Madin mentioned above. They were the mainstay of the repertoire and performed exceptionally often–I believe that Gallos made about one hundred and twenty performances a year. We can not imagine such a figure today. Everything Gallos did was very tidy and reliable, but there were two particular roles at which I have never heard him surpassed: the emperor Altoum in *Turandot* and the shepherd in *Tristan und Isolde*. The quality of his voice was tailor-made for the wistful music of *Tristan* and in *Turandot* one really had the impression that the emperor actually was the son of the heavens. Nikolaus Zec made every character he played a fully rounded

111 Maria Jeritza made her debut at the Court Opera in 1912. Here she plays Salome in Richard Strauss's opera of the same name, the premiere of which took place on 14 October 1918.

112 The composer Giacomo Puccini with Maria Jeritza, who sang the Viennese versions of Minnie in *La fanciulla del West* and *Tosca*.

113 The world premiere of the new version of Richard Strauss's *Ariadne auf Naxos* on 4 October 1916. From left to right: Julius Betetto as Truffaldin, Hermann Gallos as Scaramuccio, Maria Jeritza as Ariadne, Selma Kurz as Zerbinetta, Hans Duhan as Harlekin, and George Maikl as Brighella.

person but without excess. When I was young I saw Wiedemann play Beckmesser and Alberich, and he had the ability to make these problematic characters appear completely believable.

The monarchy was laid to rest at the end of the First World War in 1918 and the republic was proclaimed. The fate of the Court Theater was never in doubt, in spite of the natural uncertainty which prevailed. The Hofoperntheater was now called the Operntheater, the Hofburgtheater was now the Burgtheater. It was taken for granted that the general intendant who had been appointed during the monarchy should appoint the director of opera in the republic.

The general intendant of the Court Theater appointed by Emperor Karl was Leopold von Andrian, who moved in Vienna's progressive circles and was a friend of Hugo von Hofmannsthal and Richard Strauss. He simply had Gregor replaced, believing that the young republic should strive to make its presence felt internationally in the field of culture. What did little Austria have left apart from its cultural achievements? Andrian set little store by managers, concentrating instead on creative artists. On this basis he suggested the dual directorship by

114 Leo Slezak returned to the Court Opera under Hans Gregor and sang such roles as Otello in Verdi's opera.

95

Richard Strauss and Franz Schalk. This would ensure that even as a republic the Vienna Opera's artistic standards could hardly be surpassed by any theater in the world. It was inevitable that the joint direction of Strauss and Schalk was far more likely to bring the opera glory than under Gregor, who was unfairly disliked by everyone. Today we can only say that Hans Gregor carried out his task splendidly. Perhaps he was simply ahead of his time.

Richard Strauss

Born 6. 11. 1864, Munich; died 9. 8. 1949, Garmisch.
Director of the State Opera from 8. 16. 1919 to 10. 31. 1924.

Franz Schalk

Born 5. 27. 1863, Vienna; died 9. 2. 1931, Edlach (Lower Austria).
Director of the State Opera from 11. 15. 1918 to 10. 31. 1924.

The announcement of the proposed dual directorship of Strauss/Schalk was, surprisingly, not received in Vienna with unanimous enthusiasm by either the press or the opera world, but rather it was vociferously objected to. From the orchestra to the technical staff, and even the artists themselves (with the exception of Maria Jeritza, Selma Kurz, and Franz Schalk), all considered the appointment of Richard Strauss to be a damaging and dangerous step. In the background Felix von Weingartner, in particular, with his substantial influence over the orchestra of the Vienna Philharmonic, stirred up anti-Strauss feeling. The fear was widely voiced that if he became director Strauss would give too great a prominence to his own works. It should not be forgotten that there was no great enthusiasm in Vienna for modern music and at that time Strauss was largely misunderstood and considered *avantgarde*. I know from my own experience that in the twenties even Richard Wagner was looked on in many circles as a modernist; when I practiced Wagner arrangements on the piano at home my father would react furiously, even forbidding me to play "this appalling modern music."

The objections to Schalk were of a completely different order. Schalk had developed within the Court Opera–he had started there on 1 September 1901 as first conductor–and had made a reputation for himself (even with Viennese society) as a result of his excellent work. Schalk was very keen on a joint appointment with Richard Strauss. He took charge of the State Opera in mid-November 1918, while Richard Strauss waited. Although Strauss loved Vienna dearly, he was not convinced that he should ignore the storm of indignation that had greeted his proposed appointment. He remained in Garmisch and watched from there to see how matters would develop. Meanwhile, his many admirers and friends in Vienna did everything they could to ensure his nomination. Moves were also afoot at this time to persuade Strauss back to take up a leading position there. When Strauss was asked by a music fan from Berlin "What, you're going to Vienna, where people are so false?" Strauss allegedly replied "That's how they are everywhere, but in Vienna they are so elegant about it."

On 11 April 1919 a performance of *Parsifal* took place under Leopold Reichwein, who was one of Strauss's bitterest opponents. When he appeared in the orchestra pit he was met by a huge storm of protest and cries of "We want Strauss!" It was now clear that the Viennese public were on Strauss's side. He therefore decided finally to go to Vienna. He took up his post officially on 16 August 1919 but did not hold the baton until 1 January 1920 when he conducted *Lohengrin*.

115, 116 Alfred Roller's set designs for Richard Strauss's *Die Frau ohne Schatten*: the empress's bedroom, and the dyer's house. The first ever performance took place in Vienna on 10 October 1919.

HOFMANNSTHAL · STRAUSS · DIE · FRAU · OHN · SCHATTEN · DAS · FÄRBER

It was arranged that contractually Strauss was "emperor" while Schalk was "chancellor." Schalk was to be responsible for casting and, needless to say, Strauss had a say particularly in productions of his own works. However, Strauss saw the job of the director as different in practice—he took an interest in the smallest detail and it was inevitable that sooner or later he would come into conflict with Schalk. The position of Schalk (who had had sole charge of the State Opera for eight months, from 15 November 1918 until Strauss's appointment on 16 August 1919) grew in strength for the simple reason that Strauss, quite naturally, did not give up his composing and was therefore away from Vienna frequently in order to work in Garmisch. In any case, the conjunction of two major figures would never have worked in the long run. Verbal and written disputes finally lead to the premature end of the arrangement. In a letter to Schalk on 4 February 1924 Strauss wrote: "... Keep this letter as a reminder of our sincere but fruitless artistic work together. It may be the last. On my return I have decided to have a serious final discussion with the government—things cannot go on as they

117–120 Maria Jeritza as the empress, Karl Aagard Oestvig as the emperor, Lotte Lehmann as the dyer's wife, and Richard Mayr as Barak in Richard Strauss's *Die Frau ohne Schatten* in 1919.

are…" He ends the letter by saying: "I shall continue to live in Vienna as a former director. So we can play a duet or have a game of chess together at the Belvedere! The poor Opera! It is very sad!"

On paper the joint directorship of Strauss and Schalk may have been ideal, but a realist could have seen in advance that the very concept was a mistaken one. Such a structure can only succeed if one of the partners understands that he is number two and is prepared to adopt a subservient role. Schalk never had this intention and Strauss was by then a famous German composer.

In spite of the constant tension, the dual directorship did provide the musical life of Vienna with a considerable number of splendid evenings of opera. Richard Strauss made frequent appearances as conductor, the highlights of which were the *Ring, Cosi fan tutte* (his own production), *Ariadne auf Naxos*, and *Salome*; the world premiere of his Ballet *Schlagobers*, Gluck's ballet *Don Juan*, and the world premiere of his festival production of *Die Ruinen von Athen* with dance and chorus by Hugo von Hofmansthal set to his own music. Strauss's latest opera *Die Frau ohne Schatten*, his parting gift to the

121 Erik Schmedes as Palestrina and Berta Kiurina as Ighino in Hans Pfitzner's *Palestrina.* The Viennese premiere occurred on 1 March 1919.

122 Elisabeth Schumann as Susanna in Mozart's *The Marriage of Figaro.*

State Opera, had its world premiere there on 10 October 1919.

On 1 March 1919, during Schalk's interregnum, the Viennese premiere of Hans Pfitzner's *Palestrina* took place. Soon regular letters were being exchanged between the composer Pfitzner and the director Strauss, with Pfitzner complaining that *Palestrina* was not being performed often enough. The justification given for this still applies today in the case of new works, which are not easy to repeat because all the original protagonists are not always available. Palestrina was sung at the time by Erik Schmedes.

In Vienna *Die Frau ohne Schatten* had brilliant collaborators–Franz Schalk conducted, Maria Jeritza sang the part of the empress, Lotte Lehmann the dyer's wife, Lucie Weidt played the nurse, Karl Aagard Oestvig the emperor, and Richard Mayr was Barak.

A whole series of contemporary works were incorporated into the repertoire during the Strauss/Schalk period: Puccini's *Trittico* and *Manon Lescaut*, Kienzl's *Kuhreigen*, Korngold's *Die tote Stadt*, Schreker's *Schatzgräber* and *Die Gezeichneten*, Franz Schmidt's *Fredegundis*, Julius Bittner's *Die Kohlhaymerin* and *Das Rosengärtlein*. Strauss's *Josephs Legende*, which had first been performed in Paris in 1914, was added to the ballet repertoire of the Vienna State Opera in 1922 with Marie Gutheil-Schoder playing Potiphar's wife. (This persuaded me when I was director to ask Maria Callas if she was interested in the same role. She did not object to the offer in principle, but at the time she imposed impossible conditions.)

During this period the State Opera opened a subsidiary theater for small operas in the Redoutensaal of the

123 Karl Aagard Oestvig as Canio in Ruggiero Leoncavallo's *I Pagliacci*.

Hofburg, which Alfred Roller had converted. Having left in 1909 following arguments with Weingartner, Roller now returned finally to the Opera. The period also brought the conductors Karl Alwin and Clemens Krauss.

The singers from Mahler and Gregor's time were joined by the coloratura soprano Elisabeth Schumann, whose Sophie in *Der Rosenkavalier* became a world-famous bravura performance. Josef von Manowarda and Alfred Jerger very quickly became the State Opera's favorite bass baritones. Jerger was an interesting singer-actor and his Mandryka in Strauss's *Arabella* (which he had just sung a few months earlier at the world premiere in Dresden in 1933) has still to be bettered. The baritone Emil Schipper remained one of the house's busiest singers until the beginning of the Second World War. The young heroic tenor of the time was Karl

Oestvig, a favorite singer of Richard Strauss and an ideal interpreter of the roles of Baccus in *Ariadne* and the emperor in *Die Frau ohne Schatten*. I saw him myself in the role of Siegmund the first time I saw *Die Walküre*. Fritz Krenn, who actually left the State Opera in 1924 for Berlin and only returned in 1937, was the best Ochs von Lerchenau after Richard Mayr until he retired in 1958. William Wernigk, the "eternal" Wenzel in *The Bartered Bride*, went on in later life to represent the artistic staff on the management committee. He sang all the smaller comic parts (some of them very small)— hardly a performance went by in which he did not appear. I can still remember with some emotion Vienna's first Zdenka (in *Arabella*) Luise Helletsgruber, who could move us so greatly in a number of roles, Liu, for example, with her clear, bright soprano. Maria Gerhart was the

101

coloratura soprano between the wars and was the "regular" Queen of the Night and Zerbinetta.

The joint directorship of Strauss and Schalk ended on 31 October 1924—not, mercifully, with the irrevocable departure of Richard Strauss. He continued to conduct at the State Opera on many occasions and for many years, in order to fulfill the commitment he took on in accepting property on Jacquingasse offered him by the government. The house there is still owned by the great man's descendants (rented to the Netherlands embassy).

As a director of the State Opera Richard Strauss was a circumspect and possibly over-fastidious administrator, while as a conductor he has left behind unforgettable musical memories. In his youth he used to wave his hands about wildly but later with the slightest of gestures, he had complete control over the orchestra, singers, and the audience. Though he was quite plain in appearance and could not be described as having anything in the way of "artistic features," the man's magic was enormous. He radiated kindness even during the rehearsal period and hardly ever had an unfriendly word— even when he was dissatisfied with a piece of work he would indulge in gentle irony.

125 Collaborators on the world premiere of Richard Strauss's *Intermezzo* in 1927. From left to right: Margarethe Krauss as Anna, Karl Ziegler as Baron Lummer, Lotte Lehmann as Christine, Alfred Jerger as the conductor Storch, the producer Lothar Wallenstein, and (seated) the composer.

Franz Schalk

Director of the State Opera from 11. 1. 1924 to 8. 31. 1929.

The Strauss/Schalk era lasted only five years but it went down in the history of the Vienna State Opera as one of the most glittering periods. Schalk, who now had sole charge and could carry out his own plans undisturbed by Richard Strauss, ensured that a certain continuity was maintained from the previous partnership as he was still able to call on Strauss—to work for him rather than for advice as before. During this period the conducting was carried out alternately by Schalk, Richard Strauss, Clemens Krauss, Alwin, and Reichenberger, so in artistic terms not much had changed. It was only when Schalk's tenure ended that casts had to be changed. Certain singers were naturally beginning to show their age. The old system seemed to be past its best too and needed to be replaced by a young reforming spirit.

Schalk looked after Strauss's work in exemplary fashion. He introduced the Viennese versions of *Intermezzo* and of *Ägyptische Helena* (with Strauss conducting). The production had been the work of Lothar Wallerstein who had been appointed to the position of chief producer by Schalk.

Schalk's program of premieres was extremely successful. He introduced Vienna to Puccini's *Turandot*, Giordano's *André Chenier*, and Mussorgski's *Boris Godunov*. After the sensational success of Korngold's *Die tote Stadt* he managed to secure the Viennese premiere of the same composer's *Wunder der Heliane* and of Julius Bittner's *Höllisch Gold*. He also introduced Vienna to Verdi's *Forza del Destino* in the German version by Franz Werfel. It is remarkable that men whom we regard as "classical" modern compos-

126 Puccini's *Turandot* reached the Vienna State Opera when Schalk was director. Alfred Roller designed the sets and the costumes, and Lothar Wallenstein was responsible for the production.

ers—Stravinsky, Hindemith, and Krenek—were already being discussed by Schalk. The first performance of Paul Hindemith's *Cardillac* took place on 3 March 1927, but an argument took place during rehearsals; Hindemith left, and the work was only performed three times in all. Krenek's *Jonny spielt auf* was produced on 31 December in the same year, enjoying huge success: everybody wanted to see the "negro opera" and the work saw thirty-one performances in one season alone, remaining in the repertoire until 1931. Igor Stravinsky had more luck than Hindemith too, and his *Oedipus Rex*, which had its premiere on 23 February 1928, was shown six times.

Lothar Wallerstein's production of *Rheingold* was to have initiated a new *Ring*. Wilhelm Furtwängler was due to

the State Opera's Wagnerian heroine for years. There was Vera Schwarz, who became well known particularly in Berlin as a leading lady with an extensive repertoire ranging from Carmen to Lisa (in Tchaikovsky's *Pique Dame*), and Maria Nemeth, who was noted for her brilliant–though not always tidy–upper reach, above all in the part of Turandot. In addition there were the sopranos Wanda Achsel-Clemens, Margit Schenker-Angerer, who caused such a stir in the premiere of *La Forza del Destino*, and lastly Adele Kern who played soubrette roles in most Mozart productions. The tenors included Richard Schubert, who became the Wagnerians' favorite because of his dramatic power and dazzling appearance, although his heyday ended with Schalk's departure. The lyric tenor Koloman von Pataky was a mainstay of the ensemble. Another rising star among the tenors was the Roumanian Trajan Grosavescu, who had only a brief career–he was shot by his jealous wife during a performance. The lyric tenor Josef Kalenberg was the theater's regular all-purpose performer until he developed into a heroic tenor under Clemens Krauss; even in this capacity he remained an unjustifyably neglected permanent stand-in. The most important engagement, which was sadly

127 Lotte Lehmann as Turandot in Puccini's opera. The premiere took place on 14 October 1926.

128 Erich Wolfgang Korngold's *Wunder der Heliane* was performed in Lothar Wallerstein's production on 29 October 1927. A scene with Lotte Lehmann as Heliane and Jan Kiepura as the stranger.

conduct the tetralogy, and it was said that he was being groomed to take over as director when Schalk left. *Rheingold* was in fact as far as it went, and Furtwängler stayed in Berlin.

Schalk's stars Jeritza, Lehmann, and Piccaver were joined by a host of excellent new singers: the altos Rosette Anday and Maria Olczewska, and the contraltos Enid Szantho and Helene Wildbrunn, who was

short-lived, was the young Polish tenor Jan Kiepura who took Vienna by storm. He went on to enjoy an international career and even achieved popular acclaim as a film star.

The appointment of Lothar Wallerstein to the post of principle producer had a great effect on the quality of performances. He introduced the State Opera to the concept of a producer's theater. Until his arrival the audience certainly considered the musical content of opera to be paramount—it is well known that Gregor was criticized for stressing production values to the detriment of the music. In the intervening period the producer had become a more familiar figure. The undoubted crudeness of the stagecraft had gradually come to be looked on as scandalous and now audiences were no longer satisfied by a convincing musical interpretation and nothing else—they wanted to see a believable and functional production as well. Wallerstein was the first producer at the State Opera to have extra powers and to made good use of them.

Schalk's period as director saw the appointment of Robert Heger and, as well as Wilhelm Furtwängler's *Rheingold* interlude, a sensational guest performance by the whole of the Scala Milan under the baton of Arturo Toscanini, which led to closer ties between the maestro and both the Salzburg Festival and the Vienna State Opera.

129   Two stars from the Schalk era: Lotte Lehmann as Leonore and Alfred Piccaver as Florestan in Beethoven's *Fidelio* in 1927.

130   Maria Jeritza in the title role of Puccini's *Turandot*.

131 Alfred Jerger as Jonny in Ernst Krenek's jazz opera *Jonny spielt auf,* which had its premiere on 31 December 1927.

Schalk had a life-long relationship with the State Opera. He was the only man to work his way up from conductor to become a long-standing director. However, it became clear to insiders in the second half of the twenties that Schalk had had his day. In view of growing economic difficulties the government at the time took the advice of Arthur Krupp (the owner of the Berndorf steelworks) and named the hat maker Franz Schneiderhan first as general intendant and then as general director of the Austrian State Theater. This appointment caused inevitable complications with directors, who had acted with a fair degree of autonomy since the republic was established. Schneiderhan now even intervened in artistic matters, insisting for example that Schalk make the program appeal to more popular tastes. A serious artist like Schalk could not get used to such a state of affairs. His health grew worse. Finally Schalk did the only thing he could, and in view of the verbal agreement that was to have prepared the way for Wilhelm Furtwängler, his departure was welcomed. Two months before he died Schalk

appeared on the podium of the State Opera for the last time and conducted *Tristan und Isolde.*

Clemens Krauss

Born 3. 31. 1893, Vienna; died 5. 16. 1954, Mexico City.
Director of the State Opera from 9. 1. 1929 to 12. 10. 1934.

The competition for Wilhelm Furtwängler between the cities of Berlin and Vienna was eventually won by Berlin. The general director of the Austrian State Theater was now faced with the problem of finding a replacement who was equal in standing. Richard Strauss urged the appointment of Clemens Krauss, who was at the time opera director in Frankfurt. Krauss himself hesitated for a long while because he was not sure that he would be able to carry out the kind of reforming measures in Vienna which he had implemented in Frankfurt, where he had made the opera house much admired.

But Richard Strauss, who considered Clemens Krauss an outstanding interpreter and admirer of his work (as he did later with Karl Böhm), continued to recommend his appointment. The choice of Krauss brought widespread opposition in Vienna. He was thought to be too young and not famous enough for the State Opera. Nonetheless, he took up the post on 1 September 1929, and following a troubled stay, left Vienna on 10 December 1934.

Krauss made his presence felt in all spheres of activity at the State Opera. He kept rigidly to the principle that operas should only be performed by the cast who appeared in the premiere, and works which he had reserved for himself were conducted by him alone. His influence did not only cover the musical interpretation, from the initial groundwork to the mastery of a role, but also went as far as close collaboration with Lothar Wallerstein on the dramatic interpretation. He insisted on conducting all the subscription concerts of the Vienna Philharmonic (the State Opera's permanent orchestra), and from 1929 that was what happened. (As leader of the Vienna Philharmonic he introduced the New Year's concerts and also encouraged the concert work of the State Opera's chorus.) As in the time of Mahler, there was now a strong artistic personality behind decisions at the State Opera—in fact Krauss was perhaps even more rigorous in pressing home his convictions than Mahler had been. Krauss's conception of how to do things was so strong that the five years under his leadership were stamped indelibly with his mark. The period came almost to symbolize the philosophy of the ensemble.

His philosophy also caused tension. Clemens Krauss had taken on a group of new singers, but he had also promoted older members of the company of whom he thought highly, preferring to use them even if—in the opinion of the general public—there were better singers available.

The new arrivals included Viorica Ursuleac, who later became Krauss's wife; Jarmila Novotna, a stunningly beautiful singer who was a triumphant Oktavian and Giuditta; Margit Bokor, a consummate interpreter of interesting operatic character parts; the Hungarian Rose Pauly, who now played Elektra, the dyer's wife, and Marie (in Berg's *Wozzeck*); and Anny Konetzni, a Viennese soprano who played Wagnerian heroines for many years and won the audience's approval in her speciality of abandoned, melodramatic women, with her voluminous yet velvety voice. There was the lyric soprano Eva Hadrabova; the contralto Gertrud Rünger, who achieved success as Eboli in *Don Carlos*; and the tenors Helge Rosvaenge and Franz Völker, great exponents of their art who, under Krauss's proper guidance, became favorites with audiences, succeeding Leo Slezak and Erik Schmedes. To this number were added the baritone Willi Domgraf-Fassbaender, the ideal Mozart singer, Karl Hammes and

William Rode, an actor-singer of great stature who was acclaimed as Sachs in Clemens Krauss's first premiere *Die Meistersinger von Nürnberg*. He was accompanied in this performance by Erich Zimmermann, the best comic tenor of the time, in the role of David.

Conducting alongside Clemens Krauss were as before Robert Heger, Karl Alwin, and Hugo Reichenberger, and they were joined by the Viennese Josef Krips and Egon Pollack. Pollack, who had enjoyed great success in Hamburg, did not settle in completely and soon left the State Opera. As soon as he was appointed Josef Krips

132 Richard Strauss's *Arabella* was first performed at the Vienna State Opera on 21 October 1933, only months after its world premiere in Dresden. Lothar Wallerstein was the producer, and Lotte Lehmann and Alfred Jerger played Arabella and Mandryka.

embarked on an extremely successful career, which was interrupted by Austria's Anschluss with the Reich. His best time was to come in 1945 with the emergence of an independent Austria.

Krauss did particularly well by continuing very stylishly the Verdi cycle which Schalk had started, with the Wallerstein/Roller partnership and an adaptation by Franz Werfel. Their productions of *Simon Boccanegra* and *Don Carlos*, together with *Macbeth* and *Falstaff*, were the highlights of Krauss's directorship (*Macbeth* and *Don Carlos* were actually being seen at the State Opera for the first time!). Further highlights were the new production of the *Ring des Nibelungen*, which Schalk had inaugurated with *Rheingold*. For various reasons these Wagner productions were not, however, without controversy. In the first premiere, *Die Meistersinger*, the unrelieved black worn by the Mastersingers brought sneers. Also, there were complaints at first that the Walkyrie's cliff did not have a pine tree on it, and then that the pine was growing bigger and bigger with each performance. However, taken as a whole, Krauss's *Ring*

was the classic interpretation of the thirties and forties.

The task of maintaining Strauss's complete works was naturally dear to Krauss's heart. On 21 October 1933, a few days after the world premiere in Dresden, came the first performance in Vienna of *Arabella*, with Lotte Lehmann, Luise Helletsgruber, Alfred Jerger, Helge Rosvaenge (as Matteo), and Richard Mayr. The critics' prediction that *Arabella* would not remain in the repertoire was not fulfilled. *Die Frau ohne Schatten* and *Die Ägyptische Helena* received new productions, and on Krauss's recommendation Mozart's *Idomeneo* was reworked—in fact re-composed—by Richard Strauss, who also conducted.

There were new productions of Mozart's *Magic Flute* and *Cosi fan tutte*. Krauss saw Dorabella and Fiordiligi as dramatic roles and he cast them accordingly with Viorica Ursuleac and Gertrud Rünger, who were later to be admired as Chrysothemis and Elektra.

Following the *Ring*, Wagner's work was completed by a sensational new production of *Rienzi* and a new *Parsifal*.

133 Mozart's *Idomeneo* was performed in a version by Richard Strauss in 1931: Josef Kalenberg in the title role and Eva Hadrabova as Idamante in the final scene.

The bad financial situation—which on occasions even led to fears that the Opera might have to consider closing—persuaded Krauss into staging the world premiere of Lehár's *Giuditta*, playing it (with Richard Tauber and Jarmila Novotna) in rapid succession. Krauss also introduced Richard Heuberger's *Der Opernball* with Lotte Lehmann and Franz von Suppé's *Boccaccio* with Jeritza—in spite of their glittering casts neither work enjoyed great success.

In spite of the public's reservations Clemens Krauss also went in for modern opera. He premiered Alban Berg's *Wozzeck* with Josef von Manowarda and Rose Pauly, Egon Wellesz's *Bacchantinnen*, and Robert Heger's *Bettler Namenlos* (Nameless Beggar). Hans Pfitzner's last opera *Das Herz* was a failure, but Jaromir Wein-

berger's *Schwanda der Dudelsackpfeifer* was a hit, in a version by the well-known Oskar Strnad. Julius Bittner's *Das Veilchen* received its first ever performance.

Mention must be made here of another world premiere which Clemens Krauss set in motion but never produced, because of interference of one kind or another. The opera was *Karl V* and was commisioned by the Vienna State Opera from Ernst Krenek in the expectation of a similar success to that achieved by *Jonny spielt auf*. I have had close ties with this work during my opera career. When the Third Reich ended I was general secretary of the Vienna Konzerthaus and organized a version of the work in concert form. When I was appointed to the directorship of the State Opera, it was only natural that Ernst Krenek, whose work I had put on

134 Viorica Urseleac, Clemens Krauss's wife, was a celebrated Arabella.

135 Franz Lehár's *Giuditta* received its world premiere at the Vienna State Opera on 20 January 1934. The producer Hubert Marischka (left) with Jarmila Navotna and Richard Tauber.

136   The premier of Alban Berg's *Wozzeck* on 30 March 1930: Georg Maikl as the captain, Josef von Manowarda in the title role and Hermann Wiedemann as the doctor, together with the composer.

many times while I was at the Konzerthaus, should expect me to make up for the injustice of having this premiere postponed and to produce it in dramatic form at the State Opera. For various reasons, which are usually described as "technical" and which had nothing to do with the quality of the piece, I was unable to fulfill Krenek's expectations. My successor in office, Lorin Maazel, wanted to organize an opera competition and asked a number of composers to take part. Interestingly, these included Krenek. He felt he was being teased—understandably— and answered that he had been asked to submit an opera a long time ago but that it had never been produced, namely, *Karl V.* Lorin Maazel decided to schedule the work for autumn 1987. But it turned out

that he left after directing the State Opera for only a year and a half, and, as my successor's successor, it was my privilege finally to put on *Karl V* at the State Opera in the presence of the composer, in a production by Otto Schenk and with musical direction by Erich Leinsdorf. It was a great success. As Krenek can testify, "everything comes to those who wait."

Clemens Krauss was constantly on the look-out for a cheerful work for New Year's Eve, as an alternative to *Die Fledermaus.* He discovered *Ghost in the Castle* by the Czech composer Jaroslav Kricka. Although the public and the press reacted favorably to the work, it was only a passing fancy.

Krauss also looked for new places to perform besides the Redoutensaal, and found the attractive Schlosstheater at

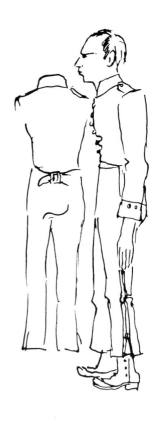

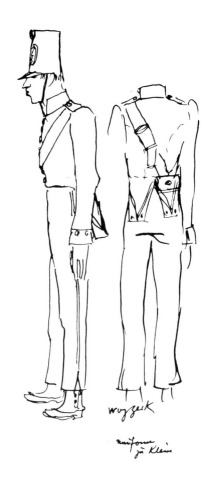

Schönbrunn, where he presented Pergolesi's *La Serva Padrona* with Elisabeth Schumann. He produced the soprano version of Rossini's *La Cenerentola* with Adele Kern.

A memorial concert at the State Opera in November 1934 commemorated the murder on 25 July of Chancellor Dollfuss. In keeping with the occasion, Arturo Toscanini conducted Verdi's *Requiem*.

Dollfuss's murder strikes the political keynote. Clemens Krauss's contract expired at the end of the 1933–34 season. The contract was to be extended for only a year, probably for political reasons. It was a time of great tension, even in Vienna, following Hitler's rise to power in Germany in 1933. Dollfuss's murder caused problems for every institution, because there were national-socialist "subversives" in every office or company. Chancellor Schuschnigg and his culture minister Hans Pernter had the impression during Krauss's last year as director that

Krauss and a number of his favorites were sympathetic towards Hitler's Germany. Krauss had in fact been asked whether he would accept an invitation to Berlin or Munich. He told me himself after the war—and this was confirmed to me by Pernter, who was a close friend—that he would have left whether or not his contract had been extended for five more years. The government could not come to a decision, and so Clemens Krauss signed for the Berlin State Opera, leaving shortly at Hitler's request for Munich to found a *Reichsoper* free of any financial constraints.

It is certainly not true that Clemens Krauss had Nazi inclinations of any kind. Unlike other major conductors he was never a party member. In my opinion, however, he failed to recognize that politics has a great bearing on art. In any case it is not true that as soon as Hitler took over in Germany he banned all works by Jewish composers from the

137 Costume sketches by Oskar Strnad for Alban Berg's *Wozzeck* in 1930.

138 Oskar Strnad's set design for the Viennese premiere of *Wozzeck* in the 1930 production by Lothar Wallenstein.

Vienna State Opera's repertoire. During Krauss's directorship the Munich State Opera offered asylum to many artists who were threatened for racial reasons. Krauss's bad reputation was due in part to the fact that the singers whom he took with him to Berlin–his wife Viorica Ursuleac, Franz Völker, Josef von Manowarda, Erich Zimmermann, Gertrud Rünger–supported national socialism.

In the course of events, in fact, the Vienna State Opera was deprived not only of its outstanding director but of its best singers. The need now was to find an appealing new director who would be able to put the ensemble back to full strength and to cope with the administrative duties which Krauss had carried out in exemplary fashion in conjunction with his permanent assistant Erwin Kerber.

114

Felix von Weingartner

Director of the State Opera from 1. 1. 1935 to 9. 1. 1936.

The most important requirement was for a big name, and Felix von Weingartner's name was suggested for a second time. He was appointed director of the Opera and Erwin Kerber became administrative director. This laid the foundations for a functional theater. Weingartner hardly had time to leave any trace in his short period in office. Events worthy of note include the premiere of Ravel's *L'Heure Espagnol*, the world premiere of Franz Salmhofer's *Dame im Traum*, and Jenö Hubay's *Anna Karenina*, which had been rejected by Krauss when he was director. There was also a very successful ballet premiere called *Der liebe Augustin* with music by Alexander Steinbrecher and choreography by Margarethe Wallmann.

As one can well imagine, the search was on in high places for an alternative director—all the more so since Bruno Walter and Hans Knappertsbusch were interested in Vienna, given the political situation in Hitler's Germany. Neither of them wanted, however, to become theater directors.

Dr. Erwin Kerber

Born 12. 30. 1891; died 2. 24. 1943, Salzburg.
Director of the State Opera from 9. 1. 1936 to 9. 1. 1940.

Erwin Kerber became the State Opera's new director on 1 September 1936. His period in office saw the Anschluss between Austria and the Third Reich. Kerber had both the difficult task of rebuilding the ensemble after Krauss's departure and of solving problems thrown up by the Anschluss even though he himself was a convinced non-Nazi.

The most notable premieres produced by Kerber were the successful one-act operas *Ivan Tarassenko* by Franz Salmhofer and *Daphne* and *Friedenstag* by Richard Strauss, Gluck's *Orfeo ed Euridice* (conducted by Bruno Walter and produced by Margarethe Wallmann, with Kerstin Thorborg playing Orfeo), and Kerber's own production of the long neglected *Das Glöckchen des Eremiten* by Louis Aimé Maillart, which had first been performed at the Court Opera in 1861.

Other additions were due to the economic situation which made it necessary to include more operettas on the program besides *Giuditta*. This led to the presentation of Franz Lehár's *Das Land des Lächelns* starring Vera Schwarz and Richard Tauber and conducted several times by the composer himself, and to a new production of Johann Strauss's *Nacht in Venedig* (in Korngold's 1929 version).

The date 1 June 1937 was an important pointer to the future: Herbert von Karajan conducted *Tristan und Isolde* as a guest, and Lotte Lehmann sang Leonore in *Fidelio* under Arturo Toscanini, who was particular admirer of hers.

Bruno Walter played an important part until 1938 for Kerber had managed to hire him as artistic adviser. In addition to *Orfeo* he also conducted Carl Maria von Weber's *Oberon*, which had received its premiere in Salzburg in the summer of 1936. Hilde Konetzni, a new acquisition from Prague and the sister of Anny Konetzni, sang the role of Rezia, with Helge Rosvaenge as Huön. *Wallenstein*, an opera by Jaromir Weinberger with Alfred Jerger in the title role, enjoyed less success and was found disappointing after *Schwanda*. Wilhelm Furtwängler conducted *Die Meistersinger von Nürnberg* a few times, and Hans Knappertsbusch became a regular guest.

It was noticeable that even Kerber made some glaring errors. He chose to produce the weak operas *Die fremde Frau* by Marko Frank and Josef Wenzel Traun-

140 *Friedenstag* (Armistice Day) by Richard Strauss had its premiere on 10 July 1939. Rudolf Hartmann was the producer.

141 Set design from 1939 by Ulrich Roller, son of Alfred Roller, for Richard Strauss's *Friedenstag*.

142 Another work by Richard Strauss: *Daphne* had its premiere on 25 April 1940 in a production by Erich von Wymetal with sets and costumes by Ulrich Roller. Marie Reining sang the title role.

fels's *Die Sühne*. On the other hand there was an interesting performance of *Carmen* at Christmas in 1937, produced by the founder of the Glyndbourne festival Carl Ebert and conducted by Bruno Walter. Jan Kiepura played Don José on several occasions.

I can still well remember a performance of *Tristan und Isolde* with Anny Konetzni singing and Bruno Walter conducting, during which stink bombs were thrown. At first the performance went on as if nothing had happened, but soon the smell became unbearable and Walter had to stop. He resumed after the theater had been thoroughly aired. The throwing of stink bombs was a consequence of the political situation that manifested itself in daily actions carried out everywhere by the illegal national socialists. Stink bombs had been thrown as early as 1934 following the appearance of Friedrich Schorr

(as Wotan), who had emigrated from Germany and come to Vienna for a brief period. Until the above-mentioned *Tristan* the opera had been like an oasis while daily life outside became increasingly dangerous, but this attack on art was a clear alarm signal, I felt, for the impending disaster. On 12 March 1938, German troops invaded, while Hans Knappertsbusch was conducting *Tristan*.

The list of singers taken on by Kerber shows how adeptly he attempted to heal the double wound struck first by the departure of Krauss and his entourage, and then by the loss of Bruno Walter, Karl Alwin, Josef Krips, Lothar Wallenstein, Hugo Reichenberg, Margarethe Wallmann, Lotte Lehmann, Vera Schwarz, Kerstin Thorberg, Rosette Anday, Alexander Sved, Richard Tauber, and many other persecuted artists.

Kerber engaged the sopranos Hilde Konetzni, Maria Reining, Margarita Perras, Esther Réthy, Else Schulz; the altos Martha Rohs and Elena Nikolaidi; the tenors Anton Dermota, Karl Friedrich, Todor Mazaroff (he and Nikolaidi had won a singing competition that also produced the future international star Tito Gobbi), Set Svanholm, and Josef Witt; the baritones Ludwig Hofmann, Karl Kamann, Alfred Poell, and Paul Schöffler; and the bass Herbert Alsen.

It seemed almost a miracle that the Anschluss had not led to the complete break-up of the State Opera. It was only to be expected, however, that the fate of the State Opera was decided more and more in Berlin, which entailed enforcing the race laws that plagued every aspect of life under the Nazi regime. While the authorities were conciliatory to the Viennese passion for opera by granting special status to artists, which spared them military service, they, nevertheless, affirmed their control of affairs by appointing appropriate persons to key positions. The affinities of directors Heinrich Karl Strohm and Lothar Müthel were representative of the Nazi era.

143 An important Viennese debut: Herbert von Karajan appeared as a guest on 1 June 1937 to conduct W gner's *Tristan und Isolde.*

144 Bruno Walter became an artistic advisor to the Vienna State Opera under Edwin Kerber. He was forced to leave the post, like so many other Jewish artists, in 1938.

Heinrich Karl Strohm

Born 2. 4. 1895, Elberfeld (Westphalia, Germany);
died 6. 9. 1959, Cologne.
Director of the State Opera from 4. 1. 1940 to January 1941.

Lothar Müthel

Born 2. 18. 1896, Szczecin (Poland); died 9. 4. 1964,
Frankfurt am Main.
Director of the State Opera from 4. 1. 1941 to 12. 31. 1942.
General intendant with overall artistic responsibility
for the State Opera until 4. 24. 1946.

So it was that the order came–influenced, no doubt, by the Third Reich's new governor in Vienna Baldur von Schirach and by his cultural official Walter Thomas–to make contact with Karl Böhm, then director of the Dresden Opera. As Böhm still had commitments in Dresden and could not be replaced just like that, Heinrich Karl Strohm was to be appointed director of the State Opera, with the director of the Burgtheater, Lothar Müthel, as general intendant. Strohm had had success in bringing the Hamburg Opera up to date. The big artistic names during his period as director in Hamburg were Oscar Fritz Schuh and Caspar Neher, both of whom Strohm brought to Vienna with him. After the war they were to help originate a new Mozart style–a new style of opera, in fact–which was to cause great interest throughout the world.

The third important figure was Ernst August Schneider, who came to Vienna as manager of the arts administration office. He had started in the book trade, then worked as a drama adviser and now he immediately made himself indispensable at the State Opera as a diligent administrator and fatherly friend to the artists. He remained the opera house's "good conscience" until his death in 1976.

The new director Heinrich Karl Strohm soon fell ill with psychiatric problems, however, and disappeared into a mental institution; so on 1 april 1941 Schneider was appointed to assist Müthel, the general intendant, and given sole responsibility for the Opera.

The biggest cultural event during this period was the festival to mark the one hundred fiftieth anniversary of Mozart's death that had its climax in the production by Schuh and Neher of *The Magic Flute* in the Redoutensaal.

One significant world premiere to take place was Rudolf Wagner-Régeny's *Joanna Balk* which, for the first time in the Third Reich, brought forth a negative reaction from opera audiences. The protestors saw in this interesting work, which was dominated by brilliant renditions by Josef Witt and Helena Braun, some sort of return to "degenerate art"; there were few performances, but it was now clear that the spirit that moved the State Opera was other than that of the official Nazi line. It should be stressed at this point that the cultural regime in Vienna under Baldur von Schirach was in any case far more liberal than Goebbels's in the Reich. Most notable among the new singers at this time were Hans Hotter, Max Lorenz, Erich Kunz, Peter Klein, and Georgine von Milinkovic. Rudolf Moralt, nephew of Richard Strauss, thoroughly deserved his engagement as conductor, going on to work at the State Opera until his death in 1958. Strohm's strange interlude came to an end when the appointment of Karl Böhm came into effect.

145 Helena Braun and Josef Witt in a scene from Rudolf Wagner-Régeny's *Johanna Balk*. The public protested against the work when it received its world premiere.

146 Caspar Neher's set design in 1941 for Rudolf Wagner-Régeny's *Johanna Balk:* "The marketplace in Hermannstadt."

147 Rehearsals for Wagner's *Tristan und Isolde* in 1942. Wilhelm Furtwängler, Anny Konetzni, and Max Lorenz.

148–153 The Richard Strauss season on the occasion of his eightieth brithday. Playbills for *Ariadne auf Naxos*, *Der Rosenkavalier*, *Capriccio*, *Arabella*, an evening of ballet with the *Couperin Suite* and *Josefs Legende*, and *Die Frau ohne Schatten*.

Karl Böhm

Born 8. 28. 1894, Graz; died 8. 14. 1981, Salzburg.
Director of the State Opera from 1. 1. 1943 until 6. 30. 1945.

Karl Böhm quickly managed to give the State Opera a new style of its own, together with the producer Oscar Fritz Schuh and the set designers Caspar Neher and Wilhelm Reinking. Böhm was particularly keen to maintain the operas of Mozart, Richard Strauss, and Richard Wagner. To celebrate Richard Strauss's eightieth birthday Böhm himself conducted *Ariadne auf Naxos* and the Viennese premiere of *Capriccio* and *Die Frau* *ohne Schatten*; Rudolf Moralt conducted *Arabella*, *Salome*, and *Der Rosenkavalier*, and on his birthday Richard Strauss himself took to the podium for *Ariadne auf Naxos*. It was a source of particular prestige that the composer should celebrate his birthday in Vienna, rather than anywhere else.

A new *Palestrina* (with Josef Witt in the title role) was produced to mark the seventieth birthday of its composer, Hans

Donnerstag, den 1. Juni 1944
Beschränkter Kartenverkauf. Preise III

RICHARD-STRAUSS-ZYKLUS
ZUM 80. GEBURTSTAG DES MEISTERS

Ariadne auf Naxos
(Neue Bearbeitung)

Oper in einem Aufzug nebst einem Vorspiel von Hugo v. Hofmannsthal
Musik von Richard Strauß

sikalische Leitung: Karl Böhm   Inszenierung: Heinz Arnold a. G.
Bühnenbilder: Wilhelm Reinking — Kostüme: Ursula Hechtenberg

Personen des Vorspiels:

Der Haushofmeister	Alfred Muzzarelli
Der Musiklehrer	Paul Schöffler
Der Komponist	Irmgard Seefried
Der Tenor (Bacchus)	Max Lorenz
Ein Offizier	Friedrich Jelinek
Ein Tanzmeister	Josef Witt
Ein Perückenmacher	Hermann Baier
Ein Lakai	Hans Schweiger
Zerbinetta	Alda Noni
Primadonna (Ariadne)	Maria Reining
Harlekin	Erich Kunz
Scaramuccio	Richard Sallaba
Truffaldin	Marjan Rus
Brighella	Peter Klein

Personen der Oper:

Ariadne	Maria Reining
Bacchus	Max Lorenz
Najade	Emmy Loose
Dryade	Melanie Frutschnigg
Echo	Elisabeth Rutgers
Zerbinetta	Alda Noni
Harlekin	Erich Kunz
Scaramuccio	Richard Sallaba
Truffaldin	Marjan Rus
Brighella	Peter Klein

Technische Einrichtung: Ferdinand Jaschke

Nach dem Vorspiel eine größere Pause

fang 18½ Uhr   Ende 21 Uhr

im Orchester zur Verfügung gelangende Flügel wurde von der Firma
Bösendorfer beigestellt

Publikum wird gebeten, sich vor Beginn der Vorstellung beim Erscheinen
erer verwundeten Frontsoldaten in der Mittelloge von den Plätzen zu erheben

---

Samstag, den 3. Juni 1944
Beschränkter Kartenverkauf. Preise III

RICHARD-STRAUSS-ZYKLUS
ZUM 80. GEBURTSTAG DES MEISTERS

Der Rosenkavalier

Komödie für Musik in drei Aufzügen von Hugo von Hofmannsthal
Musik von Richard Strauß

Musikalische Leitung: Rudolf Moralt   Inszenierung: Alfred Jerger
Bühnenbilder: Alfred Roller

Die Feldmarschallin Fürstin Werdenberg	Anny Konetzni
Der Baron Ochs auf Lerchenau	Fritz Krenn
Oktavian, genannt Quinquin, ein junger Herr aus großem Haus	Marta Rohs
Herr von Faninal, ein reicher Neugeadelter	Karl Kamann
Sophie, seine Tochter	Esther Réthy
Jungfer Marianne Leitmetzerin, die Duenna	Jarmila Barton
Valzacchi, ein Intrigant	Peter Klein
Annina, seine Begleiterin	Melanie Frutschnigg
Ein Polizeikommissär	Tomislav Neralić
Der Haushofmeister bei der Feldmarschallin	Hermann Baier
Der Haushofmeister bei Faninal	Egyd Toriff
Ein Notar	Alfred Muzzarelli
Ein Sänger	Todor Mazaroff
Ein Gelehrter	Robert Binder
Ein Flötist	Ludwig Verlik
Ein Friseur	Karl Nowak
Dessen Gehilfe	Annemarie Greger
Eine adelige Witwe	Fritzi Berthold
Drei adelige Waisen	Eva Held, Marie Langhans, Hansi Czermin
Eine Modistin	Berta Seidl
Ein Tierhändler	Erich Majkut
Ein Wirt	William Wernigk
Ein Arzt	Heinrich Berthold
Leopold, Diener des Barons	Herm. Tichavsky
Ein Hausknecht	Johann Sawka
Ein kleiner Mohr	Marie Dziewicz

Vier Lakaien der Marschallin: Leopold Männling, Franz Rouland, Franz Schramm, Franz Szkokan
Vier Kellner: Viktor Maiwald, Ludwig Fleck, Hans Hahn, Heinrich Berthold
Lakaien, Läufer, Heiducken, Küchenpersonal, Gäste, Musikanten, Kutscher, zwei Wächter, vier kleine Kinder, verschiedene verdächtige Gestalten
In Wien, in den ersten Jahren der Regierung Maria Theresias

Nach dem zweiten Aufzug eine größere Pause

Anfang 17 Uhr   Ende 20¾ Uhr

Das Publikum wird gebeten, sich vor Beginn der Vorstellung beim Erscheinen
unserer verwundeten Frontsoldaten in der Mittelloge von den Plätzen zu erheben

---

Sonntag, den 4. Juni 1944
Beschränkter Kartenverkauf. Preise III

RICHARD-STRAUSS-ZYKLUS
ZUM 80. GEBURTSTAG DES MEISTERS

CAPRICCIO

Ein Konversationsstück für Musik in einem Aufzug
von Clemens Krauß
und
Richard Strauß

Musikalische Leitung: Karl Böhm
Inszenierung: Rudolf Hartmann a. G.
Bühnenbild und Kostüme: Robert Kautsky

Die Gräfin	Maria Cebotari
Der Graf, ihr Bruder	Alfred Jerger
Flamand, ein Musiker	Anton Dermota
Olivier, ein Dichter	Erich Kunz
La Roche, der Theaterdirektor	Paul Schöffler
Die Schauspielerin Clairon	Martha Rohs
Monsieur Taupe	Peter Klein
Eine italienische Sängerin	Alda Noni
Ein italienischer Tenor	Wenko Wenkoff
Eine junge Tänzerin	Inge Hiltscher
Ein junger Tänzer	Linda Zamponi
Der Haushofmeister	Tomislav Neralić
Acht Diener	Egyd Toriff, Hans Schweiger, William Wernigk, Roland Neumann, Viktor Madin, Erich Majkut, Simon Hebein, Lothar Höberth

Ort der Handlung: Ein Schloß in der Nähe von Paris, zur Zeit, als Gluck dort
sein Reformwerk der Oper begann. Etwa um 1775
Einstudierung der Tanzszene: Erika Hanka
Technische Einrichtung: Ferdinand Jaschke

Anfang 18½ Uhr   Ende 21 Uhr

Das Publikum wird gebeten, sich vor Beginn der Vorstellung beim Erscheinen
unserer verwundeten Frontsoldaten in der Mittelloge von den Plätzen zu erheben

---

Dienstag, den 6. Juni 1944
Beschränkter Kartenverkauf. Preise III

RICHARD-STRAUSS-ZYKLUS
ZUM 80. GEBURTSTAG DES MEISTERS

ARABELLA

Lyrische Komödie in drei Aufzügen von Hugo v. Hofmannsthal

Musik von Richard Strauß

Musikalische Leitung: Rudolf Moralt
Spielleitung: Alfred Jerger
Bühnenbilder: Alfred Roller

af Waldner, Rittmeister a. D.	Fritz Krenn
elaide, seine Frau	Marta Rohs
abella, ihre Töchter	Maria Reining
enka	Else Böttcher
andryka	Alfred Jerger
atteo, Jägeroffizier	Anton Dermota
af Elemer	Josef Witt
af Dominik, Verehrer der Arabella	Georg Monthy
af Lamoral	Alfred Poell
e Fiakermilli	Alda Noni
e Kartenaufschlägerin	Dora With
elko, Leibhusar des Mandryka	Franz Szkokan
ura, Diener des Mandryka	Rudolf Daßler
nkel	Emanuel Haller
n Zimmerkellner	Karl Kolowratnik
gleiterin der Arabella	Frieda Haller
ei Spieler	Franz Polcar, Albert Piffl, Franz Schramm
n Arzt	Lothar Höberth
oom	Annemarie Ziegler

Fiaker, Ballgäste, Hotelgäste, Kellner

1. Akt: Salon in einem Wiener Stadthotel — 2. Akt: Foyer zum Ballsaal
3. Akt: Halle und Stiegenhaus im Hotel — Ort: Wien, Zeit 1860

Nach dem zweiten Aufzug eine größere Pause

nfang 17½ Uhr   Ende 20¾ Uhr

as Publikum wird gebeten, sich vor Beginn der Vorstellung beim Erscheinen
serer verwundeten Frontsoldaten in der Mittelloge von den Plätzen zu erheben

---

Donnerstag, den 8. Juni 1944
Beschränkter Kartenverkauf. Preise III

RICHARD-STRAUSS-ZYKLUS
ZUM 80. GEBURTSTAG DES MEISTERS

BALLETTABEND

Neuinszenierung

COUPERIN-SUITE

Zusammengestellt und für kleines Orchester bearbeitet von Richard Strauß
Inszenierung und Choreographie: Erika Hanka

Musikalische Leitung: Rudolf Moralt   Spielleitung: Erika Hanka
Bühnenbild: Robert Kautsky — Kostüme: Charlotte Flemming

Festlicher Einzug: Ensemble
Courante: Damen: Lucia Bräuer und Brunlechner, Greger, Klotz, Krämer, Leiter, Temple, Zamponi
Carillon: Adele Krausenecker und Damen Jezel, Kose, Macholan
Sarabande: Poldy Pokorny, Erwin Pokorny
Gavotte: Dely Kautsky, Maria Schindler, Olga Fiedler, Maria Stanitz, Toni Birkmeyer, Willy Fränzl
Wirbeltanz: Julia Drapal und Grete Dellus, Inge Hiltscher, Kl Dziewicz, Plenert
Allemande, Menuett, Marsch: Maria Graf, Erna Grübler und Corps de Ballet

JOSEPHS-LEGENDE

Handlung von Harry Graf Keßler und Hugo von Hofmannsthal
Musik von Richard Strauß
Choreographie von Heinrich Kröller
Neueinstudierung: Willy Fränzl

Musikalische Leitung: Rudolf Moralt   Spielleitung: Willy Fränzl
Bühnenbild: Alfred Roller — Robert Kautsky

Potiphar	Rudi Fränzl
Potiphars Weib	Hedy Pfundmayr
Deren Lieblingssklavin	Trude Kotz
Potiphars Haushofmeister	Robert Binder
Ein alter Scheik	Fritz Birkmeyer
Junger Orientale	Hans Kres
Joseph, ein Hirtenknabe	Carl Raimund
Sulamith, eine Tänzerin	Julia Drapal
Deren Begleiterinnen	Olga Fiedler, Anni Feix

Dienstag, den 13. Juni 1944
Beschränkter Kartenverkauf. Preise III

RICHARD-STRAUSS-ZYKLUS
ZUM 80. GEBURTSTAG DES MEISTERS

Die Frau ohne Schatten

Oper in drei Akten von Hugo v. Hofmannsthal
Musik von Richard Strauß

Musikalische Leitung: Karl Böhm   Inszenierung: Georg Hartmann a. G.
Bühnenbilder und Kostüme: Robert Kautsky

Der Kaiser	Julius Patzak, Staatsoper München
Die Kaiserin	Hilde Konetzni
Die Amme	Elisabeth Höngen
Geisterbote	Herbert Alsen
Ein Hüter der Schwelle des Tempels	Emmy Loose
Stimme eines Jünglings	Wenko Wenkoff
Die Stimme des Falken	Daga Söderqvist
Eine Stimme von oben	Melanie Frutschnigg
Barak, der Färber	Josef Herrmann
Sein Weib	Christl Goltz, Staatsoper Dresden
Der Einäugige	Georg Monthy
Der Einarmige, des Färbers Brüder	Marjan Rus
Der Bucklige	William Wernigk
Kinder- und Solostimmen	Elisabeth Rutgers, Jarmila Barton, Maria Schober, Marie Langhans, Edith Prießner, Emmy Loose, Jarmila Barton, Dora With, Melanie Frutschnigg
Die Stimmen der Wächter der Stadt	Alfred Poell, Adolf Vogel, Tomislav Neralić

Kaiserliche Diener, fremde Kinder, Dienende, Geister, Geisterstimmen
Ort der Handlung: I. Aufzug: Auf einer Terrasse über den kaiserlichen Gärten. —
Färberhaus. — II. Aufzug: Färberhaus. — Wald vor dem Pavillon des Falkners.
— Färberhaus. — Wald vor dem Pavillon des Falkners. — Färberhaus. —
III. Aufzug: Unterirdischer Kerker. — Geistertempel: Eingang. — Geistertempel:
Inneres. — Landschaft im Geisterreich.
Technische Einrichtung: Ferdinand Jaschke

Nach dem ersten Akt eine kleinere, nach dem zweiten Akt eine größere Pause

Anfang 17 Uhr   Ende nach 21 Uhr

Das Publikum wird gebeten, sich vor Beginn der Vorstellung beim Erscheinen
unserer verwundeten Frontsoldaten in der Mittelloge von den Plätzen zu erheben

154   A scene from Richard Strauss's *Capriccio* in 1944: Alfred Jerger as the Count and Martha Rohs as Clairon.

155   Maria Cebotari as the countess in the closing scene of Richard Strauss's *Capriccio* in 1944.

156   Group scene from Richard Strauss's *Capriccio* in 1944. From left to right: Martha Rohs as Clairon, Erich Kunz as Oliver, Anton Dermota as Flammand (half hidden), Maria Cebotari as the countess, Alfred Jerger as the count, and Paul Schöffler as La Roche. The sets and costumes were created by Robert Kautsky in a production by Rudolf Hartmann.

157   Richard Strauss, himself a former director of the Vienna Oper, received a fitting tribute on his birthday (oil portrait by Wilhelm Viktor Krauss).

158 Mozart operas performed in the Redoutensaal during the war, designed by Caspar Neher and produced by Oscar Fritz Schuh: *The Marriage of Figaro* with Maria Cebotari as Susanna and Maria Reining as the countess.

Pfitzner. Hans Knappertsbusch conducted the *Ring*, and Wilhelm Furtwängler occasionally *Tristan und Isolde*. Böhm also brought over a number of singers with him from Dresden and added several young performers: Irmgard Seefried, Elisabeth Höngen, Josef Herrmann, Torsten Ralph, Maria Cebotari, Christl Goltz, Daniza Ilitsch, Sena Jurinac, and Emmy Loose.

Böhm's term as director came to a brutal end in the autumn of 1944 when all theaters were shut in the interests of "total war." All that remained were individual matinee performances in concert form. On 12 March 1945, six months after it had closed, the opera house went up in flames.

159 *Cosi fan tutte* with Irmgard Seefried as Fiordiligi and Anton Dermota as Ferando in 1943.

Franz Salmhofer

Born 1. 22. 1900; died 9. 22. 1975, Vienna.
Director of the State Opera from 7. 1. 1945 to 8. 31. 1954.

After the occupation of Vienna by the Soviet army, the Russian commanding officer gave the order that opera should be resumed straight away in the Volksoper, which had not been destroyed. Alfred Jerger took over temporarily as artistic director. Ernst Schneider and Heinrich Reif-Gintl, who had been pensioned off on racial grounds during the Third Reich, managed to organize an alternative company at the Volksoper with the help of any singers who happened to be available. The first performance was *The Marriage of Figaro* on 1 May 1945 with Josef Krips conducting the following cast: Hilde Konetzni (Countess), Irmgard Seefried (Suzanne), Sena Jurinac (Cherubin), Alfred Poell (Count), and Alois Pernerstorfer (Figaro). Krips, who had been the unofficial repetiteur during the Nazi period, was now able at last to resume as conductor.

Franz Salmhofer, who had enjoyed particular success as musical director of the Burgtheater (his talent lay above all in producing incidental music very quickly), was appointed director of the State Opera at the Theater an der Wien by Egon Hilbert, who had meanwhile been put in charge of administration at the Burgtheater. The State Opera's activities at the Volksoper were managed by Hermann Juch. The administration of the two houses was split up from 1 September 1946, with Salmhofer staying at the Theater an der Wien and Juch at the Volksoper. The man with overall power was Egon Hilbert, an unofficial general intendant with overriding influence in the artistic sphere. The conductors at the Theater an der Wien (in alphabetical order—Karl Böhm, Heinrich Hollreiser, Hans Knappertsbusch, Clemens Krauss, Josef Krips, Wilhelm Loibner, and Rudolf Moralt) could call on the remaining ensemble from Böhm's time, with the addition of new singers such as Elisabeth Schwarzkopf, Ljuba Welitsch, Hilde Zadek, Leonie Rysanek, Lisa della Casa, Hilde Güden, Carla Martinis, Rita Streich,

Julius Patzak, Rudolf Schock, Murray Dickie, Josef Gostic, George London, Georg Hann, Julius Pölzer, Otto Edelmann, Oskar Czervenka, Karl Dönch, Endre Koréh, and Gottlob Frick.

The producers were Oscar Fritz Schuh, Josef Gielen, Adolf Rott, and Wymetal, together with Günther Rennert and Rudolf Hartmann. A wide-ranging repertoire was gradually built up at the Theater an der Wien—even *Elektra* was played, though it could not be presented in anything but a reduced orchestral form. The most important artistic events during Salmhofer's time included the premiere of Arthur Honegger's *Jeanne d'Arc au Bûcher* in a production by Josef Gielen conducted by Clemens Krauss; the Burgtheater's big stars, Alma Seidler and Raoul Aslan, made it a great success. On 25 April 1952 the Austrian premiere of Igor Stravinsky's *The Rake's Progress* took place in a production by Günther Rennert. Erika Hanka, the successful director of the State Opera Ballet, presented the world premiere of Theodor Berger's *Homerische Symphonie*. *Die Liebe der Danae*, Richard Strauss's penultimate opera, followed its world premiere in Salzburg by coming to Vienna (with Rudolf Hartmann producing and Krauss conducting). Gottfried von Einem's *Dantons Tod* was brought in on 25 September 1952 and his *Der Prozess* on 1 October 1953—both produced by Oscar Fritz and also transferred to Vienna from the Salzburg Festival—as well as Rolf Liebermann's *Penelope*, performed on 25 November 1954.

The idea of transferring works to Vienna after their world premiere in Salzburg was not considered again until the eighties. One interesting premiere to take place at the Theater an der Wien was the thoroughly successful *Konsul* by Gian-Carlo Menotti, sung by Hilde Zadek, produced by Adolf Rott and conducted by Meinhard von Zallinger.

I have particular memories of a performance of *Götterdämmerung* under Furtwängler, in concert form and starring

160 Opera buffa by the legendary Mozart company after 1945 at the Theater an der Wien: Erich Kunz as Papageno in Mozart's *The Magic Flute*.

161 Sena Juinac as Cherubino and Irmgard Seefried as Susanna in Mozart's. *The Marriage of Figaro*.

162 Alfred Poell as the count and Hilde Güden as Susanna in *The Magic of Figaro*.

163 Anton Dermota as Don Ottavio and Ljuba Welitsch as Donna Anna in Mozart's *Don Giovanni*.

164 Hilde Konetzni as Elisabeth in Wagner's *Tannhäuser* in 1946.

165 Helge Rosvaenge as Don José in Bizet's *Carmen* in 1948.

166 Elisabeth Schwarzkopf as Sophie in Richard Strauss's *Der Rosenkavalier* in 1948.

167 A scene from Verdi's *Falstaff*, produced by Oscar Fritz Schuh at the Theater an der Wien in 1951: the ladies are Rosette Anday, Hilde Güden, Anny Felbermayer, and Sieglinde Wagner, with Otto Edelmann in the title role.

168 The Salzburg Festival production of Richard Strauss's *Die Liebe der Danae* by Rudolf Hartmann was transferred to the Theater an der Wien in 1952. From left to right: Esther Rethy as Europa, Dorothea Siebert as Semele, Paul Schöffler as Jupiter, Sieglinde Wagner as Leda, and Georgine von Milinkovic as Alkmene.

169 Maria Reining as the Marschallin in Richard Strauss's *Der Rosenkavalier* (oil painting by Hugo Bouvard).

Anny Konetzni and Ludwig Suthaus, and of two performances of *Der Rosenkavalier* under Erich Kleiber.

Attempts were being made in Vienna at the time to make Erich Kleiber Salmhofer's successor when the opera house on the Ring was about to reopen. The names of Clemens Krauss and Karl Böhm were also touted in addition to Kleiber. I believe that Erich Kleiber overplayed his hand when at a press conference he was perhaps a little too forceful in his criticism of the general artistic standards of the State Opera at the Theater an der Wien; in my opinion he was much too premature in revealing his intention to make a clean sweep if he was appointed director.

Clemens Krauss was supported by Ernst Kolb, the culture minister, but he was rejected in favor of Karl Böhm by the Chancellor Julius Raab and by Böhm's great circle of friends led by Manfred Mautner. Another group suggested Herbert von Karajan as a possible director of the State Opera. Karajan himself felt that his time was not yet ripe, however. That time would come when he could be sure that all his wishes would be filled.

Meanwhile on the Ringstrasse reconstruction work was making rapid progress. Egon Hilbert had been moved to Rome to head the Austrian Cultural Institute as a result of a disagreement with Kolb, and in 1953 Ernst Marboe was named administrative director of the State Theater. I am convinced today that it was Marboe's intention from the start to bring Herbert von Karajan to Vienna.

Karl Böhm

Director of the State Opera from 9. 1. 1954 to 8. 31. 1956.

For the time being the man with the whip was Karl Böhm, appointed director from 1 September 1954. He hired me as his deputy and together we began to prepare for the opening of the opera house on the Ringstrasse. The opening program was originally planned by Heinrich Reif-Gintl, who did not get on particularly well with Karl Böhm, and then worked out in detail by myself. The inaugural festival, which Marboe called a "Musical Coronation" in reference to the international treaty which had just been signed, included new productions of *Fidelio* (conductor Karl Böhm, producer Heinz Tietjen, sets by Clemens Holzmeister), *Don Giovanni* (Böhm, Schuh, Neher), *Die Frau ohne Schatten*, (Böhm, Hartmann, Preetorius), *Aida* (Kubelik, Rott, Kautsky), *Die Meistersinger von Nürnberg* (Reiner, Graf, Kautsky), *Der Rosenkavalier* (Knappertsbusch, Gielen, Roller), *Wozzeck* (Böhm, Schuh, Neher), as well as an evening of ballet organized by Erika Hanka with Adolphe Adam's *Giselle* and Boris Blacher's *Othello, der Mohr von Venedig* (Hollreiser, Wakhewitsch). Bruno Walter, who now considered opera rehearsals beyond him, conducted Beethoven's Ninth Symphony.

In order to complete the existing ensemble Karl Böhm engaged, amongst others, Erika Köth, Jean Madeira (Amneris, in the inaugural *Aida*), Martha Mödl (Leonore), Wolfgang Windgassen, Hans Beirer (Stolzing), Christa Ludwig, Eberhard Wächter, and Waldemar Kmentt. The festival became an international social event of the first order, but it must be said that not all the premieres were totally convincing in artistic terms. The greatest problems, though, came when the festival ended and the day to day operation of the opera house began. Many of the major singers from the Theater an der Wien were past their peak, while the singers who had been active during the opening had completed their stays and departed, not to return until May. The subsequent meagre fare annoyed the Viennese and led to Karl Böhm's downfall. It is important to add at this point that a Viennese audience is quite able to distinguish between an unloved director and a highly

171 The glittering occasion when, on the evening of 5 November 1955, the rebuilt State Opera opened with a performance of Beethoven's *Fidelio*.

172 Spectators at the reopening of the opera house. Those who could not get a ticket wanted at least to watch from the sidelines.

173 Fortunate ticketholders in the auditiorium of the new State Opera.

174–176 Illustrious guests at the first night: John Foster Dulles, American secretary of state, Reinhard Kamitz, Austrian minister of finance and Leopold Figl, Austrian foreign minister in the interval at the State Opera (top picture), close to them Paula Wesseley, Count and Countess Schönfeldt, and Elfie Mayerhofer (middle), the leading reporter Heinz Fischer-Karwin, Bruno Walter, and Wolfgang Wagner (bottom).

177 Beethoven's *Fidelio* with its famous prisoners' chorus was a symbol of a free Austria a few weeks after the occupying forces were withdrawn. Clemens Holzmeister designed the scenery, while Heinz Tietjen was responsible for the production.

178 Martha Mödl as Leonore and Anton Dermota as Florestan in the closing scene from *Fidelio*: "Wer ein holdes Weib errungen . . ."

179 The second opening premiere followed on 6 November. Designed by Caspar Neher and produced by Oscar Fritz Schuh, Mozart's *Don Giovanni* featured Irmgard Seefried as Zerlina and George London in the title role. Karl Böhm conducted.

180 The third premiere: Verdi's *Aida* with Jean Madeira as Amneris and Leonie Rysanek as Aida. Raphael Kubelik occupied the conductor's platform.

136

181 Adolf Rott's production of *Aida* was sung by George London (Amonasro), Hans Hopf (Radames), and Leonie Rysanek (Aida). Robert Kautsky was the designer.

182 Herbert Graf produced the fourth inaugural premiere—Wagner's *Die Meistersinger von Nürnberg*—with sets and costumes by Robert Kautsky. Fritz Reiner conducted. Evchen and Hans Sachs were played in exemplary fashion by Irmgard Seefried and Paul Scöffler.

183 Hans Beirer sang the part of Stolzing in the same production.

184 Hans Knappertsbusch conducted the first *Rosenkavalier* in the new house, with Hilde Güden as Sophie and Sena Jurinac as Oktavian. The production was by Joseph Gielen and design by Adolf Rott.

185 Oskar Kokoschka painted the rebuilt Vienna State Opera to look its best during the opening festival (Museum of Modern Art, Vienna).

186 The last of the premieres on 25 November 1955 was Alban Berg's *Wozzeck*, again designed by Caspar Neher and produced by Oscar Fritz Schuh, with Walter Berry in the title role and Christl Goltz as Marie. The conductor was Karl Böhm, the director of the State Opera.

respected conductor. They booed Böhm vehemently before a performance of *Fidelio* when he had just returned from the United States and later in the same evening applauded him enthusiastically after the third Leonore overture.

As soon as Böhm had departed, negotiations were started with Herbert von Karajan, who had just enjoyed enormous success at the State Opera with a guest performance by the Scala Milan of *Lucia di Lammermoor* (with Maria Callas, Giuseppe di Stefano, and Ettore Bastianini).

187 Erika Köth was engaged by Karl Böhm. She was a virtuoso Zerbinetta in Josef Gielen's production of Richard Strauss's *Ariadne auf Naxos*.

Herbert von Karajan

Born 4. 5. 1908, Salzburg.
Artistic director of the State Opera from 9. 1. 1956 to 8. 31. 1964:
from 9. 1. 1962 to 8. 1. 1963 with Walter Erich Schäfer;
from 9. 1. 1963 with Egon Hilbert.

The musical significance of Karajan's era operates on several levels. In the first place Karajan could call on himself, as one of the world's best conductors (if not *the* best), some forty times every season. Secondly, Karajan managed to ensure that he was granted the financial resources needed to engage the best artists in the world. Thirdly, he firmly believed that opera should be sung in the original language of composition—and not just because Italian opera, for example, can never be properly orchestrated if the music is set to an artificially re-shaped libretto. Fourthly, he felt that an ensemble in the old sense, in which individual parts were sung exclusively by members of the company, was redundant and should be replaced by a type of *stagione* system. A compromise was reached whereby the Vienna State Opera obtained longer commitments from the most famous singers. Unlike the past when stars such as Caruso appeared no more than once or twice a year, all the major singers now returned on a regular basis. Karajan brought great international status to the Vienna State Opera, which until then could not compete with the Scala and the Met on this level, making it a prime tourist attraction.

Karajan's directorship was a glittering period which set standards that were hard to equal. The big problem that emerged during Karajan's time was the problem of the artistic substructure. Since then even those singers who do not enjoy star status perform as guests all over the world, so that now a program of three hundred days in a year can hardly be filled without engaging guest performers. This development was (and is) not solely due to Karajan's high standard but has only been made possible in the first place by modern airlines, simplistic though that might sound.

Karajan himself was drawn particularly to operas which had previously been conducted by repertory directors. Soon after his appointment he presented *Tosca* with Margarethe Wallmann as producer— a production which was still being performed at the State Opera in 1986. He also conducted an epoch-making *Bohème* designed and produced by Franco Zeffirelli and *Oedipus Rex* by Stravinsky, with Cocteau as the Narrator and Stravinsky himself conducting one repeat performance. He put on the *Ring der Nibelungen* with Emil Preetorius. Like Mahler, he produced it himself. Then came a new *Tristan* with Preetorius, a new *Otello* with Wilhelm Reinking (set designer) and Georges Wakhewitsch (costumes), and *Pelléas et Mélisande*, designed by Günther Schneider-Siemssen. Other important performances were a

188   International singing stars moved into the house on the Ringstrasse—here is Giuseppe Zampieri as Cavaradossi and Renata Tebaldi in the title role of Puccini's *Tosca*. Margarethe Wallmann's production remained in the repertory for over thirty years.

189 Franco Corelli as André Chenier in Umberto Giordano's opera of the same name.

190 Birgit Nilsson as Turandot in Puccini's opera of the same name.

new production by Leopold Lindtberg of *Die Fledermaus*, Monteverdi's *L'Incoronazione di Poppea* with Günther Rennert producing and decor and costumes by Stefan Hlawa, *Don Carlos* (Wallmann and Wakhewitsch), and finally the premiere of Ildebrando Pizzetti's *Assassinio nella cattedrale*.

The most important conductor, whom Karajan invited again and again, was Dimitri Mitropoulos. Karajan brought many top singers to Vienna, among them Leontyne Price, Gundula Janowitz, Mirella Freni, Renata Tebaldi, Antonietta Stella, Giulietta Simionato, Giuseppe di Stefano, Franco Corelli, Carlo Bergonzi, Giuseppe Zampieri, Mario del Monaco, Jon Vickers, Ettore Bastianini, Aldo Protti, Cesare Siepi, Tito Gobbi, Otto Wiener, Nicolai Ghiaurov, and Boris Christoff.

On taking up his post Karajan confirmed my position as deputy artistic director and general secretary. It was, I believe, a fruitful collaboration which lasted until the end of the 1960–61 season. In the spring of 1961 I received an offer from the new general intendant of the Berlin Opera Gustav Rudolf Sellner and his music director Ferenc Fricsay to join them in Berlin. I accepted because I had the feeling that I had achieved everything in Vienna that was expected of me; I was also interested in the challenge of another city and the chance to create something new. The job of a deputy general intendant at the Westberliner Oper, which was about to open, offered just that challenge.

Karajan was obliged to reorganize the directorship in light of my departure.

191 Tito Gobbi as Scarpia in Puccini's *Tosca*.

192 Leonie Rysanek and Mario del Monaco in Verdi's *Otello*.

193 Leontyn Price as Tosca in Puccini's opera.

144

194   Giulietta Simionato as
Princess Eboli in Verdi's *Don
Carlos*.

195   Christa Ludwig in the title
role and Giuseppe di Stephano as
Don José in Bizet's *Carmen*.

196   Franco Zeffirelli's famous
production of *La Bohème*. From
left to right: Rolando Panerai, Ivo
Vinco, Giuseppe Taddei, Mirella
Freni, and Gianni Raimondi.
Herbert von Karajan conducted.

197   Mozart's *The Magic Flute* in
a performance to celebrate the
reopening of the Theater an der
Wien on 30 May 1962. Herbert
von Karajan conducted, and the
singers (from left to right) were
Fritz Wunderlich, Paul Kuen,
Walter Kreppel, Wilma Lipp, and
Erich Kunz. The sets were the
work of Günther Schneider-
Siemssen and the production was
led by Rudolf Hartmann.

198 Lisa della Casa as Eva and Wolfgang Windgasse as Stolzing in Wagner's *Die Meistersinger von Nürnberg*.

199, 200 Rossini's *The Barber of Seville* in the Redoutensaal in 1957: Murray Dickie as Count Almaviva, Erika Köth as Rosina, and Hermann Prey as Figaro (right), with Karl Dönch as the notary and Oskar Czerwenka as Basilio (left).

So, after a short interval with the general intendant from Stuttgart Walter Erich Schäfer, the appointment of Egon Hilbert was announced. Although he had been an energetic organizer of the Vienna festival he was not considered a fan of Karajan by any means. There was tension between them from the start. It should have been obvious in advance that Karajan would clash with the jumpy and excitable personality of Hilbert, who loved opera fanatically but was not used to working under a major figure. Herbert von Karajan asked the culture minister Theodor Piffl-Percevic to remove Hilbert, and when this was refused he left angrily.

Egon Hilbert

Born 5. 19. 1899; died 1. 18. 1968, Vienna.
Director of the State Opera from 9. 1. 1964 to 1. 18. 1968.

With Herbert von Karajan's resignation Egon Hilbert became sole director of the State Opera, a moment which he had longed for desperately all his life. He was not put off by his inevitably hopeless position, similar to that experienced by Felix von Weingartner as Mahler's successor, and made an extremely enthusiastic start, attempting to pursue the star policy in the absence of the superstar Herbert von Karajan.

Hilbert engaged Leonard Bernstein as a counterweight to Karajan, as it were, and joined forces with Wieland Wagner and the newly-appointed chief producer at the State Opera, Otto Schenk, with the aim of creating unique, world-class theater. Wieland Wagner produced *Salome* and *Elektra* with Karl Böhm conducting. After Wieland Wagner's death his widow took over the rehearsals for his production of *Der fliegende Holländer*, which failed to please. Bernstein conducted a model *Falstaff* by Verdi in a production by Luchino Visconti and was then commissioned for a new production by Otto Schenk of *Der Rosenkavalier*,

which eventually went ahead under Hilbert's successor. Otto Schenk also produced *Jenufa*, *The Rake's Progress*, *Carmen*, and *The Tales of Hoffmann*.

Hilbert's ensemble was almost identical to Karajan's, with the exception of those stars who did not want to work at the Vienna State Opera without Karajan. Hilbert brought James King, Regina Resnik, Gwyneth Jones, and Giacomo Aragall to Vienna, and until his death in 1966 Fritz Wunderlich was heard there more often than he had been before.

Hilbert's decisions became increasingly unreliable, partly as a result of his serious illness, and this led to a progressively fierce campaign in the media. Erwin Thalhammer, chief administrator of the State Theater, suggested on behalf of the government that he should retire. With the words "So you want my death" Hilbert gave Thalhammer back the golden key to the State Opera.

The following day Hilbert did indeed die in his official car as he traveled to his beloved State Opera—a remarkably tragic and very Austrian man.

201 James King in the title role in Wieland Wagner's 1965 production of *Lohengrin*.

202 Anja Silja in the title role and Fritz Wunderlich as Naraboth in Wieland Wagner's 1965 production of *Elektra*.

203 Birgit Nilsson in the title role and Eberhard Wächter as Orest in Wieland Wagner's production of *Elektra* in 1965.

204 Igor Stravinsky's *The Rake's Progress*, with Waldemar Kmentt as Tom Rakewell in 1965.

205 As a counterweight to Karajan, Egon Hilbert engaged Leonard Bernstein, who made his debut at the Vienna State Opera with Verdi's *Falstaff*. Luchino Visconti created the sets and costumes. This picture shows a later cast with Vladimir Ganzarolli and Wilma Lipp.

206 Leonard Bernstein returned in 1968 to conduct Otto Schenk's new production of *Der Rosenkavalier* by Richard Strauss. It was sung by Gwyneth Jones (Oktavian), Walter Berry (Ochs), Erich Kunz (Faninal), and Reri Grist (Sophie).

Heinrich Reif-Gintl

Born 10. 7. 1900, Vienna; died 7. 11. 1974, Kaumberg (Lower Austria).
Director of the State Opera from 9. 1. 1968 to 8. 31. 1972.

After Hilbert's death Heinrich Reif-Gintl became the temporary and then permanent director, having been associated with the State Theater since 1923. He had been made the house's administrative secretary under Franz Schalk and artistic secretary under Clemens Krauss, deputy director (under Franz Salmhofer) in 1945, administrative director of the Burgtheater in 1962 and assistant director of the State Opera on 1 January 1965.

Reif-Gintl was extremely well-informed musically, loved chamber music and was on very close terms with the members of the State Opera's orchestra. After a lifetime waiting in the wings he reached the top job, probably too late—although he provided some interesting evenings, he was unable to give any real zest to the repertoire. He had little success with Smetana's *Dalibor*, Richard Strauss's *Ägyptische Helena*, or a revival of his *Die schweigsame Frau* in a production transferred from the Salzburg Festival. There were performances of Gluck's *Iphigenie auf Tauris* (produced by Gustav Rudolf Sellner and designed by Filippo Sanjust), Cherubini's *Medea* starring Leonie Rysanek and designed by the Viennese "fantastic realist" Arik Brauer, a new *Don Giovanni* (produced by Schenk, designed by Damiani), *Simon Boccanegra* in a production by Visconti, Einem's *Prozess* produced by Lavelli, and Berg's *Lulu* in its premiere at the State Opera (Böhm, Schenk, Schneider-Siemssen). Otto Schenk also produced the world premiere of Gottfried von Einem's *Der Besuch der alten Dame*, and Verdi's *Macbeth* and *Don Carlos*. New singers included Shirley Verrett and Sherrill Milnes.

The celebrations marking one hundred years of the State Opera took place on 25 May 1969, with Leonard Bernstein conducting the *Missa solemnis* in the morning followed later on the same day by Karl Böhm's *Fidelio*. In Austria political

207 Otto Schenk's successful production of *Fidelio* was transferred to the larger State Opera from the Theater an der Wien in June 1970. Jubilation on the first night for René Kollo, Gundula Janowitz, and the conductor Leonard Bernstein.

208 Heinrich Reif-Gintl chose the "fantastic realist" Arik Brauer to design Luigi Cherubin's *Medea*. In the foreground Lucia Popp as Glauce.

changes also tend to have ramifications for the State Theater and this happened when the Liberal Party (the Volkspartei) lost its overall majority to the Socialist Party. The new culture minister Leopold Gratz, who also ordered a reform of the administration of the State Theater towards the formation of today's State Theater Association, wanted to see the State Opera headed by Rudolf Gamsjäger, the successful general secretary of the Gesellschaft der Musikfreunde. So it was that Heinrich Reif-Gintl had finally to retire, dying two years later.

209 Otto Schenk produced Verdi's *Macbeth* in 1970 with Christa Ludwig as Lady Macbeth and Karl Böhm conducting.

210 In December 1970 Josef Krips conducted a production of *Die Ägyptische Helena* with Jess Thomas and Gwyneth Jones.

211 Gottfried von Einem's *Der Besuch der alten Dame* received its world premiere in May 1971: Hans Beirer (center), Christa Ludwig, and Eberhard Wächter (on the right in the picture) were the protagonists in Otto Schenk's production.

Rudolf Gamsjäger

Born 3. 23. 1909; died 1. 28. 1985, Vienna.
Director of the State Opera from 9. 1. 1972 to 8. 31. 1976

Rudolf Gamsjäger had run the Gesellschaft der Musikfreunde with a great degree of commercial success since 1946. He was known to be a ruthless, radical man with a talent for handling musical and, in particular, administrative problems. It was hoped that fresh impetus would now be given after Reif-Gintl's quiet–perhaps all too quiet–directorship, and Gamsjäger was considered the man to bring back Herbert von Karajan without losing Leonard Bernstein and Carlos Kleiber. The belief was that Gamsjäger,

who in our frequent conversations had shown himself to be committed to the concept of ensemble and repertory theater, would apply this principle to the opera house. It was feared this would lead to a younger ensemble, with the older, deserving singers having to make way accordingly.

In fact all these predicted changes either failed to come about, or simply failed. Karajan's system was perpetuated: guests were brought in from all over the world, not always successfully, to perform in the

212 Arnold Schönberg's *Moses und Aron* finally came to Vienna in a new production. Götz Friedrich was the producer and Christoph von Dohnanyi conducted. Rolf Boysen and Sven Olof Eliasson sang the main parts.

repertoire and in premieres. Nonetheless, Rudolf Gamsjäger does deserve whole-hearted credit for introducing Arnold Schönberg's greatest work *Moses und Aron*, which until then had only received guest performances at the State Opera, conducted by Christoph von Dohnanyi in a production by Götz Friedrich. The engagement of Carlos Kleiber for *Tristan und Isolde* in August Evering's production added a most interesting name and broad-ened the range of conductors. Gams-jäger presented *Salome*, designed by Jürgen Rose in the style of Klimt, with Karl Böhm conducting a production by Bole-slav Barlog, and the long overdue premiere of Janáček's *Katya Kabonava* in a production by Joachim Herz (who also produced *Lohengrin* and *The Magic Flute*) under the musical direction of Janos Kulka, and he scored a great success with

Schenk's production of *Boris Godunov* with Nicolai Ghiaurov in the title role. Fur-ther success came with *Die Meistersinger von Nürnberg* (Dohnanyi, Schenk, Rose) with Karl Ridderbusch as Hans Sachs, and *Cosi fan tutte* with Schenk and Böhm.

Gamsjäger introduced Vienna to sing-ers like Katia Ricciarelli, Franco Boni-solli, José Carreras, Berndt Weikl, Bengt Rundgren, Brigitte Fassbaender, and the Russians Atlantov, Mazurok, Nesterenko, and Obraztsowa. In spite of these successes however, the public was increas-ingly critical of Gamsjäger's leadership, spurred in large measure by certain mis-judged productions including *The Gypsy Baron, Aida, Der fliegende Holländer*, and *Luisa Miller*, as well as controversial pro-ductions of *Lohengrin* and *The Magic Flute*. The desire for a change at the State Opera became ever stronger.

213 The Böhm-Schenk-Rose team produced a new *Cosi fan tutte* in May 1975. Brigitte Fass-baender sang Dorabella and Bernd Weikl was Guglielmo.

214 Karl Böhm conducted
Richard Strauss's *Salome*,
produced by Boleslav Barlog and
designed by Jürgen Rose in an art
nouveau style. This photograph
features a later cast with Heinz
Zednik as Herodes, Grace
Bumbry as Salome, and Gertrude
Jahn as Herodias.

215 One of the greatest
successes during Gamsjäger's
period as director was Otto
Schenk's new production of
Modest Mussorgsky's *Boris
Godunov* with Nicolai Ghiaurov
in the title role.

Egon Seefehlner

Born 6. 3. 1912, Vienna.
Director of the State Opera from 9. 1. 1976 to 8. 31. 1982,
and from 9. 1. 1984 to 8. 31. 1986.

I had meanwhile succeeded Sellner as general intendant of the Berlin Opera and been lucky enough in my job for it to be suggested that I might come back to Vienna. My contract in Berlin had to be brought to an end a year early, which was only made possible by the culture minister Fred Sinowatz appealing to Berlin's senator for the arts, Professor Stein. I was happy to be able to return to my native land after an absence of fifteen years and set about implementing my ideas on how an opera house should be run.

The immediate priority was to create an ensemble, and my intention was that it should contain three principal groups of members. The first group was to form a base consisting of the best available young singers on permanent contracts, the second would include first-class singers on long-term engagements, while the third group of top singers would come and go on a regular basis. Point two was the cultivation of a diverse and lively repertoire in which a place would be found for operas which were seldom or never performed. Thirdly, twentieth century opera should be supported by presenting authoritative works.

Such a program can not be carried out in just a few years, obviously. I hope, however, that in my two periods as director I struck the right points of emphasis. They came in the form of my first premiere, the first performance in Vienna of Berlioz's *Les Troyens*, Bellini's *Norma* and *I Capuleti e i Montecchi*, Donizetti's *Lucia di Lammermoor*, Puccini's *Trittico*; concert versions of Mercadante's *Il Giuramento* and Halévy's *La Juive*, Verdi's *Attila*, Rossini's *La Cenerentola* (in the Italian Mezzo version with Agnes Baltsa), Verdi's *Macbeth*, Schönberg's *Erwartung*, Bartok's *Duke Bluebeard's Castle*, Korngold's *Die tote Stadt*, Einem's

Kabale und Liebe, Henze's *Der junge Lord*, Cerha's *Baal*, Menotti's *Amahl/Globolinks*, Bernstein's *Mass*, and the ballets *Josephs Legende* by Strauss, *Sheherazade*, and *Ulysses* by Haubenstock-Ramati. The productions of Berio's *Un Re in ascolto* and Krenek's *Karl V*, which were scheduled by my successor, coincided exactly with what I had in mind.

I can say with some pride that I managed to bring back Herbert von Karajan, Leonard Bernstein, and Carlos Kleiber and to introduce James Levine and George Solti for the first time to the podium of the State Opera, as well as being able to experience Karl Böhm's last years there and Giuseppe Sinopoli's first. It is very difficult now for a director to say who his favorite singers are. The major singers belong to the whole world, and if you are lucky enough to have helped young performers on their way to success such as Edita Gruberova, Agnes Baltsa, Sona Ghazarian, Marjana Lipovsek, Joanna Borovska, Llona Tokody, Patricia Wise, Mara Zampieri, Peter Dvorsky, Gottfried Hornik, Bernd Weikl, Kurt Rydl, and Thomas Moser, then you can say that you have succeeded in an important part of your job.

The extremely large number of singers on generally short-term engagements made it difficult, in fact almost impossible, to have a large repertoire constantly on tap. The State Opera had up to sixty works scheduled in a season, attempting to be a sort of museum of the opera genre. The problem is how to carry off this attempt without exposing audiences to the risk of sloppy performances. My successor in 1982, Lorin Maazel, came up with an answer to this problem—the introduction of what he called a "block system."

216, 217 The opera ball has been a glamorous occasion for over thirty years. One of the highlights is the traditional entry of the young ladies and gentlemen.

218   Edita Gruberova in Gaetano Donizetti's *Lucia di Lammermoor* in a new production by Boleslav Barlog.

219   A new production of Richard Strauss's *Ariadne auf Naxos* in November 1976 with sets and costumes by Filippo Sanjust. Edita Gruberova (Zerbinetta) and Gundula Janowitz (Ariadne) are singing, and the comic characters appear in the background.

220 Franco Zeffirelli produced Bizet's *Carmen* in 1978 with Elena Obraztsova in the title role and Placido Domingo as Don José and Carlos Kleiber conducting.

221 A new production of Verdi's *Macbeth* by Peter Wood in February 1982 with Renato Bruson and Mara Zampieri. Giuseppe Sinopoli conducted.

222 Another star-studded musical event with Carlos Kleiber. He is seen here after a performance of Puccini's *La Bohème* with Mirella Freni and Luciano Pavarotti.

Lorin Maazel

Born 3. 6. 1930, Neuilly-sur-Seine near Paris.
Director of the State Opera from 9. 1. 1982 to 6. 30. 1984.

Lorin Maazel made his debut at the State Opera way back on 26 November 1964 with *Fidelio*, and in 1966 he conducted a new production there of Bizet's *Carmen*. He was musical director of the Berlin Opera from 1965 to 1971. As director of the Vienna Opera he immediately began to reduce the repertoire substantially by presenting individual works in two blocks of four or five performances per season, intending then to let them lapse again for a few years. Maazel hoped in this way to be able to offer repertory performances which were newly rehearsed and immaculate.

It soon emerged, however, that even if performances are rehearsed they either work as badly as they did on the first day or they fail to recapture their original brilliance. The ideal system has yet to be found. You have to tread carefully before introducing a premiere or a technically complex repertory production and you are forced to make use of a small number of technically simple productions—*L'Elisir d'Amore* on Monday, for example, if *Simon Boccanegra* is to follow on Tuesday. But these "simple" pieces only sell well if they are interestingly cast with a variety of singers, rather than with the same (indifferent) performers every evening. It is also a basic truth that, although rehearsals are necessary, the quality of a performance depends ultimately on the performers themselves on the evening. A poor conductor cannot make a performance more interesting however often he rehearses his ensemble, nor does a poor singer improve in spite of any amount of rehearsals.

In the two years he was director, Maazel himself conducted new productions of

223 Verdi's *Luisa Miller* was premiered in May 1983 with Giorgio Zancanaro as Vater Miller, Katia Ricciarelli in the title role, and José Carreras as Rodolfo.

224 Puccini's *Turandot*, conducted by Lorin Maazel, with José Carreras as Calaf and Eva Marton in the title role. The production by the star Broadway producer Harold Prince was a source of controversy.

225 Luciano Pavarotti, who enjoys Viennese audiences.

226 Agnes Balsa triumphed under Lorin Maazel in January 1984 as Bizet's Carmen.

Wagner's *Tannhäuser* (produced by Otto Schenk–Reiner Goldberg was indisposed during the premiere and left the stage after only a few minutes, having to be replaced by Spas Wenkoff!), Puccini's *Turandot* (producer Harold Prince), Alban Berg's *Lulu*, produced for the first time in Vienna in the three act version completed by Friedrich Cerha, Verdi's *Aida*, and an evening of ballet with *Daphnis et Chloé/The Firebird*. He enlisted Claudio Abbado for Verdi's *Simon Boccanegra* (producer Giorgio Strehler), Riccardo Muti for Verdi's *Rigoletto* (Sandro Sequi), Dimitri Kitaenko for

Tchaikovsky's *Pique Dame* (Kurt Horres), and Zubin Mehta and Riccardo Chailly for new musical interpretations, as well as having Hassreiter's *Puppenfee* revived using designs from the old production by Anton Brioschi.

The fundamentally different philosophies of Lorin Maazel and myself led to a split between us which was unfortunate for he had come to Vienna (and years before to Berlin) to a certain extent on my recommendation. I had never even dreamt that I would succeed my successor after his premature departure form the post of director.

Double page overleaf:

227 Successful productions during Seefehlner's second term as director: the 1985 production by Jean-Pierre Ponnelle (who also designed the sets and costumes) of Pietro Mascagni's *Cavalleria Rusticana* and Ruggiero Leoncavallo's *I Pagliacci*. Placido Domingo sang the part of Canio and Ileana Cotrubas played Nedda.

228 Mirella Freni and Peter Dvorsky in Otto Schenk's 1986 production of *Manon Lescaut* by Giacomo Puccini. The conductor was Giuseppe Sinopoli.

A study of the history of the Vienna State Opera shows that it cannot be compared with the history of any other opera house. The Vienna Opera was, is, and always will be an Austrian family business, even if it takes in a lot of guests. Other opera houses (with the possible exception of the Munich Opera and the Scala Milan) are simply institutions that fulfill a purpose. The directors of the Vienna Opera, be it the Court Opera or the State Opera, have had more or less the same fate—they are carried along by the love, or the hate, of a whole city, almost a whole people. They are crowned as kings and then given the dunce's cap to wear. They flourish if allowed to bask in success, and they wither to sickly, morose creatures if they are no longer able to look after their opera house. Only a few directors of the Vienna Opera—and they must have an intimate knowledge of the Viennese soul—surrender their posts with integrity and dignity, for the pleasure of being the director of the Opera in Vienna should not be underestimated.

SET DESIGN AND COSTUMES
Wolfgang Greisenegger

In the middle of the nineteenth century the decision was taken in both Paris and Vienna to build new and prestigious opera houses which offered more space. In neither city did this decision come about as a consequence of enthusiasm for music theater or because of a deliberate cultural policy. The purpose in both cases, in fact, was to create symbols of urban development, to give the metropolis new focal points as part of an ambitious process of planned urban enlargement. In Paris the desired redevelopment was seen through consistently and effectively— streets converged in star formation on a square on which a building stood that could be glimpsed from the distance. In Vienna they made do with the usual compromises, from the choice of a low-lying location to the failure to leave any space in front of the building. A splendid opportunity to correct the mistakes of the past was missed after the Second World War, and as a result the opera house is now enclosed by streets.

Both edifices were planned as worthy temples of art in the emotional spirit of the industrial revolution and later celebrated as such, but they were above all showpieces of imperial prestige, an elegant meeting-place for high society. The showpiece foyer provides the audience place to shine by means of staircases, galleries and mirrors, while the showpiece stage attempts to disarm by means of visual sensations.

Emphasis on the visual and prestigious is traditional in music theater. The birth of opera took place in a luxurious setting full of disarming images. Vibrant colors and audacious, elegant forms in motion. The awe-inspiring scene changes offered audiences at least as much pleasure as the poetic beauty of the libretto, the musical arrangement or the interpretation by the members of the court and its artistic retinue. Opera originated at court as the elitist entertainment of an aristocracy who was eager to develop its mind. Its birth (in Florence in the late sixteenth century) was assisted by scholars and nobles who attempted putting theory into practice, which was as daring as it was unsound. Their humanistic idea that classical Greek tragedy found its form in scenic and music theater soon faded, but the activity proved an exciting stimulus for generations of creative elite.

The new genre was also influenced by its birthplace—the palace. Everything that took place within its walls, even its entertainment, served a higher purpose: the consolidation of dynastic power. So it was with opera, which soon became a regular part of courtly festivities. The unrepeatable nature of such festivities meant that every opera performance was a single, sparkling occasion. Opera's existence as a form of allegiance dictated the choice of singer-actors, the choice of material for the costumes, the decoration and the attributes, which made men into gods. Only the best was good enough for the recreation of Arcadia or ancient Rome, Olympus or the Underworld and its inhabitants.

Opera in Vienna functioned on just this basis and remained an Italian art form

229 The equestrian ballet to celebrate Leopold I's marriage to Margarita Theresa of Spain in the courtyard of the Hofburg on 24 January 1667.

230 Lodovico Ottavio Burnacini's theater curtain for Antonio Draghi's *Il Fuoco Eterno*, performed in the opera house in the Cortina in 1674.

until Mozart's time, with the Viennese espousing composers, singers, librettists and, above all, designers from Italy. During the long reign of Leopold I opera became an indispensable part of the festivities at court. Wars and epidemics could not restrain the composer-monarch's passion for opera, and even periods of mourning were shortened so that performances would not have to be sacrificed. Theaters were erected in the Hofburg and in the palaces around Vienna so that the birthdays and name days of the emperor and his wife could be celebrated in suitable fashion and the birth of the heir apparent would be put in the desired context of world history. Weddings, war and peace, receptions of important guests were all celebrated in opera houses and interpreted through a complicated codified text, music, and in particular through the décor, which made use of a refined visual language full of allegorical references.

During the high baroque period in Vienna the emperor commissioned the construction of major performance sites by Lodovico Ottavio Burnacini, the young court architect and theater engineer who had come to Vienna from Venice as a boy with his father Giovanni, one of the great masters of the new craft of theatrical scenery. The theater in the Cortina was a grand, sumptuous place, its stage equipped with a full range of technical facilities that allowed the baroque fascination for transformation effects to be indulged with apparent ease and complete lack of fuss.

Burnacini was not only an important master builder—he drew plans for parts of the Hofburg—but also a theater technician, who never ran out of new ideas for stage effects. But he was primarily a scenery and costume designer whose imaginative power, unfailing style, and compositional ability make him one of the greatest designers in the history of theater. His grandest productions (he had overall responsibility for the performance) were preserved in series of etchings, which were bound together with the libretti and score and served to make him famous throughout Europe. The Viennese court was keen for rumours of these performances to spread from country to country. This was the Austrian answer to the challenge the French posed on the battlefield where the contestants were not evenly matched. For some time the aspirations of the emperor and his people had to be satisfied with triumph scored on stage until Prince Eugen achieved lasting victories on the battlefield for the Hapsburgs.

One of the first great theatrical triumphs was the performance of Cesti's imperial opera—imperial in every sense—*Il Pomo d'Oro*. The work was intended as a wedding present from the emperor to his young wife but it reached the stage after a delay of over a year and a half. The postponement was technical as well as financial because this work brought a new dimension to theater design in Vienna, in fact in Europe as a whole. It was necessary to construct a special theater for this extraordinary production. The building work dragged on because artists and artisans, along with finances, were repeatedly withdrawn to concentrate on other scheduled items in the wedding celebrations. The complicated technical equipment, including flying machines, trapdoors, and wave effects, required testing so that the inexperienced helpers could get used to their new duties. Considerable misfortunes suffered by the imperial household did not exactly assist preparations for the celebratory opera.

Finally on 13 and 14 July 1668 everything was ready and Leopold carried out his promise to honor the empress's birthday. The performance was divided into two parts: the prologue and first and second acts on the first afternoon, the third, fourth, and fifth acts on the next. The pause in the proceedings was presumably necessary so that the scenery and flies could be completely changed, the flying machines strung up, and more lighting added. No less than twenty-three different scenes followed one after the other, each one grander than the last. The wide expanses of the stage were constantly transformed by a variety of flying and disappearing machines, making each moment an ever-changing picture.

The prologue showed clearly that baroque opera was not merely concerned with entertainment but also considered itself to be a political voice. The political aspect was brought out most clearly by the optical scenic effects. An extravagant architectural setting (which in reality the emperor could never have afforded) was created to depict "a scene of Austrian glory" featuring equestrian statues in memory of the ruler's ancestors. Before them there appeared allegorical figures in full state costume. A symbolic figure representing Austrian glory came riding through the air on Pegasus, flanked by the floating forms of Cupid and Hymenaeus. In the middle of the story, which had become a moving tableau, the emperor himself was impersonated on the stage astride his steed, while cherubs held a laurel wreath above his head.

In the audience the emperor had the best view of this elegant stage-portrayal of himself reigning on his warhorse, because the architect had planned the symmetrical perspective of the whole design from the position of the emperor's seat.

Precision of composition was a standard feature of Burnacini's designs, holding the tableaux together and bringing a sense of order to the Breugelesque underworld he created. Here grotesque demons made discretely choreographed mischief inside structures awash with flickering flames and made up of intertwined bodies of fishes, snakes, and reptiles. Burnacini made use of sharp contrasts for his effects. He loved intense colors, which he would usually combine in threes, and knew how to use sumptuous materials to execute his flamboyant ideas.

It is worth lingering on the much-praised example of the *Pomo d'Oro*. The triumphal demonstration of imperial

231, 232 Lodovico Ottavio Burnacini's sets for Antonio Cesti's *Il Pomo d'Oro* in 1668: an equestrian statue (top) and Jupiter at a banquet surrounded by the throng of Olympian gods (bottom).

233, 234 More sets from *Il Pomo d'Oro*: the entrance to Hell—the audience looks into the wide-open mouth of a monster (top)—and the storming of a fortress, assisted by two young elephants (bottom).

235 Roman costumes designed by Lodovico Ottavio Burnacini.

236 150 years later—Philipp von Stubenrauch's costumes for Ignaz Franz Mosel's *Cyrus und Astyages* in 1818.

power gave way to the contrast of a heathen hell, followed by the appearance of Jupiter, father of the gods, amid the throng of Olympian deities at a celestial wine-tasting festival in his palace in the clouds, its walls consisting of barrels brimming with nectar. The scene changed next to a bright woodland, followed by an architectural folly depicting a palace forecourt, which was very popular in the theater at the time. Then the audience found itself transported to a charming, landscaped garden, which became a harbor by a rocky shore. The next scene has fascinated generations of set designers: the spectator was now looking into the wide-open mouth of a monster. Steam poured out of its ears and three nostrils. From between its jaws hellish, torch-bearing spirits flew out at the audience. In the creature's gullet glowed the river Lethe on which Charon could be seen, ferrying the souls of the dead to Pluto's burning city like a gondolier. This effective and well-conceived horror scene was set against comic elements in the libretto and music.

Burnacini was not only an exponent of the surprise element but he also used, to amusing effect, elegant variations on the technique of the leitmotiv, incorporating into his sets (as did a large number of his contemporaries) a series of recurring images which were constantly given new interpretations: military encampments in Arcadian or desert landscapes, the windy hollow, the arsenal, various shores, palace courtyards, temples, and palaces featured again and again. Burnacini is still a source of fascination today, because he was able to present traditional ideas in a new form. His productions were full of dramatic highlights such as the storming of a fortress (in which two baby elephants took part), the destruction of Mars's castle by an earthquake, and the portrayal of the goddess Venus's floodlit domain.

Burnacini provided his master with opera festivals of this quality, if not quite so extravagantly, for half a century. Even after the great court theater and the theaters in the castles had been destroyed by the Turks, opera at court was not allowed to suffer lengthy interruptions. Such artistic continuity was a decisive factor in establishing this as Vienna's first golden operatic age and a major opera center.

Leopold I's reign also saw the appointment of Francesco Galli-Bibiena—a member of the internationally recognized North Italian family of theater architects and set designers—to build the new court theater. His auditorium was created at the turn of the seventeenth and eighteenth centuries and must have been one of Europe's most beautiful examples, with its overwhelming splendor and complete intimacy, in spite of three tiers of boxes. The decor and costumes at the Viennese Court Theater were presided over by members of his extensive and highly gifted family for the next fifty years. The designs of each of the Galli-Bibienas are so similar that only in very few cases is it possible to identify their individual contributions, particularly since several would often work together as a team. The family had an astonishing command of the laws of perspective and specialized in the invention of outlandish architectural forms. They also accepted important commissions and were masters of auditorium design. Their suites of rooms and flights of stairs gave a new sense of magnitude because they cut through spaces in such a way that the spectators had the impression of being actually in the midst of the action, feeling drawn into half-concealed areas indicated by the footlights and arrows. The audience's eye was no longer trained on a vanishing point but encouraged to roam in several directions.

Grand though they were, these palaces, dungeons, gardens, and harbors could easily be interchanged. The full range of architectural history did not impede the scenery from conveying a historical and geographical no-mans-land, in which every movement became an imperious gesture, every act a heroic deed. This heroic freedom was a substantial reason for the influence throughout Europe of this artistic family. for whom Vienna was to remain a considerable mainstay of their work until the middle of the eighteenth century.

The new spirit of the Age of Enlightenment, which coincided with a particularly low ebb in the state treasury, brought

237 Set design by Giuseppe
Galli-Bibiena representing a jail.

about a swift end to imperial grand opera after the death of the last baroque monarch, Karl I. This did not stop Maria Theresa, however, from commissioning Antonio Galli-Bibiena to reconstruct her uncle's theater in the Redoutensaal. After finishing this last work, Antonio left the city on the Danube, just as his brother Giuseppe, also a leading artist, had already done.

Audiences began to get by quite happily without an elevated visual and musical style. The purpose of the theater was now to educate and entertain: the call was for characterization, the comedy of manners, and the chance to share the destinies of people with whom the audience could relate. Theaters were made acces-

sible to a wider section of the population when they began to be leased to directors who needed to entice the paying public if they were to enjoy commerical success. If a director went bankrupt, the government or the emperor in person would step in until a new director was found, but it was difficult to expect miracles from set designers under these circumstances. Increasingly, they were asked to make do with sets from a fund of basic equipment and to adapt it to new requirements.

More care was lavished on the costumes, which for many years were designed by Philipp von Stubenrauch, a Viennese who had studied under Friedrich Füger at the Academy of Fine Arts. He was considered one of the most knowl-

238 Antonio de Pian's set for Mozart's *The Magic Flute* in 1818.

edgeable experts on the history of stage costume after he brought out four works on costumes between 1807 and 1813 with hand-colored engravings based on well-known performances in Viennese theaters. On 1 April (the State still likes to appoint its officials on this highly significant day) in 1812 he was finally named Imperial and Royal Director of Costume and Scenery, which made him responsible for designing productions in the Court Theater. In fact, he decided it was enough to plan the costumes, leaving the designing and building of the sets to his assistant Johann Ferdinand Hötzendorf von Hohenberg, who had been working for the emperor for some years and had adapted the theater in the palace of Schönbrunn. His roots were in the rococo period and he derived romantic ideas from its light and colorful design, ideas which were given concrete form in strong

architectural designs. Like the Galli-Bibienas, he loved to use curved scenery which created a sense of space, although his emotive sets avoided the monumental and grand scale of the late baroque style.

Clean lines, a front-on style, huge geometrical sets, and strong contrasts of light and shade characterized the work of Josef Platzer, the most influential classicist among the scenic artists active in Vienna at the time. He worked in Vienna until 1806 and also for palaces in Böhmen and Moravia, where his designs are still preserved in the theater in Leitomischl Palace. In spite of the monumentality of the sets used by the Paduan Lorenzo Sacchetti, who worked in Vienna between 1794 and 1810, his creations seemed delicate, cheerfully vibrant, and naturally elegant. He was followed by the Venetian Antonio de Pian, who was entitled after 1816 to call himself "Designer to the

239 Carlo Brioschi created this glasshouse for the premiere of the ballet *Satanella* in 1853.

240 "The golden tree": a set designed by Antonio Brioschi for the ballet *Tanzmärchen*.

Director of the Supreme Imperial and Royal Court Theater." This romanticist among the Court Theater's artists was responsible until the middle of the nineteenth century for an enormous body of work (and also for the theater's basic sets) that revealed a fondness for the exotic motif and also a growing interest in historical detail.

Each of these artists satisfied the demands of a city theater, but none of them had the exceptional standing of a Burnacini or of one of the Galli-Bibienas. Although they made use of the Galli-Bibienas' techniques, their work was a reaction against sumptuous sets, fantasy, and monumentality and sought to give back the full value of the poetic word by concentrating the audience's attention on the dramatic action. This new attitude to the theater never completely won through in opera. In his "Description of a Journey through Germany and Switzerland in 1781" Friedrich Nicolai praised Vienna as the leader in the field of scenery and costume design. In 1794 the *Journal of Luxury and Fashions* from Weimar reported that the magnificence of the clothes had become of the very highest quality and that Vienna's theatrical wardrobe ranked with Europe's finest. The writer did not fail to mention that (spoken) German drama tended to be less extravagant than Italian opera.

The lavishness of the costumes found a large number of critics. Accordingly, on 3 February 1820 it was brought to the notice of the chief censor, the feared Count Sedlnitzky, that the growing expenditure on sets and costumes at the Court Theater was causing resentment. There was criticism of extravagant materials, and fear was expressed that the dazzling costumes would distract the audience's attention. A confidential report to this effect was presented to the emperor on 9 February by the finance minister, Count Stadion, and made the specific point that in the past the merit of the work itself was what attracted the public, and sets, clothes, stage equipment, and the like were rarely looked on as anything more than secondary. The opposite had become the case, not just in Vienna but everywhere, and in order to fill the house

a large amount of money had to be spent in advance on creating a glittering production. The minister forgot to add that the old Viennese Volkstheater also spent huge amounts on sets, and that mechanical comedies (curious baroque tales of fairies and magic) had joined forces with romantic sensationalism, provoking set designers to produce more and more new effects. This trend found its apogee in Franz Xaver Told's *Zauberschleier* (Magic Veil), which filled the Josefstadt theater for a week in 1842 because the audience could–by means of a cyclorama–share the experience of a trip up the Danube from Valhalla to Vienna. The sets and costumes were at this time an end in themselves.

The court theaters resisted competition from the theaters in the suburbs largely by staging more lavish productions, not that the Opera or the Burgtheater intended to include mere stage spectaculars in their repertoire. The court theaters' approach is best illustrated by one of the most popular ballets Vienna has ever seen, since in ballet productions in particular the barriers between the forms of entertainment broke down most quickly. Paul Taglioni's *Satanella oder Metamorphosen* premiered at the Kärntertor theater in 1853 and until 1869 received no less than one hundred thirty-one repeat performances. It was presented in a new production at the new opera house when it opened, although its scheduled opening was postponed for several months for technical reasons. The delay was understandable when one bears in mind the estimated cost of putting on this late-romantic love story: 18,000 gulden were spent on 319 costumes, with 2,000 gulden for props. These were enormous sums when you consider that the annual subsidy for the whole of 1850 was 70,000 gulden, and that the annual salary of the man in charge of productions in 1869 was 1,560 gulden (or 1,950 if there was a large number of performances).

In fact the extraordinary effectiveness of this ballet was due in large measure to the sets and costumes, because its success continued long after Miss Taglioni, who danced the title role, had left Vienna. The efforts made prior to the first performance

241 Theodore Jachimowicz's design for act I of Wagner's *Der fliegende Holländer* in 1871.

in 1853 had been extraordinary. No less than three scenery painters were responsible for the various designs; a costume designer took care of the astonishingly diverse traditional and ethnic garments, and a specialist was summoned from Berlin to oversee the technical special effects. This concerted action was hailed by the press which applauded the ingenious use of machinery and electromagnetic equipment to elegant effect. Of particular note was the huge working fountain in the closing set that brought rousing cheers from a delighted audience.

Sharing the responsibility for this exemplary production with Lehmann were two men with completely opposing personalities: Giuseppe Brioschi, a pupil of the Milanese Alessandro Sanquirico, who was considered at that time to be one of the leading artists in the field, and Theodore Jachimovicz, the son of a Galician priest. Jachimovicz had been working at the Theater an der Wien since the eighteen thirties, creating the sensational, constantly changing set for the Josefstadt theater in 1842. He had worked in the Court Opera's scenery workshop since 1851, and was to remain there until the beginning of the eighteen seventies. With Brioschi they had commissioned a specialist of great standing in Europe, an artist who had knowledge and expertise as a modern painter of historical scenes and was now able to gather the latest technical experience at a major opera house. They put him to work with Jachimovicz, one of the Volkstheater's brilliant designers. The individual scenes were designed by one painter working on his own, so in the final analysis the production was not the product of teamwork but a jigsaw of individual efforts, which was typical of the conventions prevailing during this period.

The homogenous style which distinguished baroque productions had been fragmented, but these individual fragments—the work of various hands—remained fascinating enough. The production came increasingly to resemble a museum in which striking scenes were positioned next to each other—an educational artefact here, some precious objects there, other works of art alongside. After the middle of the century this tendency to compartmentalize work became as typical in Vienna as it was in Munich, Berlin, Paris, and London. The search went out for specialists in historical styles, in ethnic and geographial exotica, in landscapes, architecture, and accessory figures, even people who specialized in particular moods. Workshop cooperatives were formed, first at the court theaters, consisting of a partnership of specialists. These were eventually to become *ateliers*, studios using quasi-industrial methods of production, which no longer worked to cater for the needs of one theater or city but instead accepted orders from customers abroad. A workshop of this kind grew up relatively early in Vienna and spawned a few similar enterprises at the end of the century.

The Brioschi dynasty of set designers was closely identified with the scenery used in the opera house and also with a workshop which eventually supplied the whole monarchy and received commissions from Russia and Western Europe. The Brioschis had a decisive, even dominating, influence over several generations of set designers in Central Europe. The founding father, Giuseppe, had been called to Vienna in 1838 to head the Court Opera's painting workshop. His son Carlo took over the post in 1854 and contemporary critics praised the way he took set design to new artistic heights. He was not only an artist who managed to set his face against excessive specialization (he was a pupil of the landscape painter Thomas Ender but was also capable of exact reproductions of natural phenomena as well as graphic art), he was also a formidable organizer who reformed the technical system in painting workshops and introduced innovations on stage. Martinez recognized as early as 1891 in his biographical sketches that it was through Carlo Brioschi that scenery painting became a fully-fledged art which enhanced the whole of the action on stage. It appears that the leading stage designers had fallen into disrepute and needed to improve their standing once more.

Carlo Brioschi's outstanding reputation was also due to his ability to attract good collaborators. In 1863 he obtained the services of Johann Kautsky from Prague, who had also trained as a landscape painter, and in 1866 of Hermann Burghart, who could already boast long experience in Vienna's suburban theaters before he joined the court theaters. All these appointments were made in preparation for the opening of the new house, because the larger dimensions of the stage and more particularly the new technical equipment made it impossible to use the old standard sets. It was only thanks to the organizational gifts of Brioschi and Franz von Dingelstedt, the director of the opera house, that the transfer from the old Kärntnertor theater into the new house with an astonishingly diverse repertoire could be managed at all. In the first year there were already twenty productions to call on, and this figure was further increased in the following year by a number of significant ballet productions (including *Satanella*).

The workshop capacity exceeded the everyday running of the theater after the opening. It was therefore possible for the three leading artists in the Opera's workshop to form a partnership and to found a private studio which supplied innumerable sets to all countries, confirming and spreading the fame of Viennese scenery painting. The firm, which operated until 1889, also undertook work for the court theaters, making use of their experience with the latest techniques. It was only through their know-how that the change from gas lighting to electricity in 1883 could be effected without great installation problems and without giving away all the tricks of scenery-building that had been handed down over the years. This break with the past was also better handled at the Vienna Opera because Carlo Brioschi had long since gone beyond the old system of flat scenery and moved in the direction of three-dimensional designs. He created panoramas, put up walls, incorporated platforms, angles and flights of stairs, and made frequent use of set pieces which were inserted into the action.

In 1885 his thirty-year-old son Anton followed him as leader of the Court Opera's painting workshop and remained in the job until he died in 1920. The change in the type of work he did is a reflection of how the importance of set design was transformed. When Anton Brioschi was appointed, he took almost all the decisions on scenery design. His superior was Franz Gaul, who was only interested in the costumes. Brioschi's son was extravagantly praised by the critics. Unlike most of his colleagues he was the subject of detailed reviews, which were increasingly unanimous in describing him as the master of his craft. "It is difficult to conceive," confirmed the *Theaterchronik* in 1889, "what brilliant gifts, what genius the young man possesses." The magical charm of his scenery received generous praise, while the "Consortium" (Carlo Brioschi, Burghart, Kautsky, Franz Angelo Rottonara, Theodore Jachimovicz, Josef Hoffmann, etc.) had to make do with the claim that they had displayed achievements in archeology and art history to good account. In her recent work on the Brioschi family's workshops, Vana Georgila makes the following accurate observations: "In an age when what is seen on stage matches the search for historical accuracy and realistic detail, Anton Brioschi's sets—like those created by his father and the consortium—conveyed the experience of historical voyages and culture. He delivered splendid theatrical feasts that made full use of technical developments but which still managed, as it were, to respect them." Anton Brioschi was the last exponent of the voluptuous art of subtle arrangement—he had a virtuoso's feeling for the luminosity of colors, the proliferation of intriguing and surprising touches, and the visual cameo. His work represented the final flowering on stage of the Makart style that had become such a familiar part of opera since the move to the theater on the Ringstrasse, a style which achieved ever greater triumphs in the ballet, where the plot was allowed to impose few constraints.

The costume designer Franz Gaul started to compose libretti for the ballet in the 1890s. This led to a press campaign which accused him of plagiarism and criticized him for the unhealthy influence he exercised at the opera house. Gaul successfully defended himself in the courts

against "literary kleptomania" and went on working at the Court Opera.

The critics made much of the ballet pantomime *Die goldene Märchenzeit* (with a libretto by Franz Gaul), which the *Wiener Salonblatt* described as follows on 9 April 1893: "The new ballet is also well worth seeing for its décor. Messrs. Burghardt, Kautsky, Brioschi, and Rottonara have once again created something truly ideal which exactly reflects the dreams prompted by our imagination, and which brings fairytales to life. The stage hands are also kept busy in the new ballet. A large number of difficult scene changes give them ample opportunity to prove their ability, and this is what they do. Everything goes like clockwork without any hitches or interruptions to the infi-

nitely complex machinery. There is also no shortage of fine costumes to attract the eye, which turns to revel in the beauty of the forms, finding everywhere new surprises, items of genuine artistic sensitivity, a finely orchestrated symphony of agreeable colors and materials to gladden the eye."

The commanding position held by Brioschi and his co-artists, who had formed their own companies after the break-up of the cooperative workshop in 1889, came to an abrupt end at the turn of the century. Gustav Mahler appointed a pictorial artist who had had little to do with the theater up to that point, putting him in charge of scenery and costumes. Heinrich Lefler was Viennese, had studied at the academies of fine arts in

242, 243 Carlo Brioschi's 1875 staging of Karl Goldmark's *Die Königin von Saba* (act II, scene 2: the temple)—elevation and ground plan.

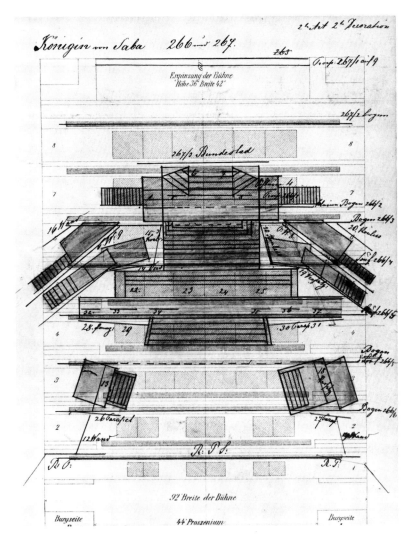

both Vienna and Munich, and had been one of the first people in the Austro-Hungarian capital to turn away from a traditional or academic approach. It was he, for example, who first put up artistically designed placards in Vienna and produced early versions of art nouveau with trend-setting book illustrations, interior furnishings, even designs for cellars of Vienna's city hall. Lefler worked with his brother-in-law Josef Urban, who achieved prominence later in the United States as a theater and cinema architect.

A community of artists, the *Hagenbund*, of which he was a co-founder, was credited with mediating between the impetuous passions of the youthful Secession movement at the turn of the century and the traditionalists, as well as encouraging art expressive of the different countries of the Austro-Hungarian Empire. Under his guidance the *Hagenbund* opened up a rich creative vein, which was in no way inferior to that of the Secession in its quality and spirit. Lefler's appointment on 1 August 1900 as "head of set design, artistic advisor and costume designer" meant the end for Gaul, whose job he now took over.

The arrival of the thirty-seven year old newcomer was the first sign of Mahler's desire to reform the way musical theater was produced. The break with tradition, which had been made long ago in the fine arts, was now to take place in theater. Demands for radical dramatic reforms filled the air during this period. All over Europe young stage designers were rebelling against the constraints which traditional realism and naturalism imposed on the imagination, looking for new ways of escaping from the all-pervasive jungle of overgrown scenery and costume. Manifestos and lists of demands for the theater were drawn up, soon becoming cult books in reform-minded circles. Critiques were organized and handed around in galleries which laid the ground for new ideas. It is noticeable that set and costume design during this period maintained its old and dignified status as an art form. Theoretical designs and workshop drafts appeared in exhibitions on an equal footing with other exhibits. For a significant number of the major theater reformers these exhibits were even to replace their practical theater work, all of which only added to the radical nature of their demands.

Adolphe Appia's book *Music and Theater Production* was published in 1899, while in London Edward Gordon Craig was experimenting as a producer and designer of music theater, drawing a large number of designs which investigated questions of light and shade, dimension and space, symbol and reality. As an actor in his own right and son of actress Ellen Terry, a star of the London stage, he had put forward ideas on the extent actors were necessary to the theatrical experience. He published his ideas and discussed his reforms with important figures in the theater. For Craig, as for Appia, these ideas, with only a few exceptions, were not to be converted into reality. Mahler's courage and broad-mindedness cannot be praised too highly when his reforms are seen in a European context. After all, Lefler had been taken on in order to rid the stage of backdrops, to take down the flies and to break down the system of maintaining a permanent stock of standard scenery. Every production was now to have completely new scenery designed for it, instead of making use of a central pool as in the past. His aim was to design a stage which created total illusion, a concept which built on Brioschi's groundwork. He achieved this perfectly, with great delicacy and complete determination. The single-minded vision of one man, who intended to give every

production its own character, set a tone to stage-designing that was a decisive step away from traditionalism. By adapting new color schemes from art nouveau and clearing the stage of everything that was merely decorative, he helped to break down old barriers.

Lefler's guiding principle, to design a set that was as practical as possible, was in tune with the spirit of the age. In Berlin Otto Brahm had insisted for some time that sets should be built and furnished as simply as possible and should minimalize the fictional aspect of the world depicted. Lefler did not go so far, deviating from naturalism above all by not filling the stage as much as possible. He attempted instead a highly poetic compromise between the three-dimensional and the self-consciously picturesque, to create the convincing effect of a slice of nature, as Leo Impekoven recommended. Lefler was the first man at the Vienna Opera consistently to remove the backdrop from the stage, thereby creating more space.

The new depth provided by three-dimensional sets required new technical equipment to move pieces of scenery on and off stage swiftly. Scene changes could be carried out instantly when two-dimensional backdrops were used, but now every new scene involved the shifting of a certain number of heavy items. Lengthy breaks were needed while the sets were changed. If this was to be avoided, either new technology was needed to move the weighty structures, or sets would have to be reduced in order to simplify operations. Lefler decided to perfect stage equipment. He created a swivel stage that could be dismantled and installed on top of the stage, and he paid particular attention to the development of the lighting system. He was one of the first theatrical designers to recognize the pictorial qualities of artificial light and to exploit them, becoming a master at creating mood from light and using it as an important method of shaping individual scenes.

But Lefler's greatest talent was costume design rather than scenery-building. In this field he again sought to combine authentic materials with historical accuracy, with his guiding principal as before

244 Anton Brioschi's set for act II of Johann Strauss's *Die Fledermaus* in 1894: "Glasshouse with winter garden."

being artistic truth. The filter between reality and what the audience sees on stage allowed the costumes to convey moods and to serve the characterization, also providing a sense of elegance and indulging tastes for fashion. Peter Pauker, who argued with Lefler over what he produced for the stage, gave this description of his work: The costumes "certainly testify to subtle psychological observations, but they are lacking in dramatic purpose. This is noticeable in the women's dresses, which are the subject of devoted attention and a most stylish imagination. Here Lefler's talents are expressed with most immediacy, his gift for the delicate, the charming, the ornate." The press rightly called his costume designs "poetry." Costume offered him more opportunity than scenery to use his refined palette to create a constant flux of colors in combination—his palette eshewed contrasts, choosing grey-violet, cream, old gold, pale pink, light green. Only when he left the Opera did Lefler discover strong colors and clearly-defined lines, and he handled them without sacrificing any of their sumptuous qualities.

Lefler's allegiance to art nouveau emerges most clearly in costume: the costume sketches perfectly captured "the soft cling of the material to the contours of the body, the supple slenderness of the proportions, the flower-like softness (...) the sinuous movements, the long flowing hair." It is certainly true that Lefler did not always succeed in making his work serve the production on stage, as Max Kalbeck observed in the *Neues Wiener Tagblatt* in connection with a new production of Tchaikovsky's *Pique Dame*. The critic pointed out the flaw that such rich and tasteful costumes were so real-looking that they did not belong on stage but on exhibition. Presumably he meant by this that the costume display resembled a lavish fashion show.

In spite of the success which accompanied Lefler's work at the Court Opera, he left there after little more than three years, taking over from Lichtenfel as professor at Vienna's Academy of Fine Arts on 3 October 1903. There he taught master classes that might have been tailor-made for Klimt. The reason for his unexpec-

tedly premature departure was more than in his decision to devote all his energy to teaching. On 21 February 1903 a premiere had taken place in the opera house, the significance of which did not escape contemporaries. The designer was Alfred Roller, a central figure in the vivid kaleidoscope of attempts to reform the fine arts which characterized Vienna's *fin de siècle*. Teacher of arts and crafts, president of the Seccession movement, he was responsible for one of the most exciting of the arts journals which were founded in Europe at that time in order to bring new artists to the attention of a wider public.

Roller was a painter, a respected graphic artist, art theoretician, and teacher when Gustav Mahler commissioned him to design a production of *Tristan und Isolde* for the Court Opera. The thirty-nine year old artist who—if we are to believe his biographer—had hardly had any contact with the theater, championed the new principles of style more radically and consistently than Lefler. The public recognized immediately that Roller's approach to music theater was new. Hermann Bahr and Ludwig Hevesi celebrated him as a reformer, and a large number of critics and (more particularly) audiences received a shock which was to prove a long-lasting one. Nobody could remain indifferent. Mahler had clearly found a complimentary partner, who would enable him to achieve the synthesis of the theatrical and musical arts which he had been seeking with his typical rigor.

In his brief biography of Roller which appeared two decades later, the writer Max Mell described the awesome visual impression which Roller's first work for the stage made: "His sets captured the spirit of the work so well that it remained unforgettable. The marvellous power of the colors blazed down from the stage—the first act was yellow-red and orange-red—with the threatening canopy structure of the sun-drenched sails, the stairs to the deck to the right hung with red, to the rear the darkness of the ship's hold with the rectangle of light from the hatch; Isolde's bed was in the center, its posts covered in black and gold pagan

245 Costume designed by Heinrich Lefler in 1901 for Marie Gutheil-Schoder in Ludwig Thuille's *Lobetanz*.

paintings and woodcuts, the shrine sheltering the poisoned drinks with lids resembling roofs, gleaming gold like little churches, studded with semi-precious stones, like the curtains and the bed with their Celtic ornamentation, showing the artist's familiarity with modern Viennese craftsmanship. The whole space is a hot, narrow interior, a seething caldron of suffocating agony which is ready to explode and in which the chants of the sailors pulse terrifyingly. It is hardly necessary to point out how this setting enhances the ensuing ecstasy and joy when love is acknowledged. The second act reveals an open starry sky. The lovers feel completely free and the only people on earth, at one with the infinite. The stage has nothing more than a narrow fringe of branches above, with a narrow piece of scenery to the left. The tree towers up against the ghostly pale wall of the tower with a gate and steep staircase on the outside. Light now breaks across this landscape heralding spiritual happenings, the heavy, dull night becomes transfigured by the harmonies of the love dream into a deep gleam, glowing in intensified nature, as if we were inside a vast blue chalice (this was the first time that a blue light had been used in Vienna); and then with Melot's betrayal a bleak, dismal day dawns with the sun weakly rising above dull clouds over low, thin ranges of blue hills. Then to the last act. A brightly-lit mountain around which a fresh sea breeze blows, bringing clear light. We can feel that we are up high, above the sea, the chalk cliffs, the surf. A sense of melancholy decay. The front of the stage is in shadow, so too is the mighty tree and the look-out, made from piled-up rocks. Between them in the background against the sky and the sea stands the fortified tower in radiance, like a broad, white block, with steep citadel walls. Isolde and the assailants enter from there, climbing up from the depths towards Tristan's bed, thereby freeing the external action, the entrance and the short fight, of theatrical banality and reinforcing the work's depth by allowing the characters to enter discretely."

This account of an overwhelming experience describes better than any analysis

of theater history the radically new interpretation of a work that until then—and, in Bayreuth, for some time to come—had been treated to a prosaic interpretation, which buried the great flights of music in a wealth of detail. Roller was searching for the essential elements of the work, which he wanted to express on several levels. His colors covered huge surfaces in a way no designer had dared before, symbolizing feelings and awaking them. The use of light conveyed the continuity of history while intimating the eternal. The story, in spite of its historical setting, was made relevant to the present. Many critics were less prepared to see the production as a concrete example of Wagner's complete "art work" than as a secessional version of *Tristan*. Immediately following the premiere, the *Hamburger Nachrichten* carried an intelligently argued polemic by Max Graf in which he wrote: "Modern impressionistic art has reached opera for the first time... Gustav Mahler's explosive genius has once again found another way of giving vent to the fireworks of the soul... When in the third act Tristan asks Kurwenal, who is looking out for the ship, 'Which flag?', the reply could so easily have been 'The flag of the Secession.' Every brush-stroke, every color combination proclaimed the watchword of the Vienna Secession: 'To the age its art, to art its freedom'."

Roller and Mahler continued seeking interpretations that conveyed the essence of the work. In his biography of Mahler, which was published in 1913, Richard Specht made a comment (in connection with *Tristan*), which applies to his productions and also to the sets which were made for them, that symbolism was enhanced by a sensitive combination of economy and imagination.

A few months after this first, decisive collaboration, Mahler went to the school of applied arts and asked Roller to work with him again. Roller stated his terms, which Mahler accepted, although they required far-reaching changes to the organizational structure at the Opera. All responsibility for design and stage equipment, including the lighting, were to be given to Roller. This opened the way for further team efforts. Their collaboration

246 Anna Bahr-Mildenburg as Amneris in Verdi's *Aida* in a costume by Alfred Roller.

reached a second landmark with *Fidelio* (1904), and a third with *Don Giovanni* (1906). These productions greatly excited the public. Long descriptions appeared in journals and people argued for and against Roller, mainly against. L. Karpath claimed in *Bühne und Welt*, for example, that the production was "simply unworthy." The same critic had loudly welcomed Lefler as a pioneer of a new perception. He was later to write: "Roller wanted to use his highly questionable creations"—he was referring to the towers, which are explained below, "in other productions but had to change his mind because the public wanted nothing of it. Unfortunately Mahler is completely under the spell of Mr. Roller, who is far too prominent."

The reason for the uproar was the so-called towers, covered scaffolding which could be manoeuvred to allow the width of the stage to be altered and the scene to be changed by turning the structures, without having to carry out arduous reorganization. Only the backdrop and a few props had to be changed. This simplified system of scenery design was considered an affront by many in the audience, who had come to expect from the opera a visual feast, an enlightening spectacle. They refused to have anything to do with the persuasive psychology behind the carefully chosen colors, nor did they understand the musicality of this new concept, which allowed the work to be presented in a concise and uninterrupted sequence by doing away with complicated structures. The sets were also notable for the effect Roller's use of velvet produced as a result of its capacity to absorb light. (Such fabric had previously been reserved for costumes.) The magnificent intensity of the colors, which was not distorted by reflections, received the general approval of the critics.

When Mahler left the Court Opera and Vienna in 1907, Roller stayed on for a time. But Mahler's departure changed Roller's relationship with the theater's administrators. They were quick to throw more and more stumbling blocks in the way of the awkward Roller, objecting to his productions on the grounds that they were too expensive, although at the same time sets for ballets were being approved which cost several times as much. Roller took the hint and returned to the field in which he had previously been active. He took over in charge of the institute of applied arts, which was making a considerable mark at the time, the effects of which are still felt today. In the five years in which he worked with Mahler, Roller was responsible for no less than twenty-one productions, which proved to have a significant influence on the history of the opera. A faithful rendering of the original, allied with a strong personal style and concentration on the essential elements without suppressing the imagination established the Mahler/Roller era as a decisive phase in the history of theater, a peak (if not *the* peak) in the history of set design at the Vienna Opera.

Before Roller turned his back on the opera house he designed the first ever production of *Elektra* by Strauss and Hofmansthal. Like the author, he rebelled against realism on the stage and anything that bordered the superficial, coincidental, trite, tasteless, hackneyed, or was irrelevant to the text, as Peter Burwik noted. This collaboration with Hofmannsthal and Strauss was to be repeated. Roller designed the world premiere of *Der Rosenkavalier* in Dresden and also its Viennese premiere. On 10 October 1919 there followed the world premiere of *Die Frau ohne Schatten* using sets and costumes which were adopted almost unchanged in the new production of 1931. The production in 1937 also used Roller's designs, nor can it be denied that the production in 1943 designed by Robert Kautsky was influenced by Roller's original.

The next appreciably different version of this opera was the work of Emil Preetorius in the series of inaugural productions in 1955. Roller's legacy is also visible in several other works and underlines the stylistic mark this artist has made on the Vienna Opera. When he left the Court Opera in 1909 Anton Brioschi came out of the shadow of the workshop again; A.D. Goltz received commissions, and Heinrich Lefler also returned.

Although it was true that the bold reforms introduced by Roller and Mahler

247 Alfred Roller's garden set for Mozart's *Don Giovanni* in 1905.

could not be undone, they were not developed either. Sets were now visually rich but stagnant. After 1919 Roller started to work on two to four operas per season, usually in productions by Lothar Wallerstein, the most important of which were transferred to the Salzburg Festival. After the First World War Roller had been responsible for the reconstruction of the Redoutensaal, a work which he carried out with great style. He designed a number of productions for this late-baroque hall, including *Figaro* and *Cosi fan tutte*. Roller died in 1934 shortly after completing his last work with Robert Kautsky.

After Roller came a series of designers who were taken on for a limited number of productions, such as Clemens Holzmeister, the architect of the Salzburg Festival Theater, who designed the sets for Lothar Wallerstein's production of *Euryanthe*. The costumes for this great romantic opera by Carl Maria von Weber were by Marielouise Luksch.

The architect and set designer Oskar Strnad—whom Roller had appointed professor at the school of applied arts before he became set designer at the German Volkstheater in Vienna after the First World War—worked on fascinating drama projects which anticipated the "total theater" of Piscador and Gropius. Employed by Reinhardt in his Josefstadt theater and at the Salzburg Festival, he made his debut at the State Opera in 1927 with Krenek's *Jonny spielt auf*. His set designs for the premiere of Alban Berg's *Wozzeck* remained effective for many years. Another significant project was his work on Jaromir Weinberger's *Schwanda der Dudelsackpfeifer*.

Before and after the Anschluss several strong figures made their appearance, such as Alfred Roller's son Ulrich, who designed productions of Strauss's *Daphne* and *Friedenstag*. The painter and cartoonist Stefan Hlawa received his first commissions and Erni Kniepert, a master of the elegant costume, also made her debut and was, like Hlawa, to stay with the State Opera for several decades. Heinrich Karl Strohm was sent from Berlin, directing the Opera for only a few months, and was joined in Vienna by the producer Oscar

Fritz Schuh and the set designer Caspar Neher from Hamburg. Neher was a pioneering designer for the stage (who as Brecht's friend and collaborator helped to shape his early creative period), and together with Schuh he laid the foundations for the Mozart style which was to become famous throughout the world after the Second World War. A few great experts in their field, such as Ludwig Sievert and Wilhelm Reinking, came from the Reich to work on a few projects but they did not leave a durable impression behind them.

The post-war style at the Theater an der Wien, while the State Opera was housed there, was marked by the work of Robert Kautsky who had quietly been maintaining standards of set design for some decades through his efforts in the workshop. Caspar Neher, Stefan Hlawa, and Erni Kniepart also played their part. The décor and costumes during this period were deliberately simple, outlined rather than stipulated, full of painterly invention, and featuring light materials rather than heavy sculptural pieces. This was not only to combat through improvisation the oppressive poverty brought on by the war, but also to oppose the hollow emotionalism, megalomania, and false nostalgia of the Third Reich by stimulating the imagination through the use of fragmentary elements.

With Clemens Holzmeister, who designed the *Fidelio* which opened the restored opera house in 1955, and Emil Preetorius, who was responsible for *Die Frau ohne Schatten*, the third festival production, a moderate form of emotionalism returned to the house, in which more and more guests artists were engaged for brief periods. They included during Karajan's era Georges Vakhevitch, whose heavily-colored designs for ballet and opera (*Otello, The Magic Flute*) did not always fit in with central European tastes. Emil Preetorius designed a production of the *Ring* for Karajan, which was very coolly received by the critics. People were no longer prepared idly to accept the emotionalism which typified Preetorius later work where he merely perpetuated the realism of the great reformer of the turn of the century, Adolphe Appia.

248 Alfred Roller (left), Robert Kautsky (center) and Lothar Wallerstein (right) discussing a production.

Audiences had come to expect a more daring approach.

A new era of scenery and costume design began in 1960 through Günther Schneider-Siemssen, who was brought over by Karajan and gradually became his preferred designer in Vienna and (in 1962) in Salzburg. Schneider-Siemssen is a painter of great vision, a demiurge to whom comic vistas open, a realist who loves opera as an intellectual spectacle, reveling in the truth and contrasting it with the fictional. His designs give visual stage directions, and it came as no surprise that he, like so many of his colleagues, went on to be a producer in his own right. Schneider-Siemssen loves a perfectly prepared experiment and is always looking out for new technical means of expression. He has been experimenting with holography for years, a form which would allow him to "build" with light.

The tragically early death of Wieland Wagner stopped short the attempt to create productions which flowed from the actual meaning of the work. His decisive productions of *Salome* and *Elektra* appeared within weeks of each other. With their abstract settings and bold use of archaic symbols, they represented a movement away from preciousness of

249 Oskar Strnad's station set for Ernst Krenek's *Jonny spielt auf* in 1927.

250 Stefan Hlawa's prison set for Verdi's *Il Trovatore* in 1951.

251 Caspar Neher's set for Violetta's bedroom in Verdi's *La Traviata* in 1940.

any kind and from attempts at realism, which had begun to be the norm in Vienna. Teo Otto, the virtuoso ascetic who had designed productions of Brecht in Zurich, provided the State Opera and the Salzburg Festival with witty, neo-baroque feasts for the eye, and Luchino Visconti and Luciano Damiani worked as guests.

Practitioners of the fine arts (Arik Brauer, Ernst Fuchs) were commissioned, generally for only one opera. There were also at this time experiments in the ballet with the recreation on stage, for example, of a Picasso masterpiece, an original design by Anton Brioschi, or Hassreiter's original choreography for the ballet pantomime *Puppenfee*. Since the deaths of Neher, Hlawa, and Teo Otto, however, design has been dominated by Günther Schneider-Siemssen. He remains a fixed point while around him people come and go, and he provides continuity by taking on productions with great aplomb, giving the house a greater sense of identity than one would guess in view of the number of works he handles. Just as he continues to work closely with Herbert von Karajan in Salzburg, he also teams up in Vienna and abroad with Otto Schenk, creating confident and effective opera.

In recent years continuity has also been reinforced by the increasing use in the program of new versions rather than new productions. This return to the old system of a basic fund of resources recalls somewhat the period before Mahler and Roller, in which all experimentation was shunned. Hardly any designs attempt to set the bounds of reality for themselves or to go beyond them. Most of the productions in the last ten years fall under the banner of hyper-realism.

Vienna showed little interest in reinterpreting the role of the opera and ballet designer. It is characteristic of this phase in the history of the Vienna Opera that one of the most significant dramatic events was Schönberg's *Moses und Aron* in the new production by Götz Friedrich. The evocatively geometrical and abstract sets were by Rudolf Heinrich, who did not live to see the work revived in December 1982. Subsequent projects did not meet with undivided support, not least because of their return to a naturalistic approach. There was little support for Jürgen Rose's *Daphnis et Chloé* or *Firebird*, which were criticized unmercifully for depicting a "picture postcard Lesbos" and a "modernistic wasteland," nor for the interpretation of *Rigoletto* by the chief designer at the State Theater workshop Pantelis Dessyllas, or Andreas Reinhardt's sets for *Pique Dame* with its light-and-dark and stage effects which were reminiscent of Caspar David Friedrich. Jean-Pierre Ponnelle ventured one step beyond the habitual realism with his vivid productions of *Bajazzo* and *Cavalleria Rusticana*, although they were full of naturalistic touches.

The story of scenery and costume design at the Court and State Opera is also the history of Viennese taste. Audiences have seldom shown themselves open to experimentation, preferring instead to put their trust in visual beauty and simply to indulge their eyes and ears. They expect opera to offer naturalism and variety, entertainment and edification—and it does. The visual character of the house has been determined by strong personalities whose expressive powers and sense of style survived successive directors. In an institution which has always concentrated on the performers, the visual aspects of a work will always be of secondary importance. The set designer is left to create a beautiful and varied framework for the singer. Scenery and costume are used less often as a means of reinforcing the understanding and meaning of a piece, than to provide an appealing backdrop to animated figures.

252   Wieland Wagner's 1965 set
for a scene in the second act of
Richard Wagner's *Lohengrin*
(with Martti Talvela as King
Heinrich, Walter Berry as Telra-
mund, Jess Thomas as Lohengrin,
Christa Ludwig as Ortrud, and
Claire Watson as Elsa).

253 Set by Günther Schneider-Siemssen—under the influence of Wieland Wagner—for the final scene of Richard Strauss's *Die Frau ohne Schatten* in 1964 (with Christa Ludwig as the dyer's wife, Leonie Rysanek as the empress, Jess Thomas as the emperor, and Otto Wiener as Barak).

254   A return to historicism:
Günther Schneider-Siemssen
designed this set of the hall in the
Wartburg for Wagner's *Tannhäuser* in 1982.

255 Jürgen Rose's set for the ballet *Daphnis et Chloé* was criticized in 1983 as showing a "picture-postcard Lesbos" and "modernistic wasteland."

256, 257 The young Austrian Hans Schavernoch designed "spiritual spheres in saturated colors" in his 1985 productions of Bela Bartok's *Duke Bluebeard's Castle* (top: Clara Takacs and Siegmund Nimsgern) and Arnold Schönberg's *Erwartung* (bottom: Karan Armstrong).

THE VIENNA OPERA BALLET
Riki Raab

The fine arts always received particular attention at the imperial court in Vienna. Besides providing entertainment they were also considered a means of education. Emperor Leopold I composed many operas, which he occasionally conducted in person from the harpsichord. It became customary to celebrate the personal feast day of the numerous members of the imperial family with a theatrical performance on the private court stage or in the gardens of the summer residences. Whether a *dramma per musica* or *festa teatrale*, the performance always had to be *con ballo*. At first these *balletti* were figurate ballroom dances and were performed by the "young ladies and gentlemen" of the ruling house, the young nobility, with rehearsals being looked after by the imperial and royal dancing master.

The theatrical arts quickly grew in popularity—the dance numbers were harmonized thematically with the main work or were given independent status in the form of a small plot. Archduchess Maria Theresa was a first-class singer and dancer. To her dismay, however, she was advised on becoming Regent not to take part in the family celebrations. In order to cope with the rehearsals for these festivities (which were becoming more and more extravagant), the dancing master was assisted by deputies. They had to dance too and were even allowed to teach commoners the stage dances, to make up the numbers of the court *corps* as required. This represented the birth of the Vienna Opera Ballet. The dancing master became the ballet master, whose responsibility it was to take dance beyond its simple function as a connecting medium and to develop it into an independent art form.

In accord with the emperor's wish a theater was built to enable the general populous also to take part in the musical spectacle. One of the first lease holders appointed by the Court Theater next to the Kärntnertor theater was Franz Hilverding von Wewen (1710–68), who was known as a dancer and ballet master. He became an important figure by preparing the way for the tragic mime ballet. Another dancer-ballet master was also placed in charge: Louis Duport (1781–1853). He and the ballet master Jean Aumer (1774–1833), who worked at the time of the Vienna Congress, introduced the Viennese Ballet to the French style of dancing. The ballet company at the Kärntnertor theater started with forty members with a French or Italian prima ballerina. At times the number of dancers had to be increased, because the company also performed at the Hofburg theater.

The Romantic age brought certain distinctive features: the ballerina moved to the prominent position formally dominated by the male dancer, and she danced on her toes for the first time. Philipp Taglioni (1777–1871) played a big part in implementing this last change, spending a great deal of time in creating a light dancing shoe until finally his daughter Marie was not only able to raise herself onto the very tips of her toes, but could also dance on them. This innovation had a fundamental effect on dancing style for it integrated romantic philosophy into dance theater.

When Vienna's city center was enlarged (with the removal of the fortifications and city walls), the young emperor Franz Josef I commissioned the building of a prestigious opera house. For some time the old Kärntnertor theater had not been equal to the demands imposed by the huge growth in the theatrical arts, although it had been the home of many major new works which later went on to be seen all over the world. It was here where the first ever mime ballet was presented in 1761, in which two reformers, the ballet master Gasparo Angiolini (1731–1803) and Christophe Willibald Gluck, together reworked the story of Don Juan. The third reformer of great style, Jean Georges Noverre (1727–1810), should be mentioned here. In seven years of working in Vienna he raised ballet to a high standard with his brilliantly choreographed work which used themes taken largely from Greek mythology. He worked at both court theaters and was the first choreographer to be allowed to receive his applause in front of the curtain. His *Lettres sur la Danse et sur les Ballets* (1760) is a seminal work. Another event worthy of mention was the first appearance of Marie Taglioni (1804–84), who went on to become the leading dancer of the Biedermeier period, having started her international career on the stage of the Kärntnertor theater in 1822. It is a charming quirk of history that on that same evening she shared the stage with Fanny Elssler (1810–84) who later became her great rival.

The opening of the new Court Opera was celebrated on 25 May 1869. The first ballet to be performed on its splendid stage was the premiere on 16 June of the historical ballet *Sardanapal* by Paul Taglioni (music by Paul Hertel), which introduced an era of grand processions. *Sardanapal* was set in Nineveh in 888 B.C. and the costumes were as sumptuous and expensive as the scenery. The production cost 25,000 thaler while the receipts for the premiere were 3,508 thaler. Taglioni received 8,000 francs and his majesty's supreme appreciation.

Since 1859 the ballet had been in the hands of the Berliner Carl Telle (1826–95). He was a hard-working ballet master who had also staged a large number of ballets by other choreographers and conscientiously rehearsed the great dance intermezzi for new operas (*Faust, Aida,* etc.). His duties also included the running of the Ballet School where he himself gave lessons; he, together with his wife, the mime Johanne Telle (1828–1906), and the solo dancer Alfred Caron (1837–99), constituted the first teaching staff. He earned great praise for drawing up the statutes of the Ballet School, in the running of which Paul Taglioni (the long-staying guest from Berlin) took a major part, presumably to ensure that his vast ballets would be recreated perfectly.

Guglielma Salvioni was the first prima ballerina to perform in the new house (from 1868 to 1873). She came from the school in Milan and showed all that was best in Italian ballet. She also took on roles in older ballets, for example Topase in Taglioni's ballet *Flick und Flock* (music again by Paul Hertel), which also featured two exponents of the *demi-charactère* style of dancing, Louis Frappart and Julius Price, who helped to make it a complete success and a dominant part of the repertoire. They both performed so marvellously in the title roles that they could not only command the highest appearance fees but also forced the theater management to grant further recognition. The two artists were each paid one hundred gulden extra after every twentieth performance, probably a unique event in the history of ballet.

There was nothing of Taglioni's magnificent style about the ballets of Pasquale Borri (1823–84), for example *Carnival's Adventures in Paris* and *The Chimney-sweep of London.* True to life personages now took over from the romantic spirit world.

Josef Hassreiter (1845–1940), first solo dancer in Stuttgart, introduced himself to Viennese audiences in a *pas de deux* with Salvioni. He was to become known as the creator of the Vienna Ballet. Born in Vienna on New Year's Eve 1845, Hassreiter was one of those people who

258 *Il Trionfo d'Amore* by Pietro Metastasio and Florian Leopold Gassmann, with choreography by Franz Hilverding, performed at the palace of Schönbrunn in 1765 with Archduke Maximilian as Cupid, Archduke Ferdinand as the shepherd Myrtil, and Princess Marie Antionette as the shepherdess Flora.

are lucky enough to know how to exploit their inate talent with humour and a cheerful attitude. He would laugh that he was a New Year's joke. His father Carl Hassreiter (1820–70) was a dancer in the company and gave his talented son tuition. At the young age of six Josef stood in the Kärntnertor theater on the same stage as the world famous Fanny Elssler as she made her much-loved guest appearances. After learning basic principles Hassreiter went to Munich for two years and then to the Court Theater in Stuttgart as first solo dancer. In 1870 he tried to earn an engagement in the city of his birth, and this he achieved after his second guest appearance. Hassreiter spent twenty years

under ballet master Telle as an uninhibited *premier danseur* who also enjoyed playing mime roles. His main job, however, was to provide lively and reliable support to a succession of invited ballerinas. For his *pas de deux* solos he would invent his own increasingly flamboyant variations, achieving the highest artistic standards.

When Salvioni left she was followed in 1873 by the Viennese prima ballerina Bertha Linda (1850–1928), who became Hassreiter's second permanent partner. She had learned her dancing in the Vienna Ballet Company of the former solo dancer Kathi Lanner (1829–1908) with whom she traveled for some years as

259 Julius Price as the slave overseer in *Sardanapal* with students Olzer, Jaksch, Fichtner, and Neumann in 1869.

260 Guglielma Salvioni, prima ballerina from 1868 to 1873.

214

261 *Flick und Flock* by Paul Taglioni with A. Stadelmeyer, Louis Frappart as Flick, Claudine Couqui, and Julius Price as Flock in 1869.

Her successor was the Milanese Luigia Cerale (1859–1937) who came from performing in London to make her Viennese debut in the ballet *Satanella* by Paul Taglioni and went on to entertain Vienna with her exceptional talents for thirteen years. Her precise Italian dancing style also greatly enhanced the nimble leg technique of her partner Hassreiter. Cerale was an elegant, refined dancer who particularly shone in the leading classical roles.

During this period there was great activity among ballet librettists and composers; it was by no means unusual for there to be as many as twenty different ballets on the program in one season. Occasionally members of the company would also compose ballet libretti. The Parisian Louis Frappart (1832–1921), who has already been referred to, proved to be particularly productive. He was an important member of the company and through the force of his expressive personality—he came to be known as the "Jupiter of lyric drama"—he influenced the stylistic direction of narrative ballet. He originated the divertissement *Saltarello*, which turned into an entertaining farce called *Saltarello, der Narr von St. Tropez*, in which he gave an opportunity to the rising musical star Franz von Suppé to compose the ballet music. This was followed by *In Versailles* and in 1884 *Vienna Waltz*, in which Josef Bayer (1852–1913), having his first contact with ballet, put together a collection of old Viennese music. On one occasion Frappart risked his life by saving one of his young female colleagues from burning to death on stage, for which the management gave him a diamond ring as a token of appreciation. At that time two mime artists from the Burgtheater, Amalie Haizinger and Carl La Roche, who ran the "First Drama College" took Frappart on to teach dance and mime. He was decorated and made an honorary member of the Court Opera Theater for his services to Viennese ballet.

Frappart had an equal in Julius Price (1833–93), who was also a great mime and dancer. The two were known as the Heavenly Twins and complimented each other in their characterization, with Frappart as a noble Flick and Price as the wan-

guest dancers. When the company broke up she went to the Court Theater in Berlin, where she soon worked her way up to the position of first dancer. Then the call went up for her to come to Vienna as prima ballerina. After the usual guest appearance she signed a four-year contract, earning twelve thousand gulden a year, tax-free. She delighted audiences in a number of title roles such as *Sylvia*, Fenella (in *La Muette de Portici*) and *Coppelia*, conducted by Leo Delibes in 1877. When her contract expired, she retired from the stage and married the painter Hans Makart, whose name is synonymous with the period in which he lived.

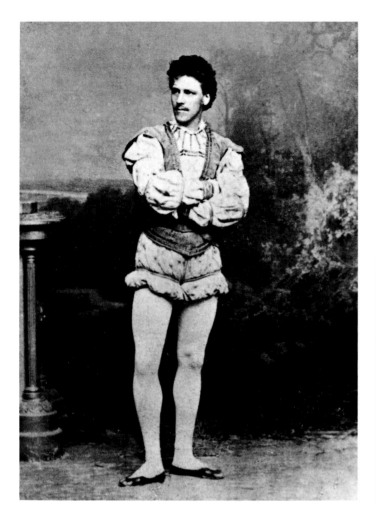

dering minstrel Flock. Price came from a famous English family of pantomime artists and circus riders. He was born in Nizhniy-Novgorod in Russia while his parents were on tour and trained as a dancer in Copenhagen under the ballet master at the court, Auguste Bournonville. This master of choreography took his pupil with him to Vienna where he had been invited to produce his sumptuous ballets, for example *Der Toreador* and *Napoli*, at the Kärntnertor theater with a company not favorably disposed towards him. Bournonville left Vienna early, disappointed and hurt. Price stayed. He danced and mimed both amusing and dignified parts, and even played the mother of the *fille mal gardée* in d'Auberval's *Lisa et Colin*. In his theater diary Price calculated that in twenty-one years he made two thousand four hundred eighty appearances on the stage of the Court Theater (and performed mime for another seventeen!). One of his own ballets was performed in 1884: *Harlekin als Elektriker*, with lively music by Josef Hellmesberger, Jr., a piece with good roles which was all that could be asked of an entertaining narrative ballet. Price taught student actors at the conservatory in Vienna for some years. He finished his career as the Englishman in the hit ballet *Die Puppenfee* and was still performing on stage twenty-one days before his death.

The mime Hans Rumpel (1853–1923) created the ballet *Die roten Dominos* to enticing music by Josef Klein, a violinist in the Court Opera Orchestra. Rehearsals were now in the hands of the leading

262 Josef Hassreiter as Hidalgo in *Fantasca* in 1878.

263 Prima ballerina Bertha Linda as Swanilda in *Coppelia*.

264   Luigia Cerale, prima ballerina from 1879 to 1892, in
Sylvia, ou la Nymphe de Diane.

mime Carl Godlevski (1862–1949), who was one of the last great mime artists at the Vienna Ballet. His appointment was revolutionary at the time, because he had been working as an acrobat–albeit a famous one–in the Zirkus Renz and moved from the circus ring to the imperial and royal Court Opera Theater. His easy personality and great artistry soon won him due recognition and he maintained his connection with the theater for thirty-one years. (A street in Vienna's twenty-second district was even named after him.)

The solo dancer and mime Voitus van Hamme (1853–1921) created and designed a ballet which gave a prominent place to national dances–*Eine Hochzeit in Bosnien* with music by Josef Bayer. It was popular with his dancers and well-received by the public, but it was only produced on this one occasion. Even so, van Hamme was not short of work. He had a hand in almost every ballet (his farmer in *Die Puppenfee* was marvellous) and was also a very popular teacher at the ballet school, where by high achievement he would earn a twenty-heller piece or even a crown. He arranged dances at other theaters and also gave instruction to aristocratic pupils in the imperial and royal Theresianum and to drama students at the conservatory, besides running his own elegant society dancing school. In 1920 van Hamme gave over teaching his classes at the conservatory to his colleague, the mime Helen Krauss (1873–1951), wife of the *Kammersänger* (a title conferred on a singer of outstanding merit) Fritz Schrödter and aunt of the director of music Clemens Krauss.

After the new opera house was opened, the *corps de ballet* took an increasing part in ballet in Europe. An important number of new works came out of the ballet centers in France and Italy which could only be mastered with application and discipline, though they received little credit. It was for this reason that the recognition given by Richard Wagner, who was known for his lack of enthusiasm for ballet, was so important. When he came to Vienna for the performance of *Lohengrin* and complained about various outrages in the opera house he exclaimed: "I have no right to object to ballet, since the correctness, precision, and vitality of their performances, here in this very opera theater, are exemplary compared with the way opera is performed."

Yet there were signs of decline which first manifested themselves in small ways. People complained that flounces on the skirts were too short and that as a result "the Princess's feelings of decency in the royal box were being insulted." It was alleged, for example, that the public was unhappy because the "negroes" were not blacking up properly, and that "the ladies of the ballet should show less interest in the audience and more interest in their own performance." Such concern over matters of morality were not new; they had already been raised in the eighteenth century, when the court police had occasionally to intervene to preserve morals and public order. The Court Opera's ballerinas were not allowed to marry, incidentally, while they were engaged by the company.

The six-act ballet *Excelsior* by Luigi Manzotti was performed in Vienna in 1885 to celebrate the completion of the St Gottard Tunnel to Milan in 1882. The very latest in technology (electricity, for example) was symbolically represented as the Goddess of Light fought for victory over the Demon of Darkness, while Grace aided Civilization in abolishing slavery. The whole company was involved including all the students and supernumeraries, so that in many scenes there were over two hundred people on the stage, which had been opened out to include the backstage area. A large number of sets and stage-hands were needed in order to set up the various dancing levels, several hundred costumes were made (many of them extremely expensive), and the total cost of the performance came to thirty-five thousand three hundred twenty-one gulden. "Civilization" was a popular guest role, and one which introduced audiences to many exceptional dancers. The most famous of these was undoubtedly Mathilde Kshesinska (1872–1971) of the imperial theater in St Petersburg.

Princess Pauline Metternich commissioned Josef Hassreiter to arrange a panto-

265 *Excelsior* by Luigi Manzotti, performed in 1885. From left to right: Julius Price, Luigia Cerale, E. Operti (guest), Louis Frappart, and Josef Hassreiter (lying).

mime for a charity performance in the Palace of Liechtenstein, to be given by the young nobility. She suggested a toy shop or something similar, so that she could possibly play a part as the shop owner. Hassreiter's imagination and talent was fired and he finished *Die Puppenfee* within two weeks. The ballet conductor Josef Bayer (who was known as the Austrian Delibes) composed the tuneful, sweeping music and the princess was able to record a great success–financial and otherwise–as the owner of the toyshop.

This success led to its transfer to the opera house, where it was first performed on 4 October 1888. The owner of the toyshop became a man and was mimed by Frappart, Hassreiter himself was his whirling factotum, the title role of the fairy doll was played by Camilla Pagliero (1859–1925), Alfred Caron was the entertaining farmer, and the "mechanical figures," as the individual dolls were called in the program, were delightfully performed by the leading solo dancers (surrounded by the other dolls played by the company and students).

Here are a few statistics: 36 rehearsals, the cost of the décor and costumes 9,305 gulden, rehearsal fees 300 gulden, royalties 20 gulden per performance. Productions were staged in all the major theaters in Europe. The fiftieth birthday of *Die Puppenfee* was celebrated in Vienna on 22 October 1938 in the presence of the ninety-three year-old Hassreiter–its six hundred seventy-fifth performance. There has been no more frequently played work in the history of ballet. Viennese children have been taken to the Court Opera to see *Die Puppenfee* since it was first presented, and for many generations this first visit to the theater has stayed in their memory into old age. The program was greatly enriched when three short ballets were incorporated into a single evening, and soon Vienna's pleasure in ballet came to be epitomized by

219

the trio of *Vienna Waltz*, *Die Puppenfee*, and Hassreiter's later work *Sonne und Erde* (with music by Josef Bayer). Hassreiter now concentrated mainly on choreography and he danced only on rare occasions, loyally filling the breach when others fell ill. He was busy enough giving dancing classes at court—he was even able to make the young aristocracy achieve a certain grace, to which end he trained the second solo dancer Leo Dubois as his assistant.

The ballet school of the Court Opera retained its structure of three groups—teachers, working male and female dancers. The ballet company was increased to one hundred twenty qualified dancers and sixty pupils.

The guest appearance of the solo dancer from Milan Irene Sironi (1872–1961) at the "International Exhibition of Music and Theater" in Vienna in 1892 caused great excitement. The management took advantage of the opportunity by taking this intelligent dancer on as prima ballerina. She could command three idioms: the wit of the French style, classical Italian and, before long, the grace of the Viennese. She also choreographed a ballet herself, which became a popular part of the repertory: *Die Perle von Iberien* with music by Josef Hellmesberger, Jr. She had the chance to shine in this piece not only thanks to her dancing talent but also because of her enormously expensive costume. Sironi had a high salary of twenty-four thousand crowns a year, but fate had prepared for her an anxious old age, however, and she ended her days in penury in her native land.

Sironi was succeeded between 1905 and 1907 by another prima ballerina from Milan, Giuseppina Gandini. It was fortunate that the engagement was short-lived because she did not bring any qualities to this leading position. Her appointment did show, though, how irrelevant the new directorship considered dance to be in the context of opera. The *corps de ballet* dropped to one hundred eight members, and resentment and humiliation raised its head at the slightest opportunity in the whole profession, having a bad effect on company morale. Hassreiter, nevertheless, had the necessary

authority to fend off attacks and—backed up by First Court Chamberlain, Prince Liechtenstein—carried on regardless.

Cäcilie Cerri (1872–1931) arrived from London in 1907. She had been recommended by Claudine Couqui (1834–1913), her former teacher at the school in Milan, who had herself been the last prima ballerina at the Kärntnertor theater. Cerri in turn became prima ballerina and was the last foreign dancer to hold this position at the imperial Court Opera Theater. She was a nimble but strict technician and had to earn the approval of audiences who, under Hassreiter, had become used to seeing easy, graceful Viennese solo dancers.

In 1909 the tsarist ballet company from St Petersburg came to Vienna for the first time on an official three-day invitation. It brought to the audience's notice the original version of the classic works *Swan Lake*, *Paquita*, and *Giselle*, and also the ballerina Anna Pavlova, whose international fame was established on this tour. These sensational guest performances had required an immense amount of diplomatic bureaucracy beforehand.

In 1912 the first guest performances took place in Vienna of Serge Diaghilev's *Ballets Russes*. Mathilde Kshesinska, who had already been guest in Vienna in 1903, and Tamara Karsavina came to Vienna with their colleagues Adolphe Bolm and Vaslav Nijinsky, teacher Enrico Cecchetti and a large *corps*, to revolutionize the ballet world completely. Here was a work of the highest artistry, a synthesis of dance, music, and décor, created by the ballet master Mikhail Fokin, the composers Nikolai Tcherepnin, and Alexander Borodin, and the set designers Nikolas Roerich, Alexander Benois, and Léon Bakst.

In the second series of guest performances in 1913 Sophie Fedorova and Lydia Kyaksht, together with Bolm and Nijinsky, also found the Viennese enthusiastic. Two exciting ballets were of particular interest to informed audiences: *Petrushka* (music by Igor Stravinsky, choreography by Mikhail Fokin) and *L'Après-midi d'un Faune* from the poem by Stéphane Mallarmé, composed by Claude Debussy and choreographed for

266 A scene from the ballet *Die Puppenfee* by Josef Bayer (a reconstruction during Lorin Maazel's directorship in 1983 of the original production).

the first time by Vaslav Nijinsky (advised by Diaghilev). Nijinsky is still identified with the figure of the faun. His sister Bronislava, who later became a famous choreographer, also took part in both ballets.

To return to the Court Opera's own company, in 1906 the old ballet *Harlekin als Elektriker* had featured a *pas de deux* involving the new solo dancer Elsa Strohl von Strohlendorf (1883–1965) and the second male soloist Leo Dubois (1876–1948). Both came from the Viennese school. Shortly afterwards a new *pas de deux* was announced, this time with Strohlendorf and the first solo dancer Carl Raimund (1871–1951). Hassreiter had picked Strohlendorf to be the new permanent prima ballerina (which she finally was in 1920), but the Italian Cerri was still under contract. The latter even took over the class of van Hamme when he left, thereby strengthening her position. Her regular partner was Carl Raimund, who also taught—their two classes produced future soloists which included Buchinger, Dirtl, Krausenecker, Pfundmayr, and Raab.

Raimund managed to have the class auditions performed on stage, before an uncritical audience consisting of relatives.

The First World War inevitably brought about a sudden interruption to activites in the opera house. No more contact with the new enemy, the Russians, no more joy in the creation of art. Remarkably, in fact, this difficult period did not mean an end to world premieres. Hassreiter produced *Wiener Legende*, the libretto of which he co-wrote with Heinrich Regel (with music by the repetiteur of the Court Opera, Raoul Mader), and *Gemma* with the libretto and music by Geza Graf Zichy. *Der 18. Lenz* (The Eighteenth Spring) with music by Archduchess Immaculata (orchestrated by Josef Kein) was to be his last ballet. He was granted honorary membership of the Court Opera Theater by order of the emperor, a mark of rare distinction at the time. Yet all his achievements on behalf of Austrian ballet seemed forgotten when the Court Opera became the State Opera. In 1920, only a few weeks short of Hassreiter's fifty-year association with the Opera, he suddenly became nothing more than a senior citizen on a pension which, during the period of inflation, did not even pay for a loaf of bread.

Ballet was not spared, needless to say, during this time of radical change. The ensemble was reduced, as were the number of evenings of ballet, and the interim leadership of Dubois-Golevski-Raimund experienced great difficulty in putting on any of their repertory performances. They eventually succeeded, principally by inserting ballet into operas.

An unusual development then occurred, which was later to become common practice: a foreign choreographer was invited. His name was Ernst Matray (1891–1978) and he created *Sheherazade*, with music by Nikolai Rimsky-Korsakov. This well-known, progressive dancer had no easy task in bringing such a demanding work to the stage with such a depleted company. The title role featured an outstanding performance from Hedy Pfundmayr (1899–1965), and Matray played the gold-slave himself. He was granted two more evenings of ballet which he

267 Irene Sironi, prima ballerina from 1892 to 1905. Her ballet *Die Perle von Iberien* was first performed in 1902.

268 Carlo Brioschi's ruin landscape for the ballet *Excelsior*.

269 Anton Brioschi's design for the ballet *Sonne und Erde*.

270 Cäcilie Cerri, prima ballerina from 1907 to 1920, in a *pas de deux* with Carl Raimund.

produced himself with the assistance of several solo dancers, and then he left Vienna. The company was again without a leader. A savior came at the last moment in the person of Heinrich Kröller (1880–1930) from Munich. He had begun his ballet studies in the Vienna Court Theater, but his dancing career did not last long. He was soon discovered as a choreographer and Germany's major theaters showed an interest in him. He was invited to Vienna in 1922 for three initial guest productions, prior to receiving a five-year contract. Because of racing inflation the contract was subject to special payments, chiefly in the form of amendments and increments. If the monthly salary was one hundred million crowns in September, the following month it would have to be revalued to one hundred twenty million–though it was difficult to talk of "value" at all.

271 Elsa Strohl von Strohlendorf, prima ballerina from 1920 to 1924 with Carl Raimund in a *pas de deux* from *Rund um Wien* in 1906.

272 Hedy Pfundmayr as Zobeide and Toni Birkmeyer as the gold slave in *Scheherazade* in 1922.

At rehearsals for *Josephs Legende* Kröller had as many problems with the company as the company had with the new work; the music and style of dancing were completely foreign to the dancers. Richard Strauss had composed the music in regular consultation with the librettists Harry Graf Kessler and Hugo von Hoffmansthal. They aimed in this way at artistic unity, which was further emphasized by dance and the brilliant set design of Alfred Roller. Unusually, the leading female role was cast with the *Kammersängerin* Marie Gutheil-Schoder. She interpreted the part of Potiphar's wife with static and austere mime and a powerful aura. Her successors were the actress from the Burgtheater Lilli Marberg and Maria Eis. Elsa von Strohlendorf also left a lasting impression when she danced this role. The part of Joseph demanded great physical expression and dancing brilliance, and the performers were the two first solo dancers Toni Birkmeyer and Willy Fränzl.

Kröller's work was characterized by the collaboration of Richard Strauss. Kröller produced the three-part *Ballettsoirée* for the newly reconstructed Redoutensaal in the Hofburg, for which Richard Strauss supplied an arrangement of music by François Couperin. Strauss never felt it was beneath him to come even to the first rehearsals in the ballet hall.

Strauss and Kröller, who both came from Munich, also let the Vienna Ballet have their entertaining two-act ballet *Schlagobers*, which is a symbol of a brotherhood of music and ballet between Munich and Vienna. Strauss usually conducted his own work. He, Kröller, the company, and audiences alike all loved this work—"his Viennese child"—although the critics did not necessarily agree.

Kröller paid his respects to Vienna's creative past in his new version of *Don Juan*, the first tragic mime ballet by Gasparo Angiolini which has already been mentioned. His ballet *Das lockende Phantom* (with music by Franz Salmhofer) showed that he was receptive to modern work. Tilly Losch (1904–75) was outstanding in the title role. She had come up through the ballet school of the Court Opera and had already caused

273   Willy Fränzl as Joseph in *Josephs Legende*.

interest as the "Green Snake" in Kröller's *Ma Mère l'Oye* (music by Maurice Ravel) and in *Tanzlegende* (music by Modest Mussorgsky).

Toni Birkmeyer (1897–1973) and Willy Fränzl (1898–1982) were the leading members of families of dancers which go back to the time of the Kärntnertor theater. For a short period in the thirties Birkmeyer was in charge of the abandoned company and staged his divertissement *Haydn-Ballett*, took the Viennese waltz style abroad with his partner Grete Wiesenthal (1885–1970),

274   Marie Gutheil-Schoder as Potiphar's wife, Toni Birkmeyer as Joseph, and Marie Buchinger as the favorite slave in *Josephs Legende* in 1922.

and founded his own school of dance. Willy Fränzl took a similar artistic path. He had also completed his ballet studies at the Opera, became a solo dancer at the same time and also toured with Grete Wiesenthal, giving guest performances; he danced as Joseph with the famous Tamara Karsavina, when she made a guest appearance in Vienna in 1923, and later took over from his father (a mime) the charge of a school for art and ballroom dancing which was well-known in the city, in which capacity he arranged the great opening dances at the Opera and Philharmonic Balls. He finished by also becoming a ballet master.

Then, however, their ways parted–Birkmeyer stayed in the ensemble as a dancer after working as ballet master, while Fränzl dedicated himself for twenty-seven years to maintaining the fabric of the Vienna Ballet through new productions. He was assisted in this endeavour by Gusti Pichler (1893–1978) of the Vienna ballet school. She had been made prima ballerina after Elsa von Strohlendorf and helped Kröller to boost support for the ballet. She retired in 1935 and was made an honorary member of the State Opera.

When Kröller left Vienna and his well-trained ensemble in 1928, the State Opera received as ballet masters three choreographers of different styles in quick succession: Georges Kyaksht (1873–1936), of the erstwhile imperial ballet in St Petersburg, Bronislava Nijinska (1891–1972), the internationally famous ballet mistress, and the modern dancer Sacha Leontyev (1897–1942).

In 1927 Vienna, like Cinderella, received another visit from its Russian prince: Diaghilev's company came to the city for the third time. On this visit two artists made themselves known who were to come to Vienna some decades later as choreographers: Leonid Massine and George Balanchine. They came as dancers, also alternating as choreographers, in a program which included *Cimarosiana*, *Le Tricorne*, *La Boutique fantasque* (conceived after *Die Puppenfee*), and *La Chatte*. Nijinska's work was also represented through *Les Biches*.

Another guest performance brought Ida Rubinstein (1888–1960) to Vienna–a rich artist obsessed by dance, she could afford her own fifty-strong company, in which she danced as prima ballerina. Nijinska was her ballet mistress and Massine choreographed for her. Rubinstein arranged for Maurice Ravel to compose *La Valse* and *Bolero* for her. The company contained two further dancers who were later to be associated with Vienna, namely Harijs Plucis and Frederick Ashton. Plucis came to the State Opera in 1961 as ballet assistant and trainer, while Ashton, who was knighted in 1962, sent his ballet *Marguerite et Armand* (music

275 Gusti Pichler, prima ballerina, 1924–35.

228

276 Grete Wiesenthal in the title role as the good-for-nothing in her ballet *Der Taugenichts in Wien*, with policemen played by Robert Casson, Bobby Binder, and Hans Weinrich in 1930.

by Franz Liszt) to Vienna in 1967 with Margot Fonteyn and Rudolf Nureyev. All these guest appearances certainly kept Vienna's interest in ballet alive, but it did not help its own *corps de ballet* escape from its Cinderella-like existence. What is more, it had to make do with ballets which were interpolated into operas.

In 1930 a new and home-grown ballet finally joined the repertoire—*Der Taugenichts in Wien*, six scenes by Grete Wiesenthal with music by Franz Salmhofer. She played the title role herself. It was a narrative ballet in the established tradition, but in her own new Viennese waltz style. (Grete Wiesenthal produced the ballet again seventeen years later, giving her part this time to Carl Raimund, Jr.)

Internal problems at the theater made it necessary at that time to cut the number of ballet personnel. Fifty dancers were left and this figure had to cover the few ballets that were staged during the season. The minor choreographers were not able to bring about a revival in the short time they were there. The exception was Margarete Wallmann, who was employed for

229

277 Margarethe Wallmann, ballet mistress from 1933 to 1938, as the bride in her ballet *Ostereichische Bauernhochzeit*, with Willy Franz as the groom in 1934.

five years. She had trained in the classical Russian style in Berlin, and in modern dance under Mary Wigman in Dresden. Wallmann managed to increase the number of dancers to meet her requirements, and her extremely energetic approach restored the company's self-confidence. Then the Second World War broke out.

During those dark days there was a ray of light in the figure of the Austrian Erika Hanka (1905–58). She had returned from Hamburg with a good reputation and became highly important for the Vienna Opera Ballet. Not only did Hanka have an extraordinary level of knowledge and ability, but she also paid particular attention to the artistic development of each individual dancer. As the doyen of Viennese ballet Josef Hassreiter (who died in 1940) had recommended, she took under her wing a third prima ballerina– Julia Drapal (b. 1917). The latter was a classically-trained dancer and an expressive mime, who achieved what she had aspired to since the age of twelve when she played the confirmation candidate in *Schlagobers*: to become a principal balle-

278 Julia Drapal, prima ballerina from 1949 to 1959, as the laundry owner in *Der liebe Augustine*.

rina. Hanka created for her *Höllische G'schicht, oder Mephistopheles seltsame Erdreise*, with music by Johann Strauss in an arrangement by Rudolf Kattnigg and Anton Paulik, in which Drapal could display her bubbly character and rich humour to the full. She could also give an interesting interpretation to dramatic roles, such as Potiphar's wife. She retired in 1959 and is an honorary member of the State Opera.

It is a measure of the lengths Erika Hanka went to towards forging a link between the Vienna *corps de ballet* and the international dance community that she commissioned Gordon Hamilton (1918–59) to rehearse full-length ballets or extracts in their original versions. He was called upon to look after this important aspect of ballet as a result of his work with Sadler's Wells Ballet and other companies. This led to Edeltraud Brexner (b. 1927) and the principal solo dancer Willy Dirtl (b. 1931) learning the famous *pas de deux* from *Don Quixote* (music by Ludwig Minkus) in the original choreography. *Giselle, Les Sylphides, The Nutcracker Suite*, and parts of *Sleeping*

279 The ballet mistress Erika Hanka and conductor Anton Paulik at a rehearsal with (from left to right) Julia Drapal, Willy Dirtl, Walter Ruess, Walter Hofer, Ewald Vondrak, Kurt Hiess, and Wilfried Fränzel.

Beauty followed. Hamilton's historical-classical style was complimented by Erika Hanka's modern narrative ballets. In the course of her seventeen years in Vienna she created thirty-eight ballets, sixteen of which used her own libretti, including *Der Mohr von Venedig* (music by Boris Blacher) and *Hotel Sacher* (music by Josef Hellmesberger, Jr.; arranged by Max Schönherr).

During this period the elite of the principal female dancers were distinctive personalities such as Margaret Bauer, Lucia Bräuer, Poldi Pokorny, and Christl Zimmerl, while the male soloists included Willy Dirtl, Erwin Pokorny, and Carl Raimund, Jr.

Edeltraud Brexner made the fourth Viennese prima ballerina. She danced with all her Viennese charm and exuberance, much as her great predecessor Fanny Elssler had done. (In fact a ring was specially made in 1960 to celebrate Elssler's one hundred fiftieth birthday, and Brexner was the first, and only, wearer.) It is interesting to note that Brexner played the farmer's child in 1938

in the six hundred seventy-fifth performance of *Die Puppenfee*. She was also a very successful and impassioned teacher. Having been forced to leave the profession as a result of a serious foot injury, she was made a professor in 1977 and an honorary member in 1980 of the State Opera.

The shock caused by the sudden death of Erika Hanka in June 1958 brought the company almost literally to its knees. The important thing then was to maintain the high standard she had set. Dimitrii Parlic (b. 1919) was the right man for the job. He had worked in Vienna once before (as a dancer at the Volksoper) and now he came to the State Opera as ballet master. He immediately recognized the company's qualities and put them to the test in his productions which included, to mention just three, *Symphony in C* (music by Georges Bizet), *Le Combat* (by Rafaello de Banfield), and *Romeo and Juliet* (by Sergei Prokofiev). The utter divergency of these three works alone shows how shrewdly he knew how to handle the company.

232

280 Edeltraud Brexner, prima ballerina between 1957 and 1972, as Sleeping Beauty at the lakeside theater in Bregenz.

281 A scene from Werner Egk's *Abraxas* with Edeltraud Brexner, Willy Dirtl, Erwin Pokorny, and Lucia Bräuer. Choreography by Erika Hanka, design by Stefan Hlawa.

Although Parlic's ballets could be understood by audiences without reading up in advance, the opposite could be said of Aurel von Milloss (b. 1906). Only the initiated knew the meaning of his work. Milloss, ballet master in 1963–66 and 1971–74, was a classically-trained dancer who traveled around the world learning and teaching, drawn more towards mythical than narrative ballet. His assistants during this period were the solo dancer Richard Novotny (b. 1926), who later embarked on a major career (with Nureyev) as a result of his work in Vienna, and Gerlinde Dill (b. 1933). Milloss also invited well-known choreographers to rehearse their works in Vienna. The result was visits from Dame Ninette de Valois with her *Check-mate* (music by Sir Arthur Bliss), George Balanchine with *Four Temperaments* (Paul Hindemith), Leonid Massine with *Tricorne* (Manuel de Falla), and Rudolf Nureyev with Marius Petipa and Lev Ivanov's *Swan Lake* (Peter Tchaikovsky). Milloss also created his own ballets, such as *Die Einöde* (music by Edgard Varese), *Per Aspera* (György Ligeti), *Relazioni Fragili* (Friedrich Cerha), and many others.

The performers represented the best of the new generation: Susanne Kirnbauer, Ully Wührer, Lisl Maar, Gisela Cech, Lilly Scheuermann, Karl and Ludwig M. Musil, Paul Vondrak, Michael Birkmeyer, and Franz Wilhelm.

Vaslav Orlikovsky (b. 1921) took over a dance company in 1966 and cultivated his luxurious style in ballets such as *Sleeping Beauty* (Tchaikovsky) and *Prince of the Pagodas* (Benjamin Britten).

After Willy Fränzl's death in 1962, responsibility for the permanent repertoire was given to the solo dancer Richard Novotny–ballet master after 1974–together with Gerlinde Dill, who in 1981 became the first woman from the Vienna ballet school to be appointed ballet mistress. The assistance she has had from famous visiting choreographers has given her ideas that she passes on to the company. She entertained audiences in 1983 with her new production of *Die Puppenfee* in the original version, contributing her own *Wiener Skizzen* (with music by Johann and Josef Strauss) to the same evening's program. In 1984 she, together with Gerhard Brunner, took sixty-two members of the Vienna Opera Ballet on an official tour of Korea and Japan, with the guest stars Yoka Morishita and Rudolf Nureyev, in his own version of *Sleeping Beauty*.

Gerhard Brunner, former dancer and music critic, was named director of the Vienna Opera Ballet in 1976. It was thanks to his initiative that the number of ballets performed has almost doubled. Along with the choreographers invited by Brunner, new works have been brought to Vienna by Rudi van Dantzig,

282 Christl Zimmerl and Willy Dirtl appearing in *The Moor of Venice* at the reopening of the State Opera in 1955.

Hans van Manen, John Neumeier, and Erich Walter.

An "older" generation of very commendable male soloists has retired from the performing side of ballet: Paul Vondrak, equally prominent as a character dancer or principal; Karl Musil, who following an international dancing career is now a choreographer; his brother Ludwig, an exceptional character dancer. Some female soloists have also withdrawn from the stage: Dietlinde Klemisch, who is still remembered for her performance in *Der Wunderbare Mandarin* or as Cupid in *Don Quixote*; Erika Zlocha, the violet girl in *Hotel Sacher*, and the mother-father doll in *Die Puppenfee*, and who was equally convincing as Juliet or Giselle; Judith Gerber, an elegant classicist, particularly memorable in *The Nutcracker*; Lisl Maar, a principal soloist and outstanding prima ballerina, who made her final appearance in 1984 in *Twilight*—in high-heeled shoes.

In 1972 three new principal ballerinas were announced. Susanne Kirnbauer's repertoire covered the full range of ballets. She was filmed in productions of *Coppelia* and *Die Puppenfee*, took her

ballet *Sommerliebelei* to Innsbruck, and presented television programs on dance and movement. From 1987 she has been director of ballet at the Volksoper. Giselle Cech is ballet's *grande dame*. She has played Giselle in both Cuba and Vienna, and in March 1985 she danced the famous *pas de quatre* in *Hommage à Fanny Elssler*, paying tribute to Elssler together with Lilly Scheuermann. Scheuermann dominated the stage majestically with her renditions of Juliet, Mélisande, and Sylvia. A principal male soloist was also appointed: Franz Wilhelm, a supple and distinctive character dancer of great merit in, for example, John Neumeier's *Don Juan* (title role) or as the Moor in *Petrushka*, in a guest production with Valery Panov (music by Igor Stravinsky). Gyula Harangozo, who had been making guest appearances since 1982, was made a first solo dancer in 1985.

The work of the company (which has eighty-five members including soloists) has become so diverse both inside the State Opera and beyond—guest performances, television broadcasts, various collaborations—that the ballet mistress alone can no longer cope with all the

283   Rudolf Nureyev in *Sleeping Beauty*.

rehearsals. She now has working with her the Cuban Carlos Gacio (b. 1937), Milan Hatala (b. 1943) from Bratislava, and from Budapest Zoltan Nagy (b. 1941).

How do they look, the leading ballerinas who will become the stars of the future? Christine Gaugusch, soloist since 1982, combines a classical technique with convincing comedy. Gabriele Haslinger, soloist since 1979, has shown a fantastic commitment to ballet by overcoming a serious foot injury. Marieluise Jaska, soloist since 1982, is a perfect ballerina whose only problems come in the classic *pas de deux*, because of her height. Jolantha Seyfried, an intellectual star, became a soloist in 1984 and is particularly remarkable for her skillful toe-work. Brigitte Stadler also moved to the soloist role in 1984, but even prior to this she had demonstrated technical brilliance dancing major roles.

The prominent men include Heinz Heidenreich and Ludwig Karl, soloists since 1982, as well as Christian Tichy and Michael Pinnisch, all of whom trained at the Viennese school after brief studies abroad. Bernd Roger Bienert combines several talents, as dancer, choreographer, set and costume designer. His dance work *Alpenglühn* (his fourth piece, with music by Thomas Pernes) was premiered at the State Opera in 1984. A year later he followed this with a ballet curiously titled *Radz-Datz* (music by Gottfried von Einem).

The future of the Opera Ballet looks secure. In 1980 a whole wing near the Opera was converted for the use of the ballet school, with seven studios, a library, and film and study rooms. At present almost one hundred fifty children are studying all forms of dance under fourteen teachers and two full-time governesses. In 1985 overall responsibility for the school was given to Toni Birkmeyer's son Michael (b. 1943), a principal soloist and *danseur noble*, who also presents music broadcasts on television.

As in life, the ballet's fortunes have gone in waves. Though often feared dead, it is as alive as ever before. Again and again the hard labor of ballet training is transformed into physical ease and grace—to the joy of Vienna's dancers and its audiences.

284 The Vienna State Opera Ballet in John Cranko's *Romeo and Juliet.*

285 *Josefs Legende* choreographed by John Neumeier, with Donna Wood, Kevin Haigen, and Ludwig Karl.

Am Ostermontag den 28. März 1842,
Mittags um halb 1 Uhr,
wird das sämmtliche
Orchester-Personal
des k. k. Hof-Operntheaters
im k. k. großen Redouten-Saale
ein großes
Concert
folgenden Inhaltes zu geben die Ehre haben.

Erste Abtheilung.

1. **Die grosse siebente Symphonie** (in A-dur), von **L. v. Beethoven.**
2. **Arie** aus der Oper: Fanisca, von **Cherubini,** gesungen von Hrn. **J. Staudigl.**
3. **Concert-Arie** „Ah perfido, spergiuro!" von **Beethoven,** gesungen von Frau **van Hasselt-Barth.**

Zweite Abtheilung.

4. **Beethoven's grosse DRITTE Ouverture** zu Leonore, (verschieden von denen bei den Vorstellungen der Oper Fidelio im k. k. Hof-Operntheater aufgeführten.)
5. **Concert-Arie** „Non temer, amato bene," von **Mozart,** gesungen von Fräulein **Jenny Lutzer,** mit obligater Violin-Begleitung, vorgetragen von Hrn. **Joseph Mayseder.**
6. **La Romanesca,** Melodie aus dem 16. Jahrhundert, auf dem Violoncell vorgetragen von Hrn. **Fr. Servais.**
7. **Grosses Duett** aus der Oper: Medea, von **Cherubini,** gesungen von Herrn **F. Wild** und Frau **van Hasselt-Barth.**
8. **Grosse Fest-Ouverture** von **L. v. Beethoven.** (Op. 124. — C-dur.)

Die genannten Künstler haben die Ausführung ihrer Solo-Parthien, so wie Herr Kapellmeister **Nicolai** die Leitung des Ganzen aus besonderer Gefälligkeit übernommen.

Sperrsitze auf der Gallerie zu 3 fl.; Sperrsitze im Parterre zu 2 fl.; Eintrittskarten in die Gallerie zu 1 fl. 30 kr. und Eintrittskarten in das Parterre zu 1 fl. C. M. sind in allen Musik-Handlungen, an der Kasse des k. k. Hof-Operntheaters, und am Tage des Concertes am Eingange zu haben.

286 The orchestra of the imperial and royal Court Opera played the inaugural concert of the Vienna Philharmonic on 28 March 1842.

THE ORCHESTRA
Otto Strasser

The orchestra of the Vienna State Opera has a special place among the many orchestras playing in opera houses and concert halls. It is probably the only opera orchestra that has managed to achieve recognition as one of the world's leading orchestras. This dual role originated before the 1848 revolution, when the members of the orchestra of the Court Opera at the Kärntnertor theater decided to escape from the restrictions of opera music and to give concerts independantly. Under the guidance of Otto Nicolai, composer and conductor at the opera theater, in 1842 the musicians founded what were known as the Philharmonic Concerts, which they continued to give in the Redoutensaal, after Nicolai left Vienna, for a further thirteen years, partly under their own instigation and partly as guests of the Gesellschaft der Musikfreunde. This irregular state of affairs came to an end when, through common consent with Carl Eckert, the director of the Opera, they organized their concerts into a subscription season. The first subscription concert took place on 1 January 1860 on the stage of the Kärntnertor theater, and the "Philharmonic" season has been going uninterrupted from that day to this.

When the imperial and royal Court Opera opened on the Ringstrasse on 25 May 1869 with Mozart's *Don Giovanni* and the Court Opera Orchestra moved in to its new home, it had to come to terms with new acoustics and dimensions. The size of the auditorium and of the stage required a considerably larger number of musicians. Franz von Dingelstedt, who had succeeded Matteo Salvi as director of the Court Opera in 1867, immediately raised the number from 86 to 111.

The Philharmonic Concerts had been developing very profitably under the leadership of Otto Dessoff, the newly chosen conductor of the Court Opera. They played an important role in the musical life of Vienna, bringing the members of the orchestra both artistic satisfaction and increased financial rewards. The social standing of the musicians was not at all good at the time, and there were also considerable differences in earnings within the orchestra. The leading players were generally members of the imperial court chapel and in this capacity they performed for church services in the Hofburg chapel, which still stands today. Many of them also taught at the conservatory, which had been founded by the Gesellschaft der Musikfreunde in 1817. Apart from a visibly enhanced position–on solemn occasions the musicians of the court chapel wore uniforms with two-cornered hats and rapiers–this also meant a substantial subsidiary income, which their less favored colleagues could only earn by giving arduous lessons.

From the very start (except for a period when there were difficulties in finding a suitable conductor) the orchestra's praises were sung by audiences and the press. Richard W gner was particularly enthusiastic when he heard *Lohengrin* for the first time in Vienna on 15 May 1861, and he did not spare any praise and recognition when he subsequently came

to stay in Vienna. After attending an opera performance in August 1863 he remarked: "Yesterday the orchestra cheered and delighted my heart again. I heard expressive and tonal beauty which no other orchestra has offered me." In his famous article "On Conducting" which was published in 1869, he called the orchestra "one of the foremost in the world."

The much-lauded Court Opera Orchestra had two special factors to thank for its status. In the first place it consisted of musicians with the same background. Almost all of them were either born in Vienna or had moved there from nearby and they had also been trained there–this made it possible for an ensemble to develop which was musically and tonally homogenous. In the second place the Philharmonic concerts represented an incentive to achieve the highest standards. This high level of achievement was passed on to the opera house and, because for several decades the conductors of the Philharmonic also conducted at the opera house, both partners carried over the Philharmonic's musical spirit into the orchestra pit. That is how it still is to a very large extent, and when Richard Wagner spoke of expressive and tonal beauty offered by no other opera orchestra, he was describing a particular characteristic of this ensemble, one which allows it in all modesty to claim certain advantages over other orchestras.

The opportunity to develop a harmonious musical style was afforded by the

287 Otto Deskoff, conductor of the imperial Court Opera at the Kärntertor theater and at the new Court Opera from 1860 to 1875.

288 Emil Wipperich, a member of the court orchestra, in his official uniform.

famous French virtuoso Pierre Rode. Böhm was taken on by the Gesellschaft der Musikfreunde as a teacher at the institute in 1819. His school produced many prominent violinists, in particular Georg Hellmesberger, the founding father of a Viennese dynasty of violinists and musicians. He became Böhm's assistant at the age of only twenty-one, was later a professor at the conservatory and then succeeded Ignaz Schuppanzigh, a friend of Beethoven's, as concertmaster at the Court Opera. He carried on Böhm's teaching and also earned recognition and respect for his conducting of the Philharmonic Concerts. One of his two sons, Georg, died in his youth while Josef (referred to as "Senior" in German because he had a son with the same name) grew into one of the most popular personalities in the Viennese music scene. In his very early years as a virtuoso violinist he earned the attention of Otto Nicolai, who chose him as a soloist at his concerts. At the age of twenty-one he formed the Hellmesberger String Quartet, named after himself, which has gone down in musical history. He later became the Gesellschaft's concert conductor, director of the conservatory, in 1860 concertmaster of the Court Opera Orchestra, and in 1877 he was promoted to court Kapellmeister. He is probably the most versatile artist ever to adorn the concertmaster's seat. His school produced Arthur Nikisch, who began his career as violinist at the Court Opera, and many other well-known names. He became almost as famous a humourist as violinist, and his *bons mots* and jokes stand comparison with the playwright Johann Nestroy for caustic wit.

The Budapest-born Jakob Grün was also appointed concertmaster shortly before the opening of the new opera house. Unlike Josef Hellmesberger, who as his father's pupil belonged to the second generation of the Böhm school, Grün had himself been Böhm's pupil and a successful professor at the conservatory like his teacher. His pupils, who were first class artists both technically and musically, still formed the kernel of the leading group of violins when I joined the State Opera Orchestra in 1922, and they made

conservatory of the Gesellschaft der Musikfreunde, where Viennese schools for string and wind players grew up over the years. In a continuous process (apart from a short break during the 1848 revolution) internationally recognized soloists as well as concertmasters, wind players, and the most highly qualified orchestra musicians were trained here, going on later to give the orchestra its particular quality. The school has changed its name twice since: in 1909 it became the State Academy for Music and the Performing Arts and not so very long ago it received university status. It continues as before to be of great benefit to the opera orchestra.

The founder of the string school in Vienna was Josef Böhm, pupil of the

289 Josef Böhm, founder of the Vienna violin school.

290 Josef Hellmesberger concertmaster of the Court Opera Orchestra after 1860, was one of the most popular figures on the Viennese music scene because of his wit and *bons mots.*

291 Arthur Nikisch began his career as a violinist in the Court Opera Orchestra and later became one of the leading conductors of his day (pastel drawing by Franz von Lenbach).

an essential contribution to the brilliance of the string section. The training of the new generation of violinists, which was so important for the orchestra of the Court Opera, thus lay in most capable hands, and there were equally good teachers in the other string groups. Reinhold Hummer, very well thought of both as a soloist and a chamber musician, was responsible for producing similar talents in the new generation of cellists. Franz Simandl, a concert soloist on the rather difficult double-bass looked after his group with no less sucess, bringing forth another double-bass virtuoso Eduard Madenski.

The sound that a musician attempts to draw from his or her instrument also depends, of course, on the quality of the instrument being played. In this respect the wind players are better off than the strings, because the design of wind instruments has made further developments, enabling the musician to buy—albeit not cheaply—the best and most modern instrument. It is different with the string section, where there is a huge, though not always unbridgeable gulf between extremely expensive and beautiful-sounding old Italian instruments and new products. But Italian violins, violas, cellos, and double-basses are many times more expensive than the best wind instruments and young people, in particular, are rarely in a position to acquire such valuable items.

In the orchestra, on the other hand, the position is different. The combined sound of as many as sixty players or more in a string section makes expensive individual instruments largely irrelevant—the opera orchestra and the essentially identical Philharmonic are proof of that. The Court Opera used to provide every member of the orchestra with a regular instrument, and in the present State Opera the practice is continued. Until 1945 the opera orchestra played instruments by such Viennese violin-makers as Thir, Stadlmann, and Geissenhof; they were good but would not have been sufficient for playing chamber music concerts. After the war these instruments went into unfamiliar hands in the course of the opera's move to alternative premises, and they were not replaced by better instruments by any means. The same was true of the Philharmonic, where at first they used instruments made by the Viennese violin-maker Gabriel Lemböck. This changed over the years for when I joined the orchestra the Philharmonic's violins were even worse than the Opera's. Nonetheless, the sound of the strings remained as extraordinary as ever, differing considerably from any other ensemble.

The only likely explanation for this phenomenon is that a beautiful sound does not only depend on the instrument, but also on the art of the player. It is precisely this art that our musicians have always mastered through training and an inately musical ear. It was Wilhelm Furtwängler, in fact, who made a most accurate assessment on this subject. When he heard the orchestra for the first time he was so fascinated by its sound that he tried to recreate it using our instruments in another orchestra. We lent them to him, but the Philharmonic sound did not materialize in other hands. Josef Hellmesberger proved that even soloists do not have to rely on old Italian instruments. Like his colleagues in the orchestra, he played a Lemböck violin all his life, both as a soloist and in quartets, and the tone and intensity of his playing were praised and admired again and again.

In the old Kärntertor theater famous concertmasters and professors at the conservatory proved themselves alongside other well-known musicians, who also performed outside the opera house as soloists and chamber musicians. Mention must be made in particular of the flutist and composer Franz Doppler, who gave concerts all over the world with his flute-playing brother Karl before settling in Vienna to work as a soloist in the orchestra and also to become one of the best conductors of ballet. The cellist David Popper, who acquired fame later as a soloist, was one of the leading performers in the orchestra, as was his colleague on the platform Heinrich Röver, who was a member of the Hellmesberger Quartet. In the first horn position sat the widely regarded Wilhelm Kleinecke. The well-known and respected horn player

Richard Lewy also enjoyed an exceptional career, leaving the orchestra in 1870 to become senior artistic overseer and solo repetiteur at the Court Opera.

There was no lack of prominent figures, and with two outstanding concertmasters leading them, Josef Hellmesberger and Jacob Grün, the highly qualified ensemble first took up their duties in the newly built theater on 25 May 1869, from which time—constantly renewing and rejuvenating itself—it has come to be looked on as one of the best, if not *the* best opera orchestra in the world.

The orchestra did not have an easy time of it when the opera house on the Ringstrasse opened. Dingelstedt, the director, had an odd aversion to concerts and particularly to the opera orchestra. He had already declared in 1868 that the new theater must bring about a new spirit and it was his wish that the Philharmonic concerts should be subsidiary to the working of the Opera. A decision on this matter was successfully postponed, but the same problem emerged again in a most unfortunate way under Dingelstedt's artistic advisor Johann Herbeck.

Herbeck, who enjoyed the admiration of the Viennese and (unlike the rather quiet conductor of the Philharmonic concerts, Otto Dessoff) made a significant impression as a virtuoso on the podium, had taken the bold jump in 1869 from the concert stage to operatic conducting although he had no experience of opera. The theater authorities immediately gave him leave to "participate in the musical organization of the Court Opera." He was denied, however, the leadership of the Philharmonic concerts, but he now tried in his own way to achieve what Dingelstedt had failed to manage in 1868. He organized concerts under the aegis of the opera house and arranged, in order to counter any opposition, for them to "benefit the Court Theater's private pension fund." There could be no objection to this praiseworthy project as such, but in the first opera season of 1869–70 he immediately offered a cycle of four subscription concerts. In this form they directly resembled the Philharmonic concerts and the orchestra was therefore obliged to compete with its own venture.

Fortunately the public did not react as Herbeck might have expected; they stayed away from the concerts in the opera house in large numbers and the experiment came to an inglorious end.

Herbeck's ambivalent relationship with the orchestra worked both ways, of course. He had opposition from the ensemble. Richard Lewy, who had risen from horn-player to take charge of training, was a particular enemy. In spite of the unfriendly attitude of individual members of the orchestra, Herbeck did, nevertheless, show an understanding of the poverty of the ensemble as a whole. In 1870 he became the director of the Court Opera in succession to Dingelstedt, who went over to the Burgtheater, and Herbeck now managed on two occasions to persuade the administrators of the Court Theater to increase the orchestra's fees. (The lowest salary at that time was less than fifty gulden a month.)

The first years after the new Court Opera opened were dominated by the figure of Richard Wagner and provided the orchestra with new and interesting problems. On 27 February 1870 the Viennese premiere of *Die Meistersinger* took place under Herbeck, which he produced in only five weeks with nineteen orchestra rehearsals. *Rienzi* followed, and in 1872 Wagner came to Vienna in person. On 12 May in the great hall of the music society he himself conducted a concert in conjunction with what was described in the program as the "Orchestra of the imperial and royal Court Opera." This was customary at the time, because the title "Philharmonic" was only applied to the orchestra's own concerts. The concert, which featured only parts of Wagner's operas together with the *Eroica*, also went down in musical history on account of a thunderstorm that occured during the magic fire from *Die Walküre*; Wagner told the audience that this represented a favorable omen for the success of the coming Bayreuth Festival.

The festival project was already well advanced by that time: ten days later on 22 May the festival theater's foundation stone could be laid. On that occasion Wagner conducted Beethoven's Ninth Symphony, having invited members of

WAGNER-CONCERT

unter **persönlicher** Leitung von

Richard Wagner

und unter gefälliger Mitwirkung

des k. k. Hofopern-Orchesters, des k. k. Hofopernsängers Herrn Dr. Kraus und eines Damenchors der k. k. Hofoper,

Sonntag den 12. Mai 1872, halb 1 Uhr Mittags,

im großen Musikvereinsfaale.

PROGRAMM.

I. Abtheilung:

Beethoven . . Eroica.

II. Abtheilung:

Wagner . . Vorspiel und neue Einleitung zu „Tannhäuser".
Wagner . . . Vorspiel und Schlusssatz aus „Tristan und Isolde".
Wagner . . . Wotans Abschied und Feuerzauber aus: „Die Walküre".

Der ganze Reinertrag diefes Concertes wird zum Ankaufe von Patronatsscheinen zu Gunften unbemittelter Mufiker und Kunftjünger verwendet.

all the great orchestras of Germany as well as the Vienna Opera's orchestra to work with him. A deputation led by the concertmaster Jakob Grün and the solo viola-player Siegmund Bachrich went to Bayreuth and received a hearty welcome from the Master. The drums were played by his favorite disciple Hans Richter, a former member of the orchestra of the Vienna Court Opera.

In Vienna the relationship between Otto Dessoff, who had been in charge of

292   The program for a concert given by the orchestra of the Court Opera under Richard Wagner on 12 May 1872.

the Philharmonic concerts since 1860, and Johann Herbeck had never been good. In the years that now followed it grew noticeably worse, and in 1874, on the occasion of the Viennese premiere of Verdi's *Aida*, rehearsals were entrusted to Dessoff and new differences arose, prompting Herbeck to turn his back on Vienna. His position had gradually become untenable in any case because of the rising deficit and in 1875 events affecting the orchestra happened thick and fast. In March and May Wagner conducted three concerts with the Vienna Opera Orchestra on behalf of Bayreuth, the performance on 6 May bringing him particularly jubilant applause. The audience was so enthusiastic that it thundered for an encore of the funeral march from *Die Götterdämmerung*–part of the orchestra refused, however, because they had to play Meyerbeer's *L'Africaine* that evening as well. Wagner was visibly upset and was obliged to inform the audience that he had to "bow to a higher will."

Herbeck had already left office on 5 April, rather unwillingly, and only a few days later Franz Jauner was named to succeed him as director of the Opera. Dessoff conducted his farewell concert, and on 1 May Hans Richter took up his post as conductor at the Court Opera with a performance of *Die Meistersinger*. This was the start of one of the finest periods in the history of the Court Opera. The orchestra's position changed fundamentally at the same time. Dingelstedt had not liked the orchestra and Herbeck had deprived the conductor of his concerts, but now in Jauner it found a sympathetic director who immediately offered the musicians the opportunity to hold their Philharmonic concerts in the opera house. The orchestra thanked him but refused because it had found a permanent and ideal home in the newly-opened building of the music society.

The concerts for the "Court Theater's pension fund" continued for decades, with Hans Richter alone conducting on eighteen occasions. They were held in the opera house and also in the great hall of the music society, but the orchestra was always very careful only to devote their official time to concerts which had a char-

itable purpose. This somewhat exaggerated concern led in 1919 to the unfortunate protest, which happily had no effect, against the appointment of Richard Strauss as director of the State Opera.

But to return to Jauner: one of his historic acts occurred immediately after he took office. He invited Giuseppe Verdi to Vienna. The maestro accepted, and on 11 June 1875 he conducted his *Requiem* at the opera house to overwhelming acclaim. It was played four times in all under his guidance. He also conducted *Aida* twice. Here was something which no other orchestra in the world had experienced: within the space of a few months, from 1 March to the end of June 1875, the orchestra of the Court Opera played on nine occasions under the greatest masters of opera in the nineteenth century–Richard Wagner and Giuseppe Verdi.

Soon after first conducting the orchestra Hans Richter was chosen to succeed Dessoff in running the Philharmonic concerts. In him the orchestra found an ideal leader for over twenty years, a man who would show them the splendors of Wagner's music, and who would also help to make a success of the works of Johannes Brahms and even the young Richard Strauss. Like many other famous musicians Richter had started out in Vienna as a choir boy, studied piano, violin, and composition at the conservatory and French horn under Wilhelm Kleinecke and then played the horn in the orchestra of the Court Opera from 1862 to 1866. Wagner took him on as a copyist for the score of *Die Meistersinger*, and Richter got to know the great composer personally at Tribschen, his private villa in Zurich, a relationship which gradually developed into genuine friendship. Wagner then brought Richter to Munich with him as chorusmaster, where he helped with preparations for the world premiere of *Die Meistersinger*. Later as conductor, he rehearsed *Lohengrin* in Brussels, became director of the Budapest Opera and then ended years of traveling when he took up his duties at the Court Opera in Vienna.

In the summer of 1875 he was in Bayreuth in charge of first rehearsals with the orchestra for the festival planned for the following year beginning on 13 August 1876 with himself conducting the world premiere of the whole *Ring* tetralogy. Jauner had won the performance rights for the *Ring* in Vienna which Richter rehearsed over and over again with the orchestra of the Court Opera. As a result a large number of the orchestra was persuaded to work with him in Bayreuth during the summer break and this brought about a partnership of top musicians (particularly the Wagnerian tuba-players) between the Court Opera Orchestra and Bayreuth, a link which was maintained until the Second World War.

Jauner was followed by Wilhelm Jahn—a musician and conductor was once again in the director's office at the Court Opera. Like Jauner he was well-disposed towards the orchestra and the combination of Jahn and Richter proved extremely beneficial to artistic development. A new generation of orchestral musicians, rigorously selected by them both, moved in during the seventeen years that Jahn was director, and with the magnificent Arnold Rosé at the concertmaster's stand, this generation was in no way inferior to the era of Georg and Josef Hellmesberger. While Josef Hellmesberger typified the Viennese violinist (and was later looked on as the precursor of Fritz Kreisler, who came to prominence from the Vienna conservatory), Rosé embodied the great classical violinist, who had none of the usual Viennese traits. With its crystal-clear tone, sparing use of vibrato, and faultless intonation, his briefest orchestral solo had something personal about it which made the audience sit up and listen. He was born in Jassy (Rumania) in 1863 and moved to Vienna when he was ten years old. Rosé studied at the conservatory with Carl Heissler, played in concerts when only fourteen and was engaged straight away as concertmaster of the Court Opera Orchestra by Jahn after making an appearance in a concert under Hans Richter in 1881. Like Hellmesberger he also made his debut, in January 1883, before he had even reached the age of twenty, in the Börsendorfersaal (a concert-room which opened in 1872) with his string quartet, which went on to achieve world fame. I myself was able to wonder at him for six-

teen years from my seat in the orchestra. His influence on the whole string section was incredible. He had such a degree of authority that each of us gave our best, from the violins to the double-basses. When he sat in the concertmaster's seat, holding his violin in an imposing manner despite his advanced years, he gave a most intense demonstration of orchestral playing.

Next to him on the platform was Josef Hellmesberger, Jr., who was appointed concertmaster in 1884 and who was cast in a different mould. As his father's pupil

K. K. Hof- Operntheater.

Freitag den 11. Juni 1875.

Abends halb 8 Uhr

Unter persönlicher Leitung des Komponisten

GIUSEPPE VERDI.

Bei aufgehobenem Abonnement.

REQUIEM

für Soli, Chor und Orchester.

(Erste Aufführung in Wien.)

Soli:

Sigra. **Teresa Stolz.**   Sigr. **Angelo Masini.**
Sigra. **Maria Waldmann.**   Sigr. **Paolo Medini.**

Chor: (150 Mitwirkende) der gesammte Chor der k. k. Hofoper, verstärkt durch Mitglieder des akademischen Gesangvereines.

Instrumentale: Das Orchester der k. k. Hofoper.

Erste Abtheilung:

Nr. 1. **Requiem und Kyrie** (Ewige Ruhe gib ihnen). 4stimmig.
Nr. 2. **Dies irae** (Soli und Chor):
  a) **Dies irae** (Tag des Schreckens). Chor.
  b) **Tuba mirum** (Die Posaune himmlisch tönend).
  c) **Liber scriptus** (Ein geschrieben Buch). Mezzo-Sopran u. Chor.
  d) **Quid sum miser** (Ach was werd' ich Armer). Sopran, Mezzo-Sopran und Tenor.
  e) **Rex tremendae** (Herr dess' Allmacht). Quartett und Chor.
  f) **Recordare** (Lieber Jesu! ach gedenke). Sopran u. Mezzo-Sopran.
  g) **Ingemisco** (Schuldvoll tönt dir). Tenorsolo.

  h) **Confutatis** (Wenn Verfluchte, wenn Verdammte). Solo für Bass.
  i) **Lacrimosa** (Thränenreichster). Quartett und Chor.

Zweite Abtheilung:

Nr. 3. **Domine Jesu** (Herr der Welt). Offertorium 4stimmig.
Nr. 4. **Sanctus** (Heilig) Doppelfuge, 2chörig.
Nr. 5. **Agnus Dei** (Lamm Gottes). Sopran, Mezzo-Sopran und Chor.
Nr. 6. **Lux aeterna** (Aetherschwingen erhellen sie). Mezzo-Sopran, Tenor und Bass.
Nr. 7. **Libera me** (Befreie mich). Sopransolo, Chor, Schlussfuge.

Die Mitglieder des akademischen Gesang-Vereines haben ihre Mitwirkung freundlichst zugesagt.

Das Textbuch in lateinischer und deutscher Sprache ist an der Kasse für 20 kr. zu bekommen.
Der freie Eintritt ist ohne Ausnahme aufgehoben.
Der Billeten-Vorverkauf zur zweiten Aufführung findet an der Tages-Kassa statt.

Morgen Samstag den 12. Juni 1875. Zweite Aufführung unter des Komponisten persönlicher Leitung.

Kassa-Eröffnung halb 7 Uhr. — Anfang halb 8 Uhr.

293 On 11 June 1875 Giuseppe Verdi conducted his Requiem Mass at the imperial Court Opera.

246

he joined the quartet at the youthful age of fifteen, served three years in the military and became the conductor at the Ringtheater—and fortunately escaped from the burning theater in 1881. He was immediately taken on as ballet conductor at the Court Opera and also conducted in the chapel at the Hofburg. As a typical Viennese he was particularly drawn to the lighter side of the Muse and composed numerous operettas. His *Veilchenmädel* enjoyed a cheerful revival in the State Opera a few years ago as the ballet *Hotel Sacher*. Josef Klein, a leading violin and also ballet conductor, was another interesting character, appointed somewhat later. His ballet *Faun und Nymphe* also played at the Court Opera. The most successful second violin the State Opera has ever had, however, must have been Josef Bayer, the composer of *Die Puppenfee*, which can still inspire feelings of nostalgia.

The wind sections also featured appointments which had a great bearing on the development of the Court Opera Orchestra. Richard Baumgärtel was from Dresden and made sure that there would always be a place in Vienna for the oboe, which is still played by his pupils and descendants and is a particular feature of the ensemble. The horns included Josef Schantl and Emil Wipperich, who kept the splendid sound of the Viennese F-horn going, which other orchestras avoided because it was "unplayable."

Although Hans Richter's twenty-five years at the Court Opera and his twenty-three years conducting the Philharmonic concerts were considered on all sides to be the Philharmonic's golden years, they were not trouble-free. The Viennese critics (notably Ludwig Speidel) soured Richter's existence and in a letter to Gustav Mahler in 1900 he expressed himself on this subject: "My whole life in the theater has been a struggle against ignorance and unreasonable attitudes… and whenever I discovered real and untroubled pleasure in my art, the ill-disposed Viennese press took care to spoil it through their abuse and their mali-

294   Viennese horn players in Bayreuth with Siegfried Wagner (center).

295 Josef Hellmesberger, Jr., imperial *Kapellmeister* and concertmaster.

feelings of those concerned, both as artists and human beings. And if that person did not comply with his frequently idiosyncratic intentions with the speed demanded by this immeasurably impatient man there were embarrassing scenes."

Playing music under this kind of pressure put a great strain on the orchestra, which sustained radical changes, some of which were volontary, others imposed. Mahler replenished it like no one before or since. He increased the number of wind-players and took on sixty-six new members during his ten-year tenure; on the other hand, fifty-five left, roughly double the usual number. This brought him enemies, naturally, but it must be said that he did try, as far as his irascible temper allowed, to create a bearable working climate. As soon as he was appointed, he managed to obtain an all-round increase in salaries, and he helped the orchestra out of a tight spot when touring in Paris by having Baron Rothschild provide twenty thousand francs to cover losses made on the trip. He also managed to resolve the question raised by members of the orchestra as to their title, winning them the right to call themselves "imperial and royal court musicians" after ten years' service.

Only on one occasion did he find words which made his musicians feel they were working in partnership with him. The orchestra had declared its readiness to play his as yet unperformed Sixth Symphony under his guidance, at which he wrote in a circular that it would fill him with pride "to feel a part of the orchestra not only in my professional capacity but also through the bond of art."

A harmonious collaboration would no doubt have been possible on such a basis, but it only came about to a limited degree, although Mahler had enormous admiration for some of the soloists in the ensemble, such as the clarinettist Franz Bartolomey, the double-bass Eduard Madenski and, especially, the harpist Alfred Holy. Time heals many wounds, and when I joined the orchestra eleven years after Mahler's death, many older colleagues described to me the brilliance of his opera performances and the effect

cious comments." He derived visible satisfaction from being the first Austrian since Josef Haydn to be made an honorary Doctor by the Universities of Oxford and Manchester, following concerts he gave in England.

The Jahn/Richter era came to an abrupt end when Gustav Mahler was named director of the imperial and royal Court Opera in 1897. His period in charge was certainly one of the most extraordinary, but also the most difficult phase in the history of the Court Opera Orchestra. It is not easy to form an objective opinion on his relationship with the orchestra which played under him. As a productive and brilliant artist he neglected, in his fanatical pursuit for perfection, to maintain customary niceties with his musicians, intimidating them to such an extent that they found it very hard to get on with him. We can see how difficult their position was from words spoken by one of his most faithful devotees, a leading violin Siegfried Auspitzer, who said at a meeting of the orchestra in 1903: "His explosive nature, which nobody could predict, inevitably had a very harmful effect on the

296 Arnold Rosé became a concertmaster at the Court Opera in 1881 at the age of eighteen, founding the world famous Rosé Quartet only two years later (oil painting by Max Oppenheimer).

297 The orchestra, painted by Max Oppenheimer. The concertmaster Arnold Rosé can be made out, and the conductor has the features of Gustav Mahler.

of his personality, which no one could deny.

His successor Felix von Weingartner, who took up his post on 1 January 1908, was left a rejuvenated and high-quality orchestra containing outstanding soloists who were to bring it status and admiration for many years. This was due in particular to the efforts of the oboist Alexander Wunderer and the horn-player Karl Stiegler who maintained the tradition of the Viennese school of wind playing, a tradition which is still upheld today by their pupils and heirs. In the string section Arnold Rosé—assisted in his teaching by his fellow concertmasters Carl Prill and Julius Stvertka, the solo cellist Friedrich Buxbaum and the previously mentioned Eduard Madenski—ensured that the Viennese string-sound was kept up and perpetuated. Franz Schmidt, who was appointed by Jahn and was in permanent disagreement with Mahler, gradually commanded attention as a composer.

If the orchestra was hard-pressed to withstand Mahler's testing reign, it quickly struck up a good relationship with Richard Strauss, who gradually entered its circle as a composer and conductor. The orchestra was already acquainted with some of his symphonic works, and in 1902 Mahler arranged a production of his *Feuersnot*—the first time the Court Opera Orchestra had played a Strauss opera. Strauss conducted the Philharmonic for the first time in August 1906 to celebrate Mozart's birth in Salzburg one hundred fifty years earlier; the orchestra's contact with him must have been successful from the very start because he was prepared there and then to agree to conduct some of their subscription concerts. Letters from this time confirm the satisfaction he found "conducting this excellent band of artists," and when his *Elektra* was produced at the Court Opera in 1909 under Weingartner this impression was reinforced to such an extent that he invited the orchestra to perform concerts with him in Munich during the first Richard Strauss Week. The Viennese premiere of *Der Rosenkavalier* followed in 1911 under the baton of Franz Schalk, who must with hindsight be acknowledged as probably the most trusty and loyal friend the Philharmonic has ever had.

The outbreak of the Great War in 1914 also exposed the orchestra to extreme danger and it can perhaps be seen as a miracle that only one of its members, the trumpeter Adolf Wunderer, lost his life. As so often happens, help arrived in a crisis, on this occasion in the form of the bandmaster of the "Hoch- und Deutschmeister" regiment, Wilhelm Wacek. Since there was no military call-up at that time, he had the majority of the Philharmonic detailed to his band, thereby ensuring their survival. With two Strauss operas, *Ariadne* and *Salome*, which eventually re-opened the Court Opera's doors, the orchestra proved itself once again as Strauss specialists. It emerged at this point that the master himself was showing an interest in the possibility of directing the Vienna Opera. The monarchy collapsed in November 1918, and shortly afterwards Richard Strauss was indeed appointed director with Franz Schalk. He had conducted a concert in aid of the Red Cross before the end of the war, and the old fear immediately grew that he would

298 The conductor Hans Richter, here as an honorary doctor of Oxford University, was involved with the orchestra for over twenty-three years.

299 When Richard Strauss was made director of the Vienna Opera, the orchestra protested against his appointment (oil painting by Wilhelm Viktor Krauss).

conduct more concerts in the opera house. This was the reason for the orchestra's deplorable protest against his appointment, which Strauss did not take at all seriously and which he no doubt ascribed to his "enemy" Weingartner. The Court Opera became the State Opera and before long Strauss and Schalk were sharing the directorship. After the magnificent world premiere of *Die Frau ohne Schatten*, both directors took the decision to augment the large house with an affiliated theater, the Kleiner Redoutensaal, which Alfred Roller had had rebuilt. I owe my engagement at the State Opera to this decision. In order to cover the activities of the two houses, the orchestra was increased by ten strings and several windplayers, and on 1 December 1922 I joined what was now known as the State Opera Orchestra.

Franz Schalk was probably the most committed director of all time, and in spite of his frequently sarcastic sense of humour and his strictness he loved our orchestra, its sound and special style, doing more than any other director to preserve it. With new musicians his word was final, he would take advice from concertmasters and soloists, and he tried to accept candidates who were not only good musicians but who also had a general cultural understanding. He would sometimes appoint someone on the basis of a teacher's recommendation, as with the flutist Josef Niedermayr, who became one of our finest artists. The same happened with Messrs. Kamesch, Wlach, and Freiberg, who came and played test pieces, admittedly, but who were accepted on his decision alone. Replacing their older predecessors, they rose to become real virtuosi of the State Opera and therefore of the Philharmonic. Richard Strauss was not very interested in test pieces—his approach to auditions was thoroughly undemocratic and based on his own appreciation. This applied in particular to the first violin Franz Mairecker, a musician through and through, whom he made concertmaster and who played all the solos in the growing number of Strauss premieres, in place of his ageing concertmaster colleagues. He also engaged Rudolf Hindemith, however, the

brother of the composer, whose virtuosity as a cellist astonished us.

Austria's economic position deteriorated appreciably and inflation shot up, but under Strauss and Schalk we carried on playing music untiringly. Nineteen twenty-four was a year full of surprises: Richard Strauss retired shortly after his sixtieth birthday, leaving Schalk in sole charge, the Austrian currency stabilized following the introduction of the schilling, and measures aimed at achieving economies hit the enlarged string section hardest. New members of the orchestra like myself feared for our existence, but Schalk stuck by us and made do by not filling any vacancies that arose. It amounted to a freeze on recruiting and some ensembles did not take on any new musicians for years.

Wilhelm Furtwängler's appearance at the opera house represented an interlude. He had taken over the Philharmonic concerts from Weingartner in 1927. The Viennese were so taken with him that they tried to have him take over at the Opera. He rehearsed *Figaro, Rheingold*, and later *Die Walküre*, providing the theater with a series of sparkling performances. The attempt to keep him in Vienna floundered, unfortunately, because of objections from Berlin.

Schalk's successor was Clemens Krauss, a virtuoso conductor and one of the best tutors an orchestra could have, who put great value on youth. Young soloists hired by Schalk gradually came to the front rows. He practiced *Wozzeck* meticulously and rehearsed a number of new productions, particularly operas by Strauss, with a care which few had ever shown. The economic crisis in 1931 gave him a lot to do: for the first and only time in the history of the orchestra salaries had to be cut, a step which the orchestra sensibly accepted. Like his predecessor, Krauss was dictatorial when it came to hearing auditions, and one of his best appointments was Willi Boskovsky, a pupil of Mairecker, who was first promoted to the position of leading second violin in 1933. He soon became first violinist and was made concertmaster shortly afterwards. Later he achieved widespread fame as conductor of the New Year's concerts.

300 Wilhelm Furtwängler rehearsed *The Marriage of Figaro, Das Rheingold,* and *Die Walküre* at the State Opera. The lengthy contact with Furtwängler came to nothing, however–Berlin was quicker.

Another new arrival was the solo cellist Richard Krotschak, whom Krauss brought to us from the Vienna Symphony Orchestra.

After a short interval under Weingartner, the opera house was taken over by Erwin Kerber, one of the orchestra's most sincere friends. It was during this period that conductors who had been driven out of Germany found a home with us. Under the leadership of Bruno Walter and Hans Knappertsbusch we experienced opera performances of the greatest accomplishment, and Arturo Toscanini himself conducted two performances of *Fidelio* and one of Verdi's *Requiem.* Kerber took on Wolfgang Schneiderhan as concertmaster in 1937. The twenty-two year old had begun his career as a boy prodigy and had been to the Vienna violin school as a pupil of Julius Winkler, a teaching colleague of Rosé. He left the orchestra in 1949 and made an international career for himself as a soloist and chamber musician.

In 1938 and during the period that followed until 1945 the orchestra went through probably the most shattering political and artistic crisis in human terms in its history. The German invasion brought the sudden introduction of the notorious Nuremberg laws, to which Arnold Rosé, our solo cellist Friedrich Buxbaum and twelve other musicians in the Philharmonic fell victims. These gentlemen were pensioned off straight away: Rosé and Buxbaum escaped to London and eight colleagues emigrated, four of whom managed to start a new life in the orchestra of the Metropolitan Opera in New York. The violinists Max Starkmann and Viktor Robitsek were not able to leave Vienna in time and died in concentration camps, like so many of their fellow-sufferers. Wilhelm Furtwängler managed to obtain "special dispensation" for nine other threatened musicians, so despite all these horrors the orchestra survived this attack on its existence.

But new dangers threatened immediately. In the Reich all orchestras were classified and rewarded according to their ability. The Berlin Philharmonic naturally belonged to the privileged group but the Viennese had to wait two years before they were finally accorded the same

253

301 Clemens Krauss, Franz Schalk's successor as opera director, was forced to cut the orchestra's fees in 1931 as a consequence of the economic crisis.

status. This was of special importance because it was only through this classification that musicians were released from military service. (Only one member of the orchestra, Hans Charwat, died, in 1943.) Operas continued to be performed undisturbed, first under Kerber and then under a director brought in from Hamburg. Kerber had employed the seventeen year-old Walter Barylli, and in the concertmaster trio of Schneiderhan-Boskovsky-Barylli, we discovered a wonderful team of a quality which had never been seen before.

In the middle of the war, on 1 January 1943, Karl Böhm took over the director's job. He had been conducting the Philharmonic's concerts and organizing opera performances since 1933, and he maintained links with our orchestra as a most faithful guardian of Viennese traditions until he died. The highlights of his work during that period were his performances of Mozart's works and the festival of Strauss operas held to celebrate the great man's eightieth birthday. Soon, however, bombing attacks started on Vienna and our performance of *Götterdämmerung* under Hans Knappertsbusch on 30 June 1944 was our last in the beautiful old opera house. The attempt on Hitler's life a few weeks later brought our involvement with opera to an end. "Total war" was proclaimed and all theaters closed.

Deprived of its purpose in this way, the orchestra was in great danger. It seems incomprehensible today that so few musicians were called upon to engage in military service. The orchestra had to play what were known as "works concerts" and film scores, and in the course of one such recording in the Rosenhügel studio

302 A successful appointment: in 1933 Willy Boskovsky started in the orchestra at the last seat of the second violins–decades later he achieved international fame as the conductor of the New Year's concerts.

303 The conductor Hans Knappertsbusch together with concertmaster Franz Mairecker.

we experienced an air-raid; it missed its target, thank God, and we got out scared but alive. On 12 March 1945 our cultural home, the State Opera, was destroyed by bombs, the Russians' march on Vienna made the situation increasingly critical, with the threat of a *Volkssturm*, the arming of civilians. It was thanks to a member of Vienna's command unit, Major Marek, that we were not called upon. He installed us in the music society building and told us to "forget ourselves" there, which is what we did. We later fled to the cellars of Vienna's main fire station, where we witnessed the entry of the Red Army.

The orchestra's continued artistic existence came under threat again after 1945. Thirteen musicians were released or retired because of their membership in the Nazi party, and others, like many a conductor, were only allowed to remain with the orchestra after appearing before a commission. Three of those who had been released were reinstated in 1950.

The State Opera Orchestra was nevertheless playing for the opera again as early as 1 May 1945, initially in the Volksoper, which had not been destroyed, and then in the hastily repaired, traditional Theater an der Wien–in spite of the hunger and cold and desperate circumstances. There were splendid opera performances nonetheless, at first under the energetic Josef Krips and subsequently with probably the leading conductors of the time, for example Furtwängler, Knappertsbusch, Erich Kleiber, and Busch. This period of reconstruction seems to those who went through it to have been one of the finest epochs in the history of the orchestra, for all the worries over the

304 Bruno Walter drew performances of the greatest perfection from the State Opera Orchestra. He lost his position and had to leave Vienna following the Anschluss in 1938.

political future of our country. The international treaty of 1955 and the opening of the restored State Opera almost immediately afterwards marked the beginning of another period. Now, as in 1869 under Dingelstedt, Karl Böhm was made responsible for the transfer of all opera activities from the Theater an der Wien, which had become so dear to us, to the new house. When we played the inaugural performance of *Fidelio* under him on 5 November 1955 our orchestra's beautiful old sound and joyful playing were there once more; the damage inflicted by the crises of 1938 and 1945 had been overcome and the structure of the ensemble remained as it was.

Böhm resigned not long after the festival performances, which lasted over a month. His successor Herbert von Karajan's eight-year stay was the last time, for the present at least, that a musician and conductor held the position of "artistic director" at the Vienna Opera. He provided an enthusiastic public with a number of great moments and in limited rehearsal time, like Toscanini, he also inspired his orchestra to playing of the

highest quality, the match of which is unlikely to be repeated.

After Karajan's departure Egon Hilbert managed to obtain the services of Leonard Bernstein. This outstanding musician introduced himself to a State Opera rich in tradition with a brilliant *Falstaff*, and our orchestra forged a link with him which continues to this day to benefit the Philharmonic.

Further decades have passed since and the State Opera Orchestra has renewed itself as never before. Hilbert increased the numbers to nearly one hundred fifty members in order to cope with the enormous volume of work which there now is. Invitation performances at operas abroad and performances throughout Austria have increased its scope—even television has made inroads into opera. The orchestra's double function continues to be a distinct advantage. If its concert activities work to the benefit of its opera playing, so equally does its opera playing enrich its concert activities. The opera musician becomes familiar with a body of work which in its range and diversity almost surpasses the concert

305, 306 Arturo Toscanini conducted Beethoven's *Fidelio* twice at the State Opera and Verdi's *Requiem* once: the conductor with Arnold Rosé and Franz Mairecker (top), and the orchestra rehearsing the *Requiem* in 1934 (bottom).

256

307 Wolfgang Schneiderhan, concertmaster of the opera orchestra from 1937 to 1949, went on to an international career as a soloist and chamber musician.

308 Karl Böhm, who had been conducting the Philharmonic concerts and operas in Vienna since 1933, became the director of the State Opera in 1943. He maintained and safeguarded the orchestra's traditions throughout his life.

309 The seventy-year-old Walter Barylli was appointed during the Second World War and formed a marvellous team of concert-masters with Wolfgang Schneiderhan and Willy Boskovsky.

310 Josef Krips, the real instigator of the legendary Mozart ensemble after the Second World War.

311 Rudolf Moralt, an opera conductor who has been one of the house's great mainstays.

312 Herbert von Karajan stamped his authority on the orchestra of the Vienna Opera in the 1960s. In the last twenty years he has concentrated his opera work almost exclusively in Salzburg.

genre, influencing and shaping it. The accompanying of singers and the changes of tempo, which are much more frequent in opera than in symphonic music, make him more flexible, versatile, and open to improvisation, which is necessary in all spheres of music. It was Wagner who in 1863 wrote in his article "The Vienna Court Opera Theater" that the "members of an excellent orchestra consist of the only musically educated players in an opera house," and although that may not be the case today, it is true nonetheless that the State Opera's orchestra commands a special position in the house. In spite of the frequent changes of conductor, which are indefensible on artistic grounds, it has remained a self-contained ensemble and for this reason represents one of the few stable elements today in the fabric of the State Opera. It has earned its international reputation as a concert orchestra by proving itself over almost one hundred fifty years, placing itself confidently in the service of opera. A universal ensemble, the Vienna Opera Orchestra has no real equal in the whole of the music world.

313   The State Opera Orchestra under Reinhard Schwarz during a performance of Wagner's *Die Walküre* in June 1986.

PREMIERES AND WORLD PREMIERES OF MAJOR OPERAS
AT THE OPERA HOUSE ON THE RING SINCE 1869

Opera titles marked with an asterisk (*) denote world premieres. Guest performances by companies from abroad are not included.

Africaine, L' (Giacomo Meyerbeer)	27 April 1870
Agyptische Helena, Die (Richard Strauss)	11 June 1928
Aida (Giuseppe Verdi)	29 April 1874
Alceste (Christoph Willibald Gluck)	4 October 1885
Andrea Chénier (Umberto Giordano)	28 January 1926
Arabella (Richard Strauss)	21 October 1933
*Ariadne auf Naxos (Richard Strauss)	4 October 1916
Baal (Friedrich Cerha)	25 September 1981
Bacchantinnen, Die (Egon Wellesz)	20 June 1931
Ballo in Maschera, Un (Giuseppe Verdi)	14 May 1870
Barber of Seville, The (Il Barbiere die Siviglia, Gioacchino Rossini)	3 April 1876
Barbier von Bagdad, Der (Peter Cornelius)	4 October 1890
Bartered Bride, The (Bedrich Smetana)	4 October 1896
Basses Terres (Eugen d'Albert)	25 February 1908
*Besuch der Alten Dame, Der (Gottfried von Einem)	23 May 1971
Bohème, La (Giacomo Puccini)	25 November 1903
Boris Godunov (Modest Mussorgsky)	24 October 1925
Capriccio (Richard Strauss)	1 March 1944
Capuleti e i Montecchi, I (Vincenzo Bellini)	21 June 1882
Cardillac (Paul Hindemith)	3 March 1927
Carmen (George Bizet)	23 October 1875
Carmina Burana (Carl Orff)	5 February 1942
Cavalleria Rusticana (Pietro Mascagni)	20 March 1891
Cenerentola, La (Gioacchino Rossini)	2 May 1881

Clemenza di Tito, La (Wolfgang Amadeus Mozart)	27 January 1880
Corregidor, Der (Hugo Wolf)	18 February 1904
Cosi fan tutte (Wolfgang Amadeus Mozart)	18 October 1872
Dalibor (Bedrich Smetana)	4 October 1897
Dantons Tod (Gottfried von Einem)	7 November 1947
Daphne (Richard Strauss)	25 April 1940
Dialogues des Carmélites (Francis Poulenc)	14 February 1959
Dido and Aeneas (Henry Purcell)	27 March 1927
Don Carlos (Giuseppe Verdi)	10 May 1932
Don Giovanni (Wolfgang Amadeus Mozart)	25 May 1869
Donna Diana (Emil Nikolaus von Reznicek)	9 December 1898
Don Pasquale (Gaetano Donizetti)	23 April 1876
Drei Pintos, Die (Carl Maria von Weber/Gustav Mahler)	18 January 1889
Duke Bluebeard's Castle (Bela Bartok)	22 November 1985
Elektra (Richard Strauss)	24 March 1909
Elisir d'Amore, L' (Gaetano Donizetti)	7 July 1876
Entführung aus dem Serail, Die (Wolfgang Amadeus Mozart)	17 January 1872
Ernani (Giuseppe Verdi)	18 May 1876
Eugene Onegin (Peter Tchaikovsky)	19 November 1897
Euryanthe (Carl Maria von Weber)	22 September 1871
Evangelimann, Der (Wilhelm Kienzl)	11 January 1896
Falstaff (Giuseppe Verdi)	21 May 1893
Fanciulla del West, La (Giacomo Puccini)	24 October 1913
Faust (Charles Gounod)	28 March 1870
Favorita, La (Gaetano Donizetti)	7 October 1871

Feuersnot (Richard Strauss) — 29 January 1902
Fidelio (Ludwig van Beethoven) — 10 June 1869
Fille du Régiment, La
(Gaetano Donizetti) — 2 April 1876
Fledermaus, Die (Johann Strauss) — 28 October 1894
Fliegende Holländer, Der
(Richard Wagner) — 27 January 1871
Florentinische Tragödie, Eine
(Alexander von Zemlinsky) — 27 April 1917
Forza del Destino, La
(Giuseppe Verdi) — 27 November 1926
Fra Diavolo (Daniel Auber) — 27 October 1869
*Frau ohne Schatten, Die
(Richard Strauss) — 10 October 1919
Freischütz, Der
(Carl Maria von Weber) — 1 January 1870
Friedenstag (Richard Strauss) — 10 June 1939
Gezeichneten, Die (Franz Schreker) — 27 February 1920
Gioconda, La (Amilcare Ponchielli) — 29 April 1884
Gianni Schicchi (Giacomo Puccini) — 20 October 1920
Giulio Cesare
(George Frideric Handel) — 3 May 1928
Götterdämmerung
(Richard Wagner) — 14 February 1879
Gypsy Baron, The
(Der Zigeunerbaron,
Johann Strauss) — 26 December 1910
Hamlet (Ambroise Thomas) — 14 July 1873
Hänsel und Gretel
(Engelbert Humperdinck) — 18 December 1894
Heure Espagnol, L' (Maurice Ravel) — 13 February 1935
Huguenots, Les
(Giacomo Meyerbeer) — 10 July 1869
Idomeneo
(Wolfgang Amadeus Mozart) — 25 October 1879
Incoronazione di Poppea, L'
(Claudio Monteverdi) — 1 April 1963
Intermezzo (Richard Strauss) — 15 January 1927
Iphigénie en Aulide
(Christoph Willibald Gluck) — 21 November 1874
Iphigénie en Tauride
(Christoph Willibald Gluck) — 2 March 1873
Jenufa (Leoš Janáček) — 16 February 1918
Jessonda (Louis Spohr) — 14 May 1887
Jonny Spielt Auf (Ernst Krenek) — 31 December 1927
Juive, La (Louis Halévy) — 12 November 1870
Junge Lord, Der
(Hans Werner Henze) — 6 June 1978
Kata Kabanova (Leoš Janáček) — 19 April 1974
Katerina Izmaylova
(Dmitri Shostakovich) — 12 February 1965
Königin von Saba, Die
(Karl Goldmark) — 10 March 1875
Kuhreigen, Der (Wilhelm Kienzl) — 18 October 1921
Lakmé (Léo Delibes) — 14 November 1904

Liebe der Danae, Die
(Richard Strauss) — 25 October 1952
Linda di Chamounix
(Gaetano Donizetti) — 11 April 1877
Lohengrin (Richard Wagner) — 4 October 1870
Lucia di Lammermoor
(Gaetano Donizetti) — 3 January 1870
Lucrezia Borgia
(Gaetano Donizetti) — 21 December 1871
Luisa Miller (Giuseppe Verdi) — 23 January 1974
Lulu (Alban Berg) — 16 December 1968
Macbeth (Giuseppe Verdi) — 28 April 1933
Madame Butterfly
(Giacomo Puccini) — 31 October 1907
Magic Flute, The (Die Zauberflöte,
Wolfgang Amadeus Mozart) — 1 September 1869
Manon (Jules Massenet) — 19 November 1890
Manon Lescaut (Giacomo Puccini) — 15 October 1923
Marriage of Figaro, The
(Le Nozze di Figaro,
Wolfgang Amadeus Mozart) — 15 October 1870
Martha (Friedrich von Flotow) — 30 December 1869
Mathis der Maler (Paul Hindemith) — 17 May 1958
Matrimonio Segreto, Il
(Domenico Cimarosa) — 15 March 1884
Medea (Luigi Cherubini) — 26 November 1880
Mefistofele (Arrigo Boito) — 18 March 1882
Meistersinger von Nürnberg, Die
(Richard Wagner) — 27 February 1870
Merry Wives of Windsor, The
(Die Lustigen Weiber von Windsor,
Otto Nicolai) — 11 February 1872
Midsummer Night's Dream, A
(Benjamin Britten) — 18 October 1962
Mignon (Ambroise Thomas) — 8 September 1870
Moses und Aron
(Arnold Schönberg) — 20 May 1973
Muette de Portici, La
(Daniel Auber) — 3 June 1869
*Musikant, Der (Julius Bittner) — 12 April 1910
Norma (Vincenzo Bellini) — 6 March 1870
Notre Dame (Franz Schmidt) — 1 April 1914
Oberon (Carl Maria von Weber) — 2 December 1873
Oedipus Rex (Igor Stravinsky) — 23 February 1928
Orfeo ed Euridice
(Christoph Willibald Gluck) — 4 February 1882
Otello (Giuseppe Verdi) — 14 March 1888
Pagliacci, I
(Ruggiero Leoncavallo) — 19 November 1893
Palestrina (Hans Pfitzner) — 1 March 1919
Parsifal (Richard Wagner) — 14 January 1914
Pelléas et Mélisande
(Claude Debussy) — 23 May 1911
Pique Dame (Queen of Spades,
Peter Tchaikovsky) — 9 December 1902

Postillon de Longjumeau, Le	
(Adolphe Charles Adam)	11 January 1871
Prince Igor (Alexander Borodin)	7 February 1941
Prophète, Le	
(Giacomo Meyerbeer)	12 December 1869
Quatro Rusteghi, I	
(Ermanno Wolf-Ferrari)	25 February 1934
Rake's Progress, The	
(Igor Stravinsky)	25 April 1952
Rheingold, Das (Richard Wagner)	24 January 1878
Rigoletto (Giuseppe Verdi)	11 February 1871
Ritter Pázmán (Johann Strauss)	1 January 1892
Robert le Diable	
(Giacomo Meyerbeer)	20 September 1870
Roméo et Juliette	
(Charles Gounod)	30 May 1869
Rosenkavalier, Der	
(Richard Strauss)	8 April 1911
Salome (Richard Strauss)	14 October 1918
Samson et Dalila	
(Camille Saint-Saëns)	11 May 1907
Schatzgräber, Der (Franz Schreker)	18 October 1922
Schauspieldirektor, Der	
(Wolfgang Amadeus Mozart)	11 December 1880
Schwanda der Dudelsackpfeifer	
(Jaromir Weinberger)	16 October 1930
Schweigsame Frau, Die	
(Richard Strauss)	1 March 1968
Siegfried (Richard Wagner)	9 November 1878
Simon Boccanegra	
(Giuseppe Verdi)	18 November 1882
Somnambula, La	
(Vincenzo Bellini)	8 February 1872
Sorochintsy Fair	
(Modest Mussorgsky)	13 February 1935
*Spielwerk und die Prinzessin, Das	
(Franz Schreker)	15 March 1913
*Sturm, Der (Frank Martin)	17 June 1956
Suor Angelica (Giacomo Puccini)	20 October 1920
Tabarro, Il (Giacomo Puccini)	20 October 1920
Tales of Hoffmann, The	
(Les Contes d'Hoffmann,	
Jacques Offenbach)	11 November 1901
Tannhäuser (Richard Wagner)	22 June 1870
Tosca (Giacomo Puccini)	28 January 1910
Tote Stadt, Die	
(Erich Wolfgang Korngold)	10 January 1921
Traviata, La (Giuseppe Verdi)	11 March 1876
Tristan und Isolde	
(Richard Wagner)	4 October 1883
Trovatore, Il (Giuseppe Verdi)	21 September 1869
Troyens, Les (Hector Berlioz)	17 October 1976
Turandot (Giacomo Puccini)	14 October 1926
Vêpres Siciliennes, Les	
(Giuseppe Verdi)	23 November 1878
Vestale, La (Casparo Spontini)	19 October 1881
Waffenschmied, Der	
(Albert Lortzing)	16 March 1872
Walküre, Die	
(Richard Wagner)	5 March 1877
*Werther (Jules Massenet)	16 February 1892
Wildschütz, Der	
(Albert Lortzing)	19 November 1888
Wozzeck (Alban Berg)	30 March 1930
Wunder der Heliane, Das	
(Erich Wolfgang Korngold)	29 October 1927
Zar und Zimmermann	
(Albert Lortzing)	25 December 1878
Zwerg, Der	
(Alexander von Zemlinski)	24 November 1923

SELECT BIBLIOGRAPHY

Opera, Opera House

Antonicek, Theophil. "Die Anfänge der Oper in Österreich." *Musik in Österreich.* Notring Yearbook. Vienna, 1971.

Christian, Hans, and Hoyer, Harald. *Die Wiener Staatsoper 1945–1980.* Vienna, n.d.

Haas, Robert. *Die Wiener Oper.* Vienna, 1926.

Hadamowsky, Franz. "Barocktheater am Wiener Kaiserhof: Mit einem Spielplan (1625–1740)." Jb. der Gesellschaft für Wiener Theaterforschung 1951/52 (Yearbook for the Vienna Theater Research Society), Vienna, 1955.

– "Theaterbauten und Bühnenkostüme für den Hof Leopolds I" (An article on the history of baroque court theater in Vienna). *Die Österreichische Nationalbibliothek.* Vienna, 1948.

Hammitzsch, Martin. *Der moderne Theaterbau.* Berlin, 1906.

Hiltl, Nora. "Die Oper am Hofe Kaiser Leopolds I. mit besonderer Berücksichtigung der Tätigkeit von Minato und Draghi." Ph. D. dissertation, Vienna, 1974.

Hoffmann, Hans-Christoph; Krause, Walter; and Kitlitschka, Werner. *Das Wiener Opernhaus. Die Wiener Ringstrasse* VIII/I. Wiesbaden, 1972 (see especially p. 99).

Holzmeister, Clemens. *Werke für das Theater.* Chosen and commented by Joseph Gregor. Vienna, 1953 (see especially p. 39).

Hundert Jahre Wiener Oper am Ring (A hundred years of the Vienna Opera on the Ring). Catalogue of the jubilee exhibition. Vienna, 1969.

Izenour, George C. *Theater Design.* New York, 1977.

Keil-Budischowsky, Verena. *Die Theater Wiens.* Vienna and Hamburg, 1983.

Kralik, Heinrich von. *The Vienna Opera* (Trans. by Richard Rickett). London, 1963.

Musikgeschichte Österreichs, vol. II. From the Baroque to the Present. Edited by Rudolf Flotzinger and Gernot Gruber. Cologne, Gratz, and Vienna, 1979.

Pirchan, Emil; Witeschnik, Alexander; and Fritz, Otto. *300 Jahre Operntheater: Werk und Werden.* Vienna, 1953.

Prawy, Marcel. *Die Wiener Oper: Geschichte und Geschichten.* Vienna, Munich, and Zurich, 1969.

Schenk, Eleonore. "Die Anfänge des Wiener Kärntnertortheaters." Ph. D. dissertation. Vienna, 1969.

Seifert, Herbert. *Die Oper am Wiener Kaiserhof im 17. Jahrhundert.* Tutzing, 1985.

Unterer, Verena. *Die Oper in Wien: Ein Überblick.* Vienna, 1970.

Weidmann, F. C. "Die fünf Theater Wiens: Von ihrer Entstehung bis zum Jahre 1847." Austria oder Österr. Universal-Kalender für das Jahr 1848. Vienna.

Weilen, Alexander von. *Geschichte des Wiener Theaterwesens von den ältesten Zeiten bis zu den Anfängen der Hoftheater.* Vienna, 1899.

Wellesz, Egon. "Die Opern und Oratorien in Wien von 1660–1708." *Studien für Musikwissenschaft* 6, 1919.

Witeschnik, Alexander. *Wiener Opernkunst von den Anfängen bis zu Karajan.* Vienna, 1959.

Set Design and Costumes

To date there is no major collected history of set design at the Vienna Court and State Opera Theaters. Most of the research on scenery and costumes has been either undertaken for doctoral theses or published in exhibition catalogues. The more significant of these are listed here.

Berger, Herbert. "Die grotesken Kostümentwürfe Ludovico Ottavio Burnacinis." Ph. D. dissertation. Vienna, 1960.

Biach-Schiffmann, Flora. *Giovanni und Ludovico Burnacini. Theater und Feste am Wiener Hofe.* Vienna, 1931.

Buchinger, Ingeborg. "Franz Gaul als Kostümzeichner." Ph. D. dissertation. Vienna, 1951.

Dietrich, Margret, and Kindermann, Heinz. *Dreihundert Jahre österreichisches Bühnenbild.* Vienna, 1959.

Ebersberger, Anna Maria. "Das Kostümwerk Antonio Bertolis: Das Bühnenkostüm der Karolinischen Oper." Ph. D. dissertation. Vienna, 1961.

Gregor, Joseph. *Wiener szenische Kunst. Die Theaterdekoration der letzten drei Jahrhunderte, nach Stilprinzipien dargestellt.* Vienna, 1924.

Greisenegger, Wolfgang. "Theater." *Clemens Holzmeister: Architekt in der Zeitwende. Sakralbau, Profanbau, Theater.* Salzburg, 1978.

Greisenegger-Georgila, Evanthia. "Naturmotive im Angebot eines Theaterdekorationsateliers des 19. Jahrhunderts: Das Atelier Brioschi." Ph. D. dissertation, Vienna, 1986.

Haase, Yorck Alexander. "Der Theatermaler Joseph Platzer." Ph. D. dissertation. Vienna, 1960.

Hadamowsky, Franz. *Stefan Hlawa und sein szenisches Werk.* Exhibition catalogue. Vienna, 1956.

Hartmann, Rudolf, ed. *Opera* (Trans. by Arnold J. Pomerans). Fribourg and New York, 1977.

Hölscher, Eberhard. *Emil Preetorius.* Collected Works. Berlin, 1943.

Kitzwegerer, Liselotte. "Alfred Roller als Bühnenbildner." Ph. D. dissertation. Vienna, 1959.

Mayerhöfer, Josef, ed. *Stefan Hlawa: 40 Jahre Bühnenbild in Österreich.* Exhibition catalogue. Vienna, 1974.

- *Der Bühnenbildner Teo Otto: Inszenierungen in Österreich.* Exhibition catalogue. Salzburg, 1977.

Pauker, Peter. "Heinrich Lefler: Sein Werk und seine Zeit." Ph. D. dissertation, Vienna, 1962.

Roboz, Peter. "Der Bühnenbildner Stefan Hlawa: Ein Beitrag zur Geschichte des modernen Bühnenbildes in Österreich." Ph. D. dissertation. Vienna, 1969.

Sbarra, Francisco. *Der guldene Apfel.* Nuremberg, 1672. Facsimile with a postface by Margret Dietrich. Vienna, 1965.

Schmid, Viola. "Studien zu Wieland Wagners Inszenierungskonzeption und zu seiner Inszenierungspraxis." Ph. D. dissertation. Munich, 1973.

Schneider-Siemssen, Günther, *30 Jahre Bühnenschaffen.* Exhibition catalogue. Salzburg, 1977.

Stoklaska, Juliane, "Oskar Strnad." Ph. D. dissertation. Vienna, 1959.

Ballet

Raab, Riki. "Vom Wiener Ballett." Yearbook for the Vienna History Society, Vol. 8. Vienna, 1950–51.

-- "Ballettreformator J. G. Noverre." Yearbook for the Vienna History Society, Vol. 13. Vienna, 1957.

-- "Wechselbeziehungen im Tanze." Österreich und die angelsächsische Welt. Vienna, 1961.

-- *Fanny Elssler: Eine Weltfaszination.* Vienna, 1962.

-- "Ballettmeister Josef Hassreiter." Notring Yearbook, Vienna, 1965.

-- "100 Jahre Wiener Opernballett." *Wiener Geschichts-Blätter,* No. 24. Vienna, 1969.

-- "Das k.k. Hofballett unter Maria Theresia." *Österreich im Europa der Aufklärung.* Vol. 2. Vienna, 1985.

Stanzl, Eva. "Das Ballett in der Wiener Barockoper." *Maske und Kothurn.* n.p. 1961.

Orchestra

Bachrich, Siegmund. *Aus verklungenen Zeiten.* Vienna, 1914.

Glasenapp, Friedrich. *Richard Wagners Leben und Wirken.* Leipzig, 1905.

Herbeck, Ludwig. *Johann Herbeck.* Vienna, 1885.

Kralik, Heinrich von. *Richard Strauss.* Vienna, Munich, and Basel, 1963.

Krebs, Carl. *Otto Dessoff.* Correspondence between Brahms and Dessoff. Berlin, 1922.

Perger, Richard von. *Geschichte der Gesellschaft der Musikfreunde.* Vienna, 1910.

Prosl, Robert Maria. *Die Hellmesberger.* Vienna, 1947.

Strasser, Otto. *Und dafür wird man noch bezahlt.* Vienna, 1974.

- *Sechse is'.* Munich, 1981.

Wagner, Richard. *Sämtliche Schriften und Dichtung.* Leipzig. n. d.

INDEX

The numbers in italics refer to the plates

Abbado, Claudio 170
Abraxus 281
Abu Hassan 15, 64
Achsel-Clemens, Wanda 105
Adam, Adolphe 30, 133
Adelina 25
Africaine, L' 30, 245
Ägyptische Helena, Die 90, 103, 109, 154; *210*
Aida 64, 68, 133, 158, 170, 212, 245; *68, 69, 72, 246*
Albert, Eugen d' 89
Alceste (Draghi) 14
Alceste (Gluck) 22; *13*
Allessandro Stradella 30
Alpenglühn 236
Alsen, Herbert 118
Alt, Franz *34*
Alwin, Karl 103, 108, 117
Amahl und die nächtlichen Besucher 162
Anday, Rosette 105, 117; *167*
André Chenier 103; *189*
Andrian, Leopold von 95
Andromeda 9
Angelica Vincitrice 16; *10, 11*
Angliolini, Gaspara 22, 212, 226
Anna Karenina 115
Aphrodite 90
Appia, Adolphe 192, 200
Après-midi d'un Faune, L' 220
Arabella 101, 109, 122; *132, 151*
Aragall, Giacomo 150
Ariadne auf Naxos 90, 99, 101, 122, 250; *133, 148, 187, 219*
Armstrong, Karan *257*
Ashton, Frederick *228*
Asplan, Raoul 127
Aspelmayer, Franz 24
Assassinio nella cattedrale 144
Atlantow, Vladimir 158
Attila 162
Auber, François 28, 30
Auberval, Jean d' 216
Aumer, Jean 211
Auspitzer, Siegfried 248
Axur (Tarare) 24

Baal 162
Bacchantinnen, Die 110
Bachrin, Siegmund 244
Badia, Carlos Agostino 14
Bahr, Hermann 82
Bahr-Mildenburg, Anna 77, 82; *96, 105, 246*
Bajazzo, Der 74, 204; *123, 227*
Baklanoff, George 90
Bakst, Léon 220
Balanchine, George 228, 233
Ballets Russes 220
Ballo in Maschera, Un 30
Baltsa, Agnes 162; *226*
Banfield, Rafaello de 232
Barbaja, Domenico 25, 28
Barbier von Bagdad, Der 74, 89
Barber of Seville, The 25; *199, 200*
Barber of Severing, The 30
Barlog, Boleslav 158; *214, 218*
Barry, Edward 39
Bartered Bridge, The 77, 101
Bartok, Bela 162; *256*
Bartolaia, Ludovico 11
Bartolomey, Franz 250
Barylli, Walter 254; *309*
Bastianini, Ettore 140, 144
Bauer, Margaret 232
Baumgärtel, Richard 247
Bayer, Josef 215, 218, 219, 247; *266*
Beaumarchais, Pierre Augustini Caron de 24
Beck, Johann Nepomuk 64
Beduzzi, Antonio 16; *12*
Beethoven, Ludwig van 25, 68, 78, 86, 133; *24, 106, 129, 171, 177, 178, 305*
– *Missa solemnis* 154
– Symphony No. 3 ("Eroica") 68, 244
– Symphony No. 9 ("Choral") 133, 244
Beirer, Hans 133; *183, 211*
Bellini, Vincenzo 28, 162
Benois, Alexander 220
Benvenuto Cellini 89
Berg, Alban 110, 154, 170, 200; *136, 137, 186*
Berger, Theodor 127
Bergonzi, Carlo 144
Berio, Luciano 162
Berlioz, Hector 89, 162

Bernstein, Leonard 150, 154, 157, 162; *205, 206, 207*
– *Mass* 162
Bertalli, Antonio 11, 14; *6*
Besuch der alten Dame, Der 154; *211*
Bettler Namenlos 110
Bianchi, Bianca 68
Biches, Les 228
Bienert, Bernd Roger 236
Binder, Bobby *276*
Birkenmeyer, Michael 233, 236
Birkmeyer, Toni 226, 228, 236; *272, 273*
Bittner, Julius 89, 103, 110
Bizet, Georges 68, 168, 232; *79, 144, 165, 195, 220, 226*
– *Symphonie in C* 232
Blacher, Boris 133, 232
Bliss, Sir Arthur 233
Boccaccio 110
Bohème, La (Leoncavallo) 82
Bohème, La (Puccini) 82, 141; *94, 196, 222*
Böhm, Josef 241; *289*
Böhm, Karl 58, 59, 62, 107, 119, 122, 127, 133, 140, 150, 154, 158, 162, 254, 256; *179, 186, 187, 209, 213, 214, 308*
Boieldieu, François-Adrien 28
Boito, Arrigo 74
Bokor, Margit 108
Bolero 228
Bolm, Adolphe 220
Boltenstern, Erich 40, 42, 44, 50; *50*
Bonisolli, Franco 158
Bononcini, Giovanni 16
Boris Godunov 103, 158; *215*
Borodin, Alexander 220
Borosini, Francesco 16
Borovska, Joanna 162
Borri, Pasquale 212
Boskovsky, Willi 252, 254; *302, 309*
Bournonville, Auguste 216
Boutique fantasque, La 228
Bouvard, Hugo *169*
Boysen, Rolf *212*
Brahm, Otto 192
Brahms, Johannes 68, 82, 245
– *German Requiem* 68
Bräuer, Lucia 232; *281*
Braun, Baron 25

Braun, Helena 119; *145*
Brecht, Berthold 200
Breuer, Hans 82; *91*
Brexner, Edeltraud 231, 232; *280, 281*
Brioschi, Anton 170, 189, 198, 204; *75, 103, 240, 244, 269*
Brioschi, Carlo 58, 188, 189, 190, 192; *62, 81, 239, 242, 243, 268*
Brioschi, Giuseppe 188
Britten, Benjamin 233
Bruckner, Anton 82
Bruckwald, Otto 37
Brunner, Gerhard 234
Bruson, Renato 221
Buchinger, Marie 222; *273*
Bumbry, Grace 214
Burghart, Hermann 189, 190; *68, 69*
Burnacini, Giovanni 11, 177, 186; *2, 6*
Burnacini, Lodovico Ottavio 12, 177, 178, 182; *7, 8, 230–5*
Busch, Fritz 255
Buxbaum, Friedrich 250, 253

Caccia felice, La 11
Caldara, Antonio 16
Callisto et Arcade 9
Callas, Maria 100, 140
Calzabigi, Ranieri da 22
Capriccio 122; *150, 154–6*
Capuleti e i Montecchi, I 28, 162
Cardillac 104
Carmen 68, 117, 150, 168; *79, 144, 165, 195, 220, 226*
Carmina Burana 43
Carnival's Adventures in Paris 212
Caron, Alfred 212, 219
Carreras, José 158; *223, 224*
Caruso, Enrico 90, 141; *97*
Casa, Lisa della 127; *198*
Casson, Robert *276*
Cavalli, Francesco 11
Cavalleria, Rusticana 74, 204; *227*
Cebotari, Maria 126; *155, 156, 158*
Cecchetti, Enrico 220
Cech, Gisela 235
Cenerentola, La 112, 162
Cerale, Luigia 215; *264, 265*
Cerha, Friedrich 162, 170, 233
Cerri, Cäcilie 220; *270*
Cesti, Antonio 12, 13, 178; *7, 231–4*
Chailly, Riccardo 170
Charwat, Hans 254
Chatte, La 228
Check-mate 233
Cherubini, Luigi 25, 254; *208*
Chimneysweep of London, The 212
Christoff, Boris 144
Cid, Le 77
Cimarosa, Domenico 24
Cimarosiana 228
Clemenza di Tito, La 25
Cocteau, Jean 141
Colbran, Isabella 25
Combat, Le 232
Conti, Francesco 16
Copellia 215, 235; *263*
Corelli, Franco 144; *189*

Cornelius, Peter 77, 89
Cosi fan tutte 24, 99, 109, 158, 200; *18, 159*
Constanze e Fortezza 16; *15*
Cotrubas, Ilena *227*
Couperin, François 226
Couperin Suite 152
Couqui, Claudine 220; *261*
Craig, Edward Gordon 192
Cranko, John *284*
Cyrus und Astyages 236
Czerwenka, Oskar 127; *199*

Dalibor 154
Dame Blanche, La 28
Dame im Traum 115
Danaïdes, Les 24
Dantons Tod 127
Danzig, Rudi van 234
Daphne 115, 200; *142*
Daphnis et Chloé 170, 204; *255*
Debussy, Claude 90, 220
Delibes, Leo 215, 219
Demuth, Leopold 82; *98*
Dermota, Anton 118; *156, 159, 163, 178*
Dessoff, Otto 243, 244, 245; *278*
Dessyllas, Pantelis 204
Deux journées, Les 25
Diaghilev, Serge 220, 228
Diana rappacificata con Venere e con l'Aurora 14
Dickie, Murray 127; *200*
Dill, Gerlinde 233, 234
Dingelstedt, Franz von 30, 57, 58, 59, 62, 64, 68, 189, 239, 243, 244, 245, 256; *60*
Dirtl, Willy 222, 231; *279, 281, 282*
Ditters von Dittersdorf, Karl 24, 25
Dohnanyi, Christoph von 158; *212*
Dollfuss, Engelbert 112
Domgraf-Fassbaender, Willi 108
Domingo, Placido *220, 227*
Don Carlos 108, 109, 144, 154; *194*
Don Giovanni 24, 25, 30, 58, 62, 82, 133, 198, 239; *19, 60, 62, 163, 179, 247*
Don Juan (Gluck) 22, 99, 226, 235
Don Pasquale (Donizetti) 28
Don Quixote 231, 235
Donizetti, Gaetano 28, 162; *88, 218*
Doppler, Franz 243
Doppler, Karl 243
Dori, La 14
Draghi, Antonio 12; *8, 230*
Drapal, Julia 230, 231; *278, 279*
Drei Pintos, Die 74
Dubois, Leo 220, 222
Due Foscari, I 28
Duhan, Hans 94; *113*
Duke Bluebeard's Castle 162; *256*
Dulles, John Foster 62; *174*
Duport, Louis 211
Durazzo, Jakob Count 20, 22
Dustmann, Louise 64; *61*
Dvorsky, Llona 162; *228*
Dyck, Ernest van 77

Ebert, Carl 43, 117
Eckert, Carl 239
Edelmann, Otto 127; *167*

Ehnn, Bertha 64; *64, 65*
Einem, Gottfried von 127, 154, 162, 236; *211*
Einöde, Die 233
Eis, Maria 226
Eisenmenger, Rudolf 45; *53*
Elektra 82, 89, 127, 150, 198, 201, 250; *103–5, 203*
Eliasson, Sven Olof *212*
Elisier d'Amore, L' 168
Elizabeth, Emperess 68
Elizza, Elisa 77
Elssler, Fanny 212, 214, 232, 235
Emilia Galotti 24
Ender, Thomas 188
Entführung aus dem Serail 24, 82
Ernani 28
Erwartung 162; *257*
Eugene Onegin 82
Euristhemo 16
Euryanthe 28, 200; *26*
Evangelimann, Der 77
Evering, August 158
Excelsior 77, 218; *265, 268*

Faistauer, Anton *107*
Falla, Manuel de 233
Falstaff 82, 109, 150, 256; *99, 167, 205*
Fanciulla de West, La 50
Fanisca 25
Fantasca 66; *262*
Fassbaender, Brigitte 158; *213*
Fato monarchico, Il 14
Faun und Nymphe 247
Faust (Gounod) 30; *64, 65*
Faust (Spohr) 28
Federova, Sophie 220
Felbermeyer, Anny *167*
Ferdinand, Archduke *258*
Ferdinand I, Emperor 38
Ferdinand II, Emperor 9, 11; *1*
Ferdinand III, Emperor 9, 11; *3*
Fernand Cortez 25
Feuersnot 82, 250
Fidelio 14, 25, 43, 78, 90, 115, 133, 140, 154, 168, 198, 200, 253, 256; *25, 106, 129, 171, 177, 178, 207, 305*
Figl, Leopold *174*
Fille du Régiment, La 88
Firebird, The 170, 204
Fischer-Karwin, Heinz *176*
Fledermaus, Die 111, 144; *244*
Flick und Flock 212; *261*
Fliegende Holländer, Der 30, 150, 158; *29*
Flotow, Friedrich von 30
Fokin, Mikhail 220
Fonteyn, Margot 229
Forster, Bertha 82
Forza del Destino 103, 105
Four Temperaments 233
Francescini, Girolamo *29*
Francis I, Emperor 25
Frank, Marko 115
Franz Joseph 31, 38, 212
Fränzl, Willy 226, 228, 234; *274, 277*
Fränzel, Wilfried *279*
Frappart, Louis 212, 215, 219; *261, 265*

Frau ohne Schatten, Die 90, 99, 100, 101, 109, 122, 133, 198, 200, 252; *115–20, 153, 253*
Fredegundis 100
Freischütz, Der 28; *25*
Fremde Frau, Die 115
Freni, Mirella 144; *196, 222, 228*
Freysinger, Caspar 11
Frick, Gottlob 127
Fricsay, Ferenc 144
Friedenstag 115, 200; *140, 141*
Friedrich, Caspar David 204
Friedrich, Götz 158, 204; *212*
Friedrich, Karl 118
Füger, Friedrich 183
Fuoco eterno, Il 14; *230*
Furtwängler, Wilhelm 104, 105, 107, 115, 126, 127, 243, 252, 253; *147, 300*
Fux, Johann Joseph 14, 16; *10, 11, 15*

Gacio, Carlos 236
Galli-Bibiena, Family 35, 186
Galli-Bibiena, Antonio 35, 183
Galli-Bibiena, Ferdinando *10, 11*
Galli-Bibiena, Francesco 14, 35, 182
Galli-Bibiena, Giuseppe 16, 183; *10, 11, 15, 237*
Gallos, Hermann 94; *113*
Galuppi, Baldassare 22
Gamsjäger, Rudolf 156–8
Gandini, Giuseppina 220
Ganzarolli, Vladimir *205*
Gara, La 9, 11; *2*
Gassmann, Florian Leopold 22, 24, 25; *258*
Gaugusch, Christine 236
Gaul, Franz 58, 62, 189–91; *72*
Gazza Ladra, La 25
Genoveva 64
Genueserin, Die 28
Georgila, Vana 189
Gerber, Judith 235
Gerhart, Maria 101
Gezeichneten, Die 100
Ghazarian, Sona 162
Ghiaurov, Nicolai 144, 158; *215*
Ghost in the Castle 111
Gilly, Frederick 36
Giordano, Umberto 103; *189*
Giselle 133, 220, 231
Giuditta 110, 115; *135*
Giuramento, Il 162
Globolinks, Hilfe! Die 162
Glöckchen des Eremiten, Das 115
Gluck, Christophe Willibald 20, 22, 24, 25, 30, 115, 154, 212; *13, 144*
Gobbi, Tito 119, 144; *191*
Godlevski, Carl 218
Goebbels, Joseph 119
Goldberg, Reiner 170
Goldene Märchenzeit, Die 190
Goldmark, Karl 64; *71, 242, 243*
Goltz, Christl 126; *186*
Gonzaga, Princess Eleonore I 9; *1*
Gonzaga, Princess Eleonore II 11; *3*
Gonzaga, Maria *3*
Gossec, François Joseph 24
Gostic, Josef 127
Götterdämmerung 127, 245, 254; *74*

Gounod, Charles 30, 66; *64, 65*
Graf, Herbert 133; *182*
Graf, Max 196
Gratz, Leopold 156
Gregor, Hans 90, 92, 94–6, 101, 106
Gregor, Joseph 42, 44
Grétry, André Ernest Modeste 24
Grist, Reri *206*
Gropius, Walter 42, 204
Grosavescu, Trajan 105
Gruberova, Edita 162; *218, 219*
Grün, Jakob 241, 244
Güden, Hilde 127; *162, 167, 184*
Guglielmi, Pietro Alessandro 24
Gutheil-Schrode, Marie 82, 100, 226; *94, 101, 108, 245, 273*
Gryowetz, Adalbert 25
Gypsy Baron, The 158

Hadrabova, Eva 108; *139*
Hähnel, Ernst Julius 54
Haigen, Kevin *285*
Haizinger, Amalie 215
Halévy, Jacques François Fromental Elias 28, 162
Halm, Friedrich von 58
Hamilton, Georg 231, 232
Hamlet 64
Hamme, Voitus van 218
Hammes, Karl 108
Hanka, Erika 127, 133, 230–2; *279, 281*
Hann, Georg 127
Hans Heiling 30, 215
Hänsel und Gretel 77; *85, 86*
Hansen, Theophil 40
Hanslick, Eduard 62
Harangozo, Gyula 235
Harlekin als Elektriker 222
Harrach, Ferdinand 16
Hartmann, Rudolf 127, 133; *140, 156, 168, 197*
Hasemauer, Carl 39
Haslinger, Gabriele 236
Hasse, Johann Adolf 22
Hassreiter, Carl 204, 214
Hassreiter, Josef 170, 204, 212, 214, 215, 218–20, 222, 230; *262, 265*
Hatala, Milan 236
Haubenstock-Ramati, Roman 162
Haydn, Josef 24, 248
Haydn-Ballet 226
Hegel, Georg Friedrich Wilhelm 25
Heger, Robert 106, 108
Heidenreich, Heinz 236
Heinrich, Rudolf 204
Heissler, Carl 246
Helletsgruber, Luise 101, 109
Hellmesberger, Georg 241, 246
Hellmesberger, Josef 241, 243, 246; *290*
Hellmesberger Jr., Josef 220, 231, 241, 243, 247; *295*
Henze, Hans Werner 162
Herbeck, Johann von 62, 64, 66, 68, 243–5
Herold, Ferdinand 28
Herrmann, Joseph 126
Hertel, Paul 212
Herz, Das 110
Herz, Joachim 158

Hesch, Wilhelm 77; *99*
Heuberger, Richard 110
Heure Espagnole, L' 115
Hiess, Kurt *279*
Hilbert, Egon 127, 133, 141, 150, 154, 256
Hilgermann, Laura 82
Hilverding van Wewen, Franz 22, 211; *258*
Hindemith, Paul 104, 233, 252
Hindemith, Rudolf 252
Hitler, Adolf 92, 112, 115, 254
Hlawa, Stefan 144, 200, 204; *250, 281*
Hochzeit in Bosnien, Eine 218
Hofer, Walter *279*
Hoffmann, Hans Christoph 40
Hoffmann, Josef 40, 64, 189; *63*
Hofmann, Leopold Friedrich Freiherr von 72
Hofmann, Ludwig 118
Hofmannsthal, Hugo von 95, 198, 226
Höllisch Gold 103
Höllische G'schicht, oder Mephistopheles seltsame Erdreise 231
Hollreiser, Heinrich 127, 133
Holy, Alfred 248
Holzmeister, Clemens 42–4, 200; *48, 177*
Homersche Symphonie 127
Hommage à Fanny Ellsler 235
Honegger, Arthur 127
Höngen, Elisabeth 126; *170*
Hopf, Hans 170, 181
Horeau, Hector 39
Hornik, Gottfried 162
Hotel Sacher 232, 235, 247
Hotter, Hans 119
Hötzendorf von Hohenberg, Johann Ferdinand 184; *16*
Hubay, Jenö 115
Huguenots, Les 28, 72; *66*
Hummer, Reinhold 242
Humperdinck, Engelbert 77; *85*

Idomeno 25, 109; *133*
Ilitsch, Daniza 126
Impekoven, Leo 192
Incoronazione di Poppea, L' 144
Inganni di Polinesso, Gli 11
Inganno d'amore, L' 11; *6*
Intermezzo 103; *125*
Iphigenie auf Tauris 154
Ivan Tarassenko 115
Ivanov, Lev 233

Jachimovicz, Theodore 188, 189; *241*
Jahn, Gertrude *214*
Jahn, Wilhelm 77, 78, 246, 248, 250; *86*
Janáček, Leoš 82, 90, 158
Janowitz, Gundula 144; *207, 219*
Jaska, Marieluise 236
Jauner, Franz von 62, 66, 68, 72, 245, 246; *76*
Jean de Paris 28
Jeanne d'Arc au Bûcher 127
Jenufa 82, 90, 150
Jerger, Alfred 101, 109, 115, 127; *125, 131, 132, 154, 156*
Jeritza, Maria 62, 90, 92, 96, 100, 105, 110; *111–3, 117, 130*
Jessonda 28

Joanna Balk   119; *145, 146*
Jolantha   82
Jones, Gwyneth   150; *206, 210*
Jonny spielt auf   104, 110, 200; *131, 249*
Joseph   28
Joseph I, Emperor   16, 57; *12*
Joseph II, Emperor   22, 24, 25; *16*
Josephs Legende   100, 162, 226; *152, 273, 274, 285*
Juck, Hermann   127
Juive, La   28, 162
Junge Lord, Der   162
Jurinac, Sena   126; *161, 184*

Kabale und Liebe   162
Kain und Abel   86
Kalbeck, Max   194
Kalenberg, Josef   105; *133*
Kamann, Karl   118
Kamitz, Reinhard   *174*
Karajan, Herbert von   115, 133, 140, 141, 144, 150, 157, 162, 200, 204, 256; *143, 196, 197, 205, 312*
Karl I, Emperor   95, 183
Karl IV, Emperor   16; *15*
Karl V   110, 111, 162
Karl, Ludwig   236; *285*
Karsavina, Tamara   220, 228
Kattnigg, Rudolf   231
Katya Kabanova   158
Kautsky, Johann   189, 190
Kautsky, Robert   133, 198, 200, 204; *156, 181, 182, 248*
Kerber, Erwin   114, 115, 118, 253, 254; *144*
Kern, Adele   105, 112
Kessler, Harry   222
Kienzl, Wilhelm   77, 100
Kiepura, Jan   106, 117; *128*
King, James   150; *201*
Kirnbauer, Susanne   233
Kitaenki, Dimitri   170
Kittel, Hermine   82; *100*
Kiurina, Berta   *121*
Kleiber, Carlos   157, 158, 162; *220, 222*
Kleiber, Erich   133, 255
Klein, Josef   216, 247
Klein, Peter   119
Kleinecke, Wilhelm   243, 245
Klemisch, Dietlinde   235
Klimt, Gustav   158, 194
Kmentt, Waldemar   133; *204*
Knappertsbusch, Hans   115, 117, 126, 253–5; *184, 303*
Kniepert, Erni   200
Kohlhaymerin, Die   100
Kokoschka, Oskar   *185*
Kolb, Ernst   133
Kollo, René   *207*
Konetzni, Anny   108, 115, 117, 133; *147*
Konetzni, Hilde   118, 127; *164*
Königin von Saba, Die   64; *71, 242, 243*
Konsul, Der   127
Korngold, Erich Wolfgang   89, 90, 100, 103, 162; *128*
Kossak, Zeno   50
Köth, Erika   133; *187, 200*
Krauss, Clemens   103, 105, 107–9, 112, 154, 218, 252; *134, 301*

Krauss, Helene   218
Krauss, Margarethe   *125*
Krauss, Wilhelm Viktor   *157, 299*
Kreisler, Fritz   246
Krenek, Ernst   104, 110, 111, 162, 200; *131, 249*
Krenn, Fritz   101
Kreppel, Walter   *197*
Kreutzner, Konradin   28, 30
Kricka, Jaroslav   111
Kringsteiner, Ferdinand   *30*
Krips, Joseph   108, 117, 255; *210, 310*
Kröller, Heinrich   224, 226, 228
Krotschak, Richard   253
Krupp, Arthur   107
Kshesinska, Mathilde   218, 220
Kubelik, Paul   133; *180*
Kuen, Paul   *197*
Kuhreigen   100
Kulka, Janos   158
Kunz, Erich   119; *156, 160, 197, 206*
Kurz, Selma   82; *94, 95, 113*
Kyaksht, George   228
Kyaksht, Lydia   220

La Roche, Carl   215
Land des Lächelns, Das   115
Langhans, Carl Ferdinand   36
Lanner, Kathi   214
Laske, Oskar   *51*
Lavelli, Jorge   154
Lefler, Heinrich   190, 191, 192, 198; *100, 245*
Lehár, Franz   110, 115; *135*
Lehmann, Lily   *85*
Lehmann, Lotte   90, 92, 100, 105, 109, 110, 117, 118; *119, 125, 127–9, 132*
Leinsdorf, Erich   111
Lemböck, Gabriel   243
Lenbach, Franz von   *291*
Leoncavallo, Ruggiero   74, 82; *123, 227*
Leontyev, Sacha   228
Leopold I, Emperor   11, 12, 16, 35, 57, 177, 182, 211; *4, 229*
Leopold II, Emperor   25
Lessing, Gotthold Ephraim   24
Leuer, Hubert   82, 94
Levine, James   162
Lewy, Richard   244
Liebe Augustin, Der   115; *278*
Liebe der Danae, Die   127
Ligeti, György   233
Linda, Bertha   214
Linda di Chamonix   28
Lindpainter, Peter   28
Lindtberg, Leopold   144
Lipovsek, Marjana   162
Liszt, Franz   229
Lockende Phantom, Das   226
Lohengrin   30, 68, 96, 158, 218, 239, 245; *29, 92, 201, 252*
Lombardi, I   28
Loose, Emmy   126
Lorenz, Max   119; *147*
Lortzing, Albert   30
Losch, Tilly   226
Lucca, Pauline   66, 68; *79*
Lucia di Lammermoor   140, 162; *218*

Ludwig, Christa   133; *195, 209, 211, 252, 253*
Luisa Miller   158; *223*
Luksch, Marielouise   200
Lulu   154, 170
Lutzer, Jenny   58

Maar, Lisl   233, 235
Maazel, Lorin   111, 162, 168, 170; *224, 226, 266*
Macbeth   109, 154, 162; *221*
Madame Butterfly   95
Madeira, Jean   133; *180*
Madenski, Eduard   242, 248
Mader, Raoul   222
Madin, Victor   88, 94
Magic Flute, The   24, 25, 62, 109, 119, 158, 200; *20–3, 63, 70, 160, 197, 238*
Mahler, Gustav   74, 77, 78, 82, 84, 88–90, 101, 108, 150, 190–2, 194, 196, 204, 247, 248, 250; *297*
– *Kindertotenlieder*   82
– *Leid von der Erde, Das*   82
– Symphony No. 6   248
Maikl, Georg   82, 94; *113, 136*
Maillart, Louise Aimé   115
Mairecker, Franz   252; *303, 306*
Makart, Hans   58, 62, 74, 189, 215
Mallarmé, Stéphane   220
Manen, Hans van   235
Manon   74; *84*
Manon Lescaut   100; *228*
Manowarda, Joseph von   101, 110, 114; *136*
Mantua-Nevers, Prince Karl von   *3*
Manzotti, Luigi   218; *265*
Marberg, Lilly   226
Marboe, Ernst   62, 133
Marcel, Lucille   89; *104*
Margherita of Spain   11, 12; *2, 5, 229*
Marguerite et Armand   228
Maria Anna of Spain   9
Maria Antonio, Archduchess   12
Maria di Rohan   28
Maria Theresa, Empress   20, 22, 24, 183, 211
Marie Antoinette, Princess   *258*
Marriage of Figaro, The   24, 127, 200, 252; *17, 67, 158, 161, 162, 300*
Marischka, Hubert   *135*
Mark, Paula   77; *85, 88*
Marschner, Heinrich   30
Martha   30
Martin y Soler, Vincenzo   24, 25
Martinis, Carla   127
Marton, Eva   *224*
Mascagni, Pietro   74; *227*
Massenet, Jules   74, 90; *84*
Massine, Leonid   228, 233
Materna, Amalie   64, 68; *66, 71, 77, 83*
Matray, Ernst   222
Matsch, Franz   *96*
Maximilian I, Emperor   9
Maximilian, Archduke   258
Mayerhofer, Carl   72; *67*
Mayerhof, Elfie   *175*
Mayr, Richard   82, 84, 88, 89, 100, 101, 109; *102, 107, 120*
Mazaroff, Todor   118
Mazurok, Jurij   158

Medea 154; *208*
Medici, Elenore de *1*
Mehta, Zubin 170
Métul, Etienne-Nicolas 28
Meistersinger von Nürnberg, Die 43, 62, 108, 109, 115, 133, 158, 244, 245; *51, 80, 98, 182, 198*
Melchior, Lauritz 82
Mell, Max 194
Melusine 28
Mendelssohn-Bartholdy, Felix 68
– *Athalia*, Ouverture 68
Menotti, Gian Carlo 127, 162
Mephistopheles 74
Mercadante, Saverio 162
Mère L'Oye, Ma 226
Merelli, Bartolomeo 38
Merry Wives of Windsor, The 30
Metastasio, Pietro 16; *258*
Metternich, Princess Pauline 218
Meyerbeer, Giacomo 28, 30, 72, 245; *66*
Michalek, Margarethe 100
Mignon 30, 62
Mildenburg, Anna von see Bahr-Mildenburg, Anna
Milinkovic, Georgine von 119; *168*
Milloss, Aurel von 233
Milnes, Sherrill 154
Minato, Nicolo 14
Minkus, Ludwig 231
Mitropoulos, Dimitri 144
Mödl, Martha 133; *178*
Mohr von Venedig, Der 232; *282*
Monaco, Mario del 144; *192*
Monarchia latina trionfante 14; 8
Montecchi e i Capuletti, I 28
Monteverdi, Claudio 11, 144
Moralt, Rudolf 119, 122
Morelli, Bartolomeo 38; *40*
Morishita, Yoka 234
Mosel, Ignaz Franz *236*
Moser, Thomas 162
Moses und Aron 158, 204; *212*
Mottl, Felix 86
Mozart, Wolfgang Amadeus 24, 25, 30, 58, 62, 82, 105, 109, 122, 177, 239, 250, 254; *17–23, 60, 62, 63, 67, 70, 122, 133, 158–63, 179, 197, 213, 238, 247, 310*
Muette di Portici 28, 30, 215
Müller, Wenzel 25
Musikant, der 89
Musil, Karl 233, 235
Musil, Ludwig R. 233, 235
Mussorgsky, Modest 103, 226; *215*
Müthel, Lothar 118, 119
Muti, Riccardo 170

Nabucco 28
Nacht in Venedig, Eine 115
Nachtlager von Granada 28
Nagy, Zoltan 236
Napoleon 25
Natale di Giunono, Il 16
Neher, Caspar 119, 122, 133, 200, 204; *146, 158, 159, 179, 186, 251*
Nemeth, Maria 105
Nesterenko, Jewgenij 158
Nestroy, Johann 241

Neumann, Angelo 64
Neumeier, John 235; *285*
Nicolai, Friedrich 186
Nicolai, Otto 30, 239, 241
Niedermayr, Josef 252
Nijinska, Bronislava 222, 228
Nijinsky, Vaslav 220, 222
Nikisch, Arthur 241; *291*
Nikolaidi, Elena 118
Nilsson, Birgit *190, 203*
Norma 26, 162
Notre Dame 90
Noverre, Jean Georges 22, 212
Novotna, Jarmila 108; *135*
Novotny, Richard 233, 234
Nüll, Eduard van der 31, 39; *31, 39, 41–3*
Nureyev, Rudolf 229, 233, 234; *283*
Nutcracker Suite, The 231, 235

Oberleithner, Max 90
Oberon 30, 64, 115
Obraztsowa, Elena 158; *220*
Oedipus Rex 104, 141
Oestvig, Karl Aagard 100, 101; *118, 123*
Offenbach, Jacques 30, 72
Olczewska, Maria 105
Opernball, Der 110
Operti, E. *265*
Oppenheimer, Max *296, 297*
Orfeo 9
Orfeo ed Euridice 22, 115; *13, 144*
Orff, Carl 43
Orlikovsky, Vaslav 233
Otello (Rossini) 25
Otello (Verdi) 74, 141, 200; *87, 114, 192*
Othellerl, der Mohr von Wien 30; *30*
Othello, der Mohr von Venedig 133
Otto, Teo 204

Paalen, Bella 82
Pacassi, Nikolaus Franz Leonhard von *16*
Pagliero, Camilla 219
Paisiello, Giovanni 24
Palestrina 43, 100, 122; *121*
Palladio, Andrea 32
Palladio 16
Panerai, Rolando *196*
Panov, Valery 235
Papier, Rosa 77; *73*
Paquita 220
Pariati, Pietro 14
Paride ed Helene 22; 13
Parlic, Dimitrii 232, 233
Parsifal 43, 64, 90, 96, 109; *83*
Pataky, Koloman von 105
Patzak, Julius 127
Pauker, Peter 194
Paulik, Anton 231; *279*
Pauly, Rose 108, 110
Paumgartner, Hans 77
Pausinger, Clemens von *84*
Pavarotti, Luciano *222, 225*
Pavlova, Anna 220
Pelléas et Mélisande 90, 141
Penelope 127
Per Aspera 233
Pergolesi, Giovanni Battista 112
Perle von Iberien, Die 220; *267*

Pernerstorfer, Alois 127
Pernes, Thomas 236
Pernter, Hans 112
Perras, Margarita 118
Petipa, Marius 233
Petrushka 220, 235
Pfitzner, Hans 43, 100, 110, 126; *121*
Pfundmayr, Hedy 222; *272*
Philidor, François André 24
Pian, Antonio de 184; *238*
Piccaver, Alfred 92, 105; *129*
Piccini, Nicola 22
Pichler, Gusti 228; *275*
Piffl-Percevic, Theodor 150
Pinnisch, Michael 236
Pio, Prince of Savoy 16
Pique Dame (Queen of Spades) 82, 105, 170, 194, 204; *100*
Piscator, Erwin 204
Pizzetti, Ildebrando 144
Platzer, Josef 184
Plucis, Harijs 228
Poell, Alfred 118, 127; *162*
Pokorny, Edwin 232; *281*
Pokorny, Poldi 232
Pollack, Egon 108
Pölzer, Julius 127
Pomo d'Oro, Il 12, 178; *4, 5, 7, 231–4*
Ponnelle, Jean-Pierre 204; *227*
Ponte, Lorenzo da 24
Popp, Lucia 208
Popper, David 243
Porsile, Giuseppe 16
Postillion of Enzersdorf Barn, The 30
Postillion de Longjumeau, Le 30
Preetorius, Emil 133, 141, 198, 200
Price, Julius 212, 215; *259, 262, 265*
Price, Leontyne 144; *193*
Prill, Carl 250
Prince, Harold 170; *224*
Prince of the Pagodas 233
Prokofiev, Sergei 232
Prophète, Le 30
Prossinger, Otto 50
Protti, Aldo 144
Prozess, Der 127, 154
Puccini, Giacomo 82, 89, 90, 100, 103, 162, 170; *94, 95, 112, 126, 127, 130, 188, 190, 191, 193, 222, 224, 228*
Puppenfee, Die (The Fairy Doll) 77, 170, 204, 218–20, 232, 234, 235, 247; *266*

Quaglio, Giovanni Maria 22
Queen of Spades see *Pique Dame*

Raab, Julius 133
Raab, Riki 222
Radz-Datz 236
Raimondi, Gianni *196*
Raimund, Carl 222; *270, 271*
Raimund Jr., Carl 229
Rake's Progress, The 127, 150; *204*
Ralph, Torsten 126
Ratto delle Sabine, Il 12
Ravel, Maurice 115, 226, 228
Re in ascolto, Un 162
Regel, Heinrich 222
Reichenberger, Hugo 89, 103, 108, 117

Reichmann, Theodor   77; *82*
Reichwein, Leopold   96
Reif-Gintl, Heinrich   127, 133, 154, 156, 157
Reiner, Fritz   133; *182*
Reinhardt, Andreas   204
Reinhardt, Max   200
Reining, Maria   118; *142, 158, 169*
Reinking, Wilhelm   122, 141
Relazioni Fragili   233
Renard, Marie   77; *84, 85*
Rennert, Günther   127, 144
Resnik, Regina   150
Réthy, Ester   118; *168*
Rheingold, Das   104, 105, 109, 252; *75, 90, 300*
Ricciarelli, Katia   158; *223*
Richter, Hans   66, 68, 72, 78, 244, 245, 248; *298*
Ridderbusch, Karl   158
Rienzi   65, 109, 244
Rigoletto   30, 170, 204
Rimsky-Korsakov, Nikolai   222
Ring des Nibelungen, Der,   64, 99, 109, 126, 141, 200, 246; *76, 78, 82*
Ritter, Josef   77
Robitsek, Viktor   253
Rode, Pierre   241
Rode, William   108
Roerich, Nikolas   220
Rohs, Martha   118; *154, 156*
Rokitansky, Hans von   64
Roller, Alfred   78, *82, 90, 100, 109, 194, 196, 200, 204, 226, 252; 89, 90, 103, 110, 115, 116, 126, 141, 246-8*
Roller, Ulrich   200; *141, 142*
Romeo and Juliet (Prokofiev)   232
Roméo et Juliette (Gounod)   30
Rosamunda   30
Rosé, Arnold   246, 250, 253; *296, 297, 305*
Rose, Jürgen   158, 204; *213, 214, 255*
Rosengärtlein, Das   100
Rosenkavalier, Der   82, 90, 101, 122, 150, 198, 250; *107, 109, 110, 149, 166, 169, 184, 206*
Rossini, Gioacchino   25, 28, 30, 112, 162; *28, 199, 200*
Rosvaenge, Helge   108, 109, 115; *165*
Roten Dominos, Die   216
Rothschild, Baron   248
Rott, Adolf   127, 133; *181, 184*
Rottonara, Franz Angelo   189, 190
Röver, Heinrich   243
Rubinstein, Ida   *105*
Ruinen von Athen, Die   99
Rumpel, Hans   216
Rundgren, Bengt   158
Rünger, Gertrud   108, 109, 114
Rydl, Kurt   162
Rysanek, Leonie   127, 154; *181, 182, 192, 253*

Sacchetti, Paduan Lorenzo   184
Salieri, Antonio   22, 24, 25
Salmhofer, Franz   115, 127, 154, 226, 229
Salome   84, 90, 99, 122, 150, 158, 201, 250; *11, 202, 214*
Saltarello   215

Salvi, Matteo   30, 59, 68, 239
Salvioni, Guglielma   212, 214; *260*
Sanjust, Filippo   154; *219*
Sanquirico, Alessando   188
Sardanapal   64, 212; *259*
Sarti, Giuseppe   24
Satanella oder Metamorphosen   186, 215; *239*
Sbarra, Francesco   14
Scamozzi, Vincenzo   32
Scaria, Emil   72; *78*
Schäfer, Walter Erich   150
Schalk, Franz   84, 90, 96, 98, 99, 100, 102, 103, 105, 107, 109, 154, 252; *124*
Schatzgräber, Der   100
Schavernoch, Hans   *256, 257*
Schenk, Johann   25
Schenk, Otto   111, 150, 158, 170, 204; *206, 207, 209, 211, 213, 214, 228*
Schenker-Angerer, Margit   105
Scheuermann, Lilly   233, 235
Schikaneder, Emanuel   24; *20–3*
Schinkel, Karl Friedrich   36, 40
Schipper, Emil   101
Schirach, Baldur von   119
Schittenhelm, Anton   68; *80*
Schläger, Antonie   87
Schlagobers   99, 226, 230
Schmedes, Erik   82, 100, 108; *91, 93, 121*
Schmelzer, Johann Heinrich   12; *8*
Schmidt, Franz   90, 100, 250
Schneemann, Der   89
Schneider, Ernst August   119, 127
Schneider-Siemssen, Günther   141, 201, 204; *197, 253, 254*
Schneiderhan, Franz   107
Schneiderhan, Wolfgang   253, 254; *307, 309*
Schock, Rudolf   127
Schöffler, Paul   118; *156, 168, 182*
Schönberg, Arnold   158, 162, 204; *212, 257*
Schönerer, Alexandrine von   82
Schönerer, Count and Countess   *175*
Schönherr, Max   232
Schönpflug, Fritz   97
Schorr, Friedrich   117
Schreker, Franz   100
Schröder-Devrient, Wilhelmine   *26*
Schrödter, Fritz   218; *94*
Schubert, Franz   30, 64
Schubert, Richard   105
Schuh, Oscar Fritz   119, 122, 127, 200; *158, 159, 167, 179, 186*
Schulz, Else   118
Schumann, Elizabeth   82, 101
Schumann, Robert   28
Schuppanzigh, Ignaz   241
Schuschnigg, Kurt   112
Schwanda der Dudelsackpfeifer   110, 115, 200
Schwarz, Josef   88
Schwarz, Richard   *313*
Schwarz, Vera   105, 115, 117
Schwarzkopf, Elisabeth   127; *166*
Schweigsame Frau, Die   154
Schwind, Moritz von   54; *55–7*
Seefehlner, Egon   162; *227*
Seefried, Irmgard   126; *159, 161, 179, 182*

Seidler, Alma   127
Selliers, Josef Carl   16, 20
Sellner, Gustav Rudolf   150
Semiramis   20; *13*
Semper, Gottfried   36, 39
Sequi, Sandro   170
Serlio, Sebastiano   32
Serva Padrona, La   112
Seyfried, Jolantha   236
Sheherazade (Haubenstock-Ramati)   162
Sheherazade (Rimsky-Korsakov)   222; *272*
Siccard von Siccardburg, August   31, 39; *32, 41–3*
Sidonio, Il   11
Siebert, Dorothea   *168*
Siepi, Cesare   144
Silja, Anja   *202*
Simandl, Franz   242
Simionato, Giulietta   144; *194*
Simon Boccanegra   109, 168, 170
Sinopoli, Giuseppe   162; *221, 228*
Sinowatz, Fred   162
Sironi, Irene   220; *267*
Sleeping Beauty   231, 233, 234
Slezak, Leo   82, 108; *92, 114*
Smetana, Friedrich   77, 154
Solti, George   162
Sommerliebelei   235
Somnambula, La   28
Sonne und Erde   200; *269*
Specht, Richard   196
Speidel, Ludwig   247
Spohr, Louis   25, 28
Spontini, Gasparo   25
Sprenger, Paul   38
Stadelmayer, A.   *261*
Stadler, Brigitte   236
Starkmann, Max   254
Stefano, Giuseppe di   144; *195*
Stehmann, Gerhard   *94*
Steinbrecher, Alexander   115
Stella, Antonietta   144
Stiegler, Karl   250
Stranitzky, Joseph Anton   16; *14*
Strauss, Johann   115, 231, 234; *244*
Strauss, Josef   234
Strauss, Richard   82, 89, 90, 95, 96, 98–103, 107, 109, 115, 119, 122, 127, 162, 198, 200, 226, 245, 250; *103–5, 107, 109–11, 113, 115–20, 124, 125, 132, 133, 140–2, 148–57, 166, 168, 169, 184, 187, 206, 210, 214, 219, 253, 299*
Stravinsky, Igor   104, 127, 141, 220, 235; *204*
Strehler, Giorgio   170
Streich, Rita   127
Strnad, Oskar   42, 110, 200; *137, 138, 249*
Strohl von Strohlendorf, Elsa   222, 226, 228; *271*
Strohm, Heinrich Karl   118, 119, 200
Stubenrauch, Philipp von   183; *236*
Stvertka, Julius   250
Sühne, Die   117
Suppé, Franz von   110, 215
Süssmayer, Franz Xaver   24, 25
Suthaus, Ludwig   133
Svanholm, Set   118
Sved, Alexander   117

Swan Lake 220, 233
Sylphides, Les 231
Sylvia, ou la Nymphe de Diane 215; *264*
Szantho, Enid 105

Taddei, Giuseppe *196*
Taglioni, Marie 186, 212
Taglioni, Paul 186, 212, 215; *261*
Taglioni, Philipp 211
Takacs, Clara *256*
Tales of Hoffmann, The 72, 150
Talvela, Martti *252*
Tancred 25
Tannhäuser 30, 92, 170; *27, 29, 164, 254*
Tanzlegende 226
Tanzmärchen 240
Tauber, Richard 117; *135*
Taugenichts in Wien, Der 229
Tchaikovsky, Peter 82, 105, 170, 194, 233
Tcherepnin, Nikolai 220
Tebaldi, Renata 144; *188*
Telle, Carl 212, 214
Telle, Johanne 212
Tellheim, Caroline 67
Terres Basses 89
Terry, Ellen 192
Thalhammer, Erwin 150, 154
Thomas, Ambroise 30, 62, 64
Thorberg, Kerstin 117
Thuille, Ludwig *245*
Tichy, Christian 236
Tietjen, Heinz 133; *177*
Tokody, Ilona 162
Told, Franz Xaver 186
Tosca 89, 141; *188, 191, 193*
Toscanini, Arturo 106, 112, 115, 253; *305, 306*
Tote Stadt, Die 100, 162
Traunfels, Josef Wenzel 115
Traviata, La 30; *251*
Tricorne, Le 228, 233
Trionfo d'amore, Il 258
Tristan und Isolde 62, 64, 74, 84, 94, 107, 115, 117, 126, 141, 162, 194, 196; *81, 93, 102, 143, 147*
Trittico 100, 162
Trovatore, Il 30; *250*
Troyans, Les 162
Turandot 94, 103, 170; *126, 127, 130, 190, 222*
Twilight 235

Ulysses 162
Umlauf, Ignaz 24
Undine 30
Urban, Josef 191
Ursuleac, Viorica 108, 109, 114; *134*
Uthal 28

Vakhevitch, Georges 200

Valois, Dame Ninette de 233
Valse, La 228
Vampyr, Der 28
Varese, Edgar 232
Veilchen, Das 110
Veilchenmädel see *Hotel Sacher*
Verdi, Giuseppi 30, 64, 68, 74, 78, 82, 103, 109, 154, 162, 170, 245, 253; *68, 69, 72, 87, 99, 114, 167, 170, 180, 181, 192, 194, 205, 209, 221, 223, 246, 250, 251, 293, 305, 306*
—— *Messa da Requiem* 68, 112, 245, 253; *293, 306*
Verrett, Shirley 154
Versailles, In 215
Vestale, La 25
Vickers, Jon 144
Vienna Waltz 215, 220
Violanta 90
Visconti, Luchino 150, 154, 204; *205*
Völker, Franz 108, 114
Vondrak, Erwald *279*
Vondrak, Paul 233, 235

Wacek, Wilhelm 250
Wächter, Eberhard 133; *203, 211*
Waffenschmied, Der 30
Wagner, Cosima 78, 82
Wagner, Richard 30, 35–7, 62, 64, 68, 78, 90, 96, 122, 170, 196, 218, 239, 240, 245; *27, 29, 73–5, 77–83, 90–3, 98, 102, 143, 147, 164, 182, 198, 241, 252, 292, 313*
Wagner, Siegfried *294*
Wagner, Sieglinde 167, 168
Wagner, Wieland 150, 201; *201–3, 252, 253*
Wagner, Wolfgang *176*
Wagner-Régeny, Rudolf 119; *145*
Wakhewitsch, Georges 133, 141
Walküre, Die 101, 244, 252; *73, 77, 300, 313*
Wallenstein 115
Wallerstein, Lothar 103, 104, 106, 108, 109, 117, 200; *125, 126, 128, 132, 138, 248*
Wallman, Margarethe 115, 117, 118, 141, 229; *188, 277*
Walter, Bruno 84, 115, 117, 133, 253; *144, 176, 304*
Walter, Erich 235
Walter, Gustav 64, 72
Watson, Claire 252
Weber, Carl Maria von 25, 28, 64, 74, 115, 200; *27, 28, 144*
Weidemann, Friedrich 82, 95; *93*
Weidt, Lucie 82, 100; *106, 109*
Weigl, Joseph 25
Weikl, Berndt 158, 162; *213*
Weinberger, Jaromir 110, 115, 200
Weingartner, Felix von 86, 88, 90, 96, 101, 115, 150, 250; *104, 106*

Weinrich, Hans *276*
Welitsch, Ljuba 127; *163*
Wellesz, Egon 110
Wenkoff, Spas 170
Werfel, Franz 103, 109
Wernigk, William 101
Werther 74, 90
Wertheimer, Gustav 79
Wessely, Paula 175
Wiedemann, Hermann 94; *136*
Wiener, Otto 144; *253*
Wiener Legende 222
Wiener Skizzen 234
Wiesenthal, Grete 226, 228, 229; *276*
Wigman, Mary 230
Wildbrunn, Helene 105
Wilhelm, Franz 233, 235
William Tell 28
Wilt, Maria 64; *70*
Windgassen, Wolfgang 133; *198*
Winkelmann, Hermann 77; *83, 87*
Winkler, Julius 253
Winter, Peter von 25
Wipperich, Emil 247; *288*
Wise, Patricia 162
Witt, Josef 118, 119; *145*
Witzmann, Karl 42
Wood, Donna *285*
Wotuba, Fritz 45, 50; *54*
Wozzeck 108, 110, 133, 200; *136–8, 186*
Wrbna, Rudolf Graf 64
Wührer, Ully 233
Wunder der Heliane 103; *128*
Wunderbare Mandarin, Der 235
Wunderer, Alexander 250
Wunderlich, Fritz 150; *197, 202*
Wymetal, Wilhelm von 89

Yolanta 82

Zadek, Hilde 127
Zallinger, Meinrad von 127
Zampa 28
Zampieri, Giuseppe 144; *188*
Zampieri, Mara 162; *221*
Zancanaro, Giorgio *223*
Zar und Zimmermann 30
Zauberharfe, Die 30
Zauberschleier 186
Zec, Nikolas 94
Zednik, Heinz *214*
Zeffirelli, Franco 141; *196, 200*
Zemire und Azor 28
Zemlinsky, Alexander von 84, 85
Ziani, Marc Antonio 14
Zichy, Geza Graf 222
Zimmerl, Christl 232; *282*
Zimmermann, Erich 114
Zlocha, Erika 235

PHOTO CREDITS

The publishers wish to thank all the photographers who collaborated on this book, as well as the museums, archives, and other institutions which supplied additional photographic material. The illustrations not listed below were kindly put at our disposal by the Oesterreichischen National-bibliothek, Vienna (Theatersammlung and photo archives). The numbers refer to the plates.

Graphische Sammlung Albertina, Vienna 13, 41
Osvaldo Böhm, Venice 35
G. Brandenstein page 167
Bundesdenkmalamt, Vienna 50
Enkelmann, Munich 280
Fayer, Vienna 179, 180, 188, 189, 190, 191, 193, 196, 197, 199, 200, 201, 202, 203, 206, 208, 209, 210, 211, 219, 252, 253; pages 122, 133, 141, 154
Johanna Fiegl, Vienna 56, 57, 58
Foto Vouk, Vienna 54
Gesellschaft der Musikfreunde, Vienna 287, 289, 307, 310, 312
Elfriede Hanak, Vienna 308
Elisabeth Hausmann, Vienna (State Opera) 192, 194, 195, 198, 212, 213, 218, 220
Historisches Museum der Stadt Wien 12, 14, 28, 29, 39, 157
Kunsthistorisches Museum, Vienna 1, 3, 4, 5, 16, 258
Siegfried Lauterwasser, Ueberlingen 312
Erich Lessing, Culture and Fine Arts Archives, Vienna 205
Margit Münster, Vienna 256, 313
Museum Moderner Kunst, Vienna 185
Oesterreichische Galerie, Vienna 297
Richard Pietsch & Co., Vienna 53, 55
Pressebilddienst Votava, Vienna 172, 174, 175, 176, 178, 207, 216; page 157

Private collections, Vienna 27, 33, 34, 97, 124, 245, 282
Riki Raab (archives), Vienna 262, 264, 265, 267, 270, 271, 275, 282
Schikola, Vienna 301
Setzer-Tschiedel (archives), Vienna 95, 108, 111, 112, 117, 118, 119, 120, 123, 130, 134, 272, 274
Stadtgeschichtliche Museen, Nuremberg 296
State Opera, Vienna 45; page 162
Richard Strauss-Archiv, Garmisch-Partenkirchen 299 (photo: Photohaus Beckert, Inh. Hans Auer, Garmisch-Partenkirchen)
Vienna Philharmonic (archives), Vienna 286, 288, 291, 292, 294, 298, 300, 303, 304, 305, 309
Lukas Walter, Lofer 169
Axel Zeininger, Vienna (State Opera) 214, 215, 221, 222, 223, 224, 225, 226, 227, 228, 254, 255, 257, 266, 283, 284, 285

Copyright:
© Dr. F. Borges, Prague 137, 138, 249
© COSMOPRESS, Geneva 185
© Dr. Peter Faistauer, Saalfelden 107
© Boosey & Hawkes Music Publishers Ltd., London 110, 115, 116
© Martin Hochstetter, Bad Aussee 250
© Gunda Holzmeister, Salzburg 48
© Renée Klezl-Norberg 169
© Therese Matsch, Vienna 96
© Dr. Clemens Pausinger, Vienna 84
© Dr. Dietrich Alfred Roller, Vienna 89, 90, 103, 141, 247
© Helen Schönpflug-Sagunt, Vienna 97
© Lilly Schulz-Laske, Vienna 51
© Dr. Frank Tornquist, Graz 146, 251
© Legacy Lucy Wotruba, represented by Karl Leutgeb, Vienna 54

This book was printed and bound in March, 1987 by Druckerei Carl Ueberreuter Ges.m.b.h., Korneuburg
Photolithography (color): Photolitho Bienna AG, Biel, Switzerland (black and white): look graphic sa,
Acacias, Geneva
Setting: Typobauer Filmsatz GmbH, Ostfildern (Scharnhausen), West Germany
Coordination: Hubertus von Gemmingen
Editorial: Martha Swiderski-Ritchie
Design and production: Emma Staffelbach

Printed and bound in Austria